Analog Automation and Digital Feedback Control Techniques

Series Editor
Jean-Paul Bourrières

Analog Automation and Digital Feedback Control Techniques

Jean Mbihi

WILEY

First published 2018 in Great Britain and the United States by ISTE Ltd and John Wiley & Sons, Inc.

ISTE Ltd
27-37 St George's Road
London SW19 4EU
UK

www.iste.co.uk

John Wiley & Sons, Inc.
111 River Street
Hoboken, NJ 07030
USA

www.wiley.com

Library of Congress Control Number: 2018930828

British Library Cataloguing-in-Publication Data
A CIP record for this book is available from the British Library
ISBN 978-1-78630-248-9

Contents

Preface

Analog automation is a multidisciplinary science that studies techniques, tools and technologies for the design and implementation of analog controllers for dynamic processes, the controller being a device for automatic correction of possible errors between the set point quantity and the corresponding response.

Therefore, in an uncertain operating environment that is subjected to unknown disturbances or unpredictable noise, a dynamic process equipped with an appropriate controller can provide good dynamic performances (stability, overshoot, rapidity) and static performances (precision, robustness).

According to the history of automation, the first mechanical controller, known as the "water clock", was invented in Greece by Ktesibios around 270 BC [STU 96]. After 23 centuries, in 1956, analog electronic controllers were developed [FRI 82, THO 07]. The first computer-aided digital feedback control processes were then implemented in major industries in the United States starting from 1950 [BAK 12]. Moreover, starting from the 1970s, the digital automation techniques assisted by microprocessor and PLC (programmable logic controller) have progressively occupied the wide SMI (small and medium-sized industries) sector, which had been beyond the reach of these computers until that time. They were, indeed, bulky, expensive and difficult to program. Furthermore, they had high maintenance costs and were sensitive to industrial environments.

Nevertheless, after the emergence of the first PC (*personal computer*) generations in the 1980s, followed by the development of microcomputer models featuring increasingly high performances at low costs (industrial PC, multimedia PC, PC/pad and PC/panel), the range of application of computer-aided digital control technology has rapidly extended to SMIs in various fields: manufacturing, textile, food-processing industry, chemical industry, energy, robotics, telescopic devices, avionics, bio-mechatronics, home automation, etc.

Given the lack of reference manuals intended to serve as a learning bridge between analog and digital control systems, this book will allow the readers to easily master analog automation skills and then to rapidly become introduced to the techniques for design and simulation of modern PC-aided digital control systems. The book is mainly addressed to students and teachers of engineering schools, to teachers' training schools for technical education and to vocational training centers for applied sciences.

Indeed, readers will discover in this book the following relevant main elements:

– the stakes of computer-aided control in the set of control technologies for dynamic processes;

– a summary of the theory of analog control systems;

– a clear presentation of the experimental modeling of dynamic processes, with or without input delay;

– modern tools for the rapid design of optimal PID controllers;

– techniques for computer-aided synthesis and simulation of digital control loops, with a detailed case study of speed and position servomechanisms;

– methods for the discretization of dynamic process state models;

– Matlab® programs for teaching purposes, allowing the convenient introduction, if needed, of the digital and graphic results presented;

– a variety of corrected exercises at the end of each chapter.

The analog and digital control systems presented in this book are the result of the continuously enhanced teaching of the "Computer-aided automation of feedback control systems" course, which the author has taught since 2000 in the "Electrical Engineering" department of ENSET (École Normale Supérieure d'Enseignement Technique), a technical higher education school of the University of Douala, and in the "Computer Science Engineering" department of ESSET (Écoles Supérieures des Sciences et Techniques), scientific and technical higher education schools of Douala and Nkongsamba.

The author acknowledges the favorable effects of the scientific research grant offered by MINESUP (Ministry of Higher Education) of Cameroon. It has facilitated the access to support and scientific and technical research resources needed for editing activities involved in this book project.

Moreover, the author sincerely thanks his close collaborators in the scientific field of industrial automation and computing who have offered their constructive suggestions concerning both technical and teaching aspects, as follows:

– Prof. Womonou Robert, director and promoter of ESSET at Douala and Nkongsamba;

– Prof. Nneme Nneme Léandre, director of ENSET at the University of Douala;

– Pauné Félix, PhD, lecturer in the "Computer Science" department of ENSET at the University of Douala;

– Moffo Lonla Bertrand, PhD, lecturer at ENSET at the University of Buea.

The author also wishes to thank:

– The students of the second cycle of the "Electrical Engineering" department, ENSET, at the University of Douala and of ESSET at Douala and Nkongsamba, who have followed his "Computer-aided automation of feedback control systems" course with great interest. Thanks to their many relevant questions, which have allowed him to identify certain obscure didactic aspects of basic automation that have been clarified in this book.

– His wife, Mrs. Mbihi born Tsafack Pélagie Marthe, and her entire family, who have all offered him continuous and comforting support, as well as unforgettable close assistance.

– Mr. Ajoumissi Jean's and Nkongli Teuhguia's families, who motivated him to initiate and complete this book project.

– The ISTE editorial team, who provided him with the tools and means that facilitated this book's content restructuring and improvement.

January 2018

Introduction

I.1. Architectural and technological context

I.1.1. *Analog automation*

In automation, dynamic processes are part of a class of analog power systems that can be controlled in an open or closed loop. This is why the characteristic input, state and output signals of a dynamic process, are continuous time functions. Therefore, the architecture of an analog control loop of a dynamic process is homogeneous as regards the nature of signals involved, in which case the connection between the controller and the dynamic process does not require A/D (analog/digital) and D/A (digital/analog) conversion devices of signals involved.

In practice, the study of analog feedback control systems relies on design techniques available in automation, as well as on implementation technologies used in analog electronics. Nevertheless, in demanding application fields, analog control technology presents technical problems, the most important of which are [MBI 17]:

– large dimensions (volume, weight), especially for a significant number of control loops;

– aging of the controller components, which can lead to long-term parameter variations beyond acceptable thresholds;

– high sensitivity to noise and disturbances in the environment;

– lack of flexibility in terms of extension of the control device;

– complexity of advanced control strategy implementation;

– poor performance of the analog devices for monitoring, log book development, data archiving, etc.

I.1.2. *Computer-aided control*

A computer-aided control loop is a "hybrid" dynamic system. In fact, it involves continuous signals related to the dynamic process, while the signals involved in the computer operation are characterized by discrete quantities. In automated process engineering, this hybrid nature consequently generates the following new problems:

– the requirement to install between the computer and the analog process an interfacing device for combined A/D (analog/digital) and D/A (digital/analog) conversions [BOL 04, MBI 12];

– the need to train automation experts in the field of fundamental techniques and tools for the study of sampled signals and dynamic systems;

– the need for the automation experts to adapt to the computer science environment;

– the ongoing retraining of automation professionals faced with the rapid evolution of computer technologies and tools for the development of software applications for teaching and professional purposes.

Despite the above-mentioned technical problems, computer-aided controllers [FAD 09] offer new perspectives. In the class of digital processors, computers play an increasingly key role in industrial automation [MBI 05]. Indeed, modern technology for computer-aided control offers the following specific advantages:

– tremendous possibilities in terms of multitasking, with simultaneous services for video processing and virtual instrumentation with data monitoring [MBI 15a, MBI 15b]. Moreover, industrial automation computers can also be used for the monitoring of industrial LAN (local area network), nano-systems [DUR 15] and embedded bio-systems [SAL 16] that are equipped at the field level of PIC (*programmable integrated circuit*) [SHA 13], FPGA (*field programmable gate array*) [MAS 10, JAS 11, ZAH 11, GÜR 16], CPLD (*complex programmable logic device*) [GRO 08] and PLC (programmable logic controller) [BIA 85];

– a wide variety of high-performance machine models: standard PCs/laptops, PCs/Pads, industrial PCs/laptops with a compact or rackable case and protection index of the order of IP68 [PAR 07];

– a wide range of ports and extension slots;

– numerous advanced devices for operator dialog: touchscreen, giant screen and mobile terminal;

– a wide availability of free device drivers for popular development tools such as Visual C++, Visual Basic, Visual C#, Matlab® and LabVIEW. These drivers allow a significant reduction of efforts required for the implementation of instrumentation and control functions;

– a wide variety of advanced resources and implementations of new structures of intelligent digital controllers;

– impressive memory capacity of data storage media of programs and data: DVD of the order of Go (Gigaoctet), USB drive and memory card of the order of Go and internal or external hard disk of the order of To (Teraoctet);

– huge multitasking possibilities (control loop monitoring, screen, digital control processor, virtual instrument, etc.);

– advanced means for easy realization of remote feedback control systems.

I.2. Scientific and teaching context

I.2.1. *Analog automation*

The scientific tools used in analog feedback control for the mathematical representation of dynamic processes and controllers are:

– the transfer function (of Laplace variable s) defined in the frequency domain;

– the continuous state model.

The analog control structures that can be synthesized in the frequency domain, in order to obtain good indicators of closed-loop dynamic and static performances, vary from simple proportional controller to PID (proportional–integral–derivative) controller, passing through phase-lead or phase-delay controllers. Morcover, the control structures that can be synthesized in the space state vary from simple state feedback controller to LQR (*linear quadratic regulator*) controller with partial or full state observer, passing through the state controller with full set point tracking error.

I.2.2. *Computer-aided control*

Computer-aided control involves similar scientific constituents and tools, created from those available in analog automation. This is the case for:

– dynamic and static performance indicators;

– transfer function in z (where $z = e^{Ts}$, T being the sampling period);

– discrete PID controller;

– discrete state model;

– discrete state feedback;

– discrete LQR, etc.

Given these similarities, the purpose of this book can now be stated.

I.3. Purpose of the book

This is an original textbook, designed for readers of Master 1 and Master 2 levels who are interested in a detailed study of analog automation solutions and in the discovery and rapid understanding of the elements of computer-aided control technology.

I.4. Organization of the book's content

The book is organized into two parts, each of which is structured in coherent chapters.

Part 1 deals with analog control systems. It is in fact a summary of processes and results of the theory of analog control systems. In this part, the models of dynamic processes are detailed in Chapter 1, followed, in Chapter 2, by a clear presentation of the experimental modeling technique. Finally, Chapter 3 presents a summary of analog feedback control systems.

Part 2 presents techniques for the synthesis and simulation of digital control systems. Synthesis elements in the frequency domain of digital control systems are described in Chapter 4. Then, Chapter 5 focuses on computer-aided simulations of digital control systems. Moreover, Chapter 6 is an introduction to discrete state models of dynamic processes. The constituent elements of this part can be generalized in the case of digital control systems with more complex architecture [FOU 87, KYR 16].

It is worth remembering that the corrected exercises in this book can be found at the end of each chapter, in order to consolidate the acquired knowledge. Appendix 1 provides a table of the z-transforms of simple transfer functions that are commonly used in practice for the accurate discretization of transfer functions. Finally, a descriptive table of Matlab commands used in the teaching programs presented in this book can be found in Appendix 2.

Part 1

Analog Feedback Control Systems

Models of Dynamic Processes

1.1. Introduction to dynamic processes

1.1.1. *Definition, hypotheses and notations*

From an input and output perspective, a dynamic process, as illustrated in Figure 1.1, represents a controllable physical system, whose law governing the joint evolution in time of characteristic input variables $U(t)$ and output variables $Y(t)$, for example, can be algebraically modeled by a differential equation [LUE 79].

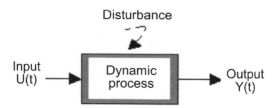

Figure 1.1. *Controllable dynamic process*

According to the simplifying hypotheses adopted for the mathematical representation of the dynamic processes studied in this book, these processes have the following traits:

a) They can be modeled using ordinary differential equations.

b) They are univariate, or, in other words, $U(t)$ and $Y(t)$ are scalar quantities.

c) They are of finite order, in which case the highest degree of the differential term (of the output quantity) contained in the characteristic dynamic equation is equal to n, with $1 \le n < \infty$.

d) They have constant parameters, and therefore, the response profile to an input signal does not depend on the instant when the input signal is applied.

e) They are linear in the vicinity of the fixed operating point, which means that the dynamic behavior to be studied is additive and homogeneous in the space of small variations $u(t)$ of $U(t)$ and $y(t)$ of $Y(t)$.

f) They are deterministic, in the sense that the characteristic quantities of the dynamic behavior are not probabilistic.

g) They are slightly disturbed, in which case the quantitative effect of an unknown disturbance at the output to be controlled is sufficiently limited and it can consequently be compensated in closed-loop by a robust control strategy.

h) They can be with or without pure input delay, in which case $\tau_0 \geq 0$. If $\tau_0 > 0$, an input quantity applied to the process at instant t has no effect until the previous instant $t + \tau_0$. This type of pure input delay phenomenon (or dead time) is quite present in processes in biology, ecology, transportation, signal processing and transmission, etc.

The basic notations employed are defined as follows:

$-\, U(t) \in \Re$: main scalar input;

$-\, Y(t) \in \Re$: scalar output;

$-\, \tilde{P} = \{\tilde{U}, \tilde{Y}\}$: rated operating point;

$-\, u(t), y(t), w(t)$: variations of $U(t)$ and $Y(t)$, respectively, around $\tilde{P} = \{\tilde{U}, \tilde{Y}\}$.

The following relation can therefore be written:

$$u = U - \tilde{U}, \quad y(t) = Y - \tilde{Y} \tag{1.1}$$

1.1.2. *Implications of hypotheses*

Hypotheses (a), (b) and (c) defined in section 1.1.1 entail that the general structure of the differential equations of the dynamic processes considered can be written as:

$$\frac{d^n Y(t)}{d\,t^n} = F\left(U(t-\tau_0), ..., \frac{d^m U\,(t-\tau_0)}{dt^m}, \ Y(t), ..., \frac{d^{n-1} Y\,(t)}{dt^{n-1}} \right) \tag{1.2}$$

with τ_0: pure delay time or dead time of input U.

Therefore, the rated operating point $\tilde{P} = \{\tilde{U}, \tilde{Y}\}$ defined by [1.1] is necessarily a solution of [1.2]. Consequently, relation [1.2] leads to relation [1.3]:

$$\frac{d^n \tilde{Y}(t)}{d\,t^n} = F\left(\tilde{U}(t - \tau_0), ..., \frac{d^m \tilde{U}(t - \tau_0)}{dt^m}, \tilde{Y}(t), ..., \frac{d^{n-1}\tilde{Y}(t)}{dt^{n-1}} \right) \qquad [1.3]$$

Hypothesis (e) stated in section 1.1.1 entails that expression [1.2] can be linearized around $\tilde{P} = \{\tilde{U}, \tilde{Y}\}$. Therefore, a first-order Taylor series expansion of [1.2], followed by the simplification of the result by replacing the right term of [1.2] with the equivalent left term, leads to the linear differential equation [1.4]:

$$\frac{d^n Y(t)}{dt^n} - \frac{d^n \tilde{Y}(t)}{dt^n} = \sum_{i=0}^{m} \left. \frac{\partial F(.)}{\partial\left(\dfrac{d^i U(t - \tau_0)}{dt^i} \right)} \right|_{\tilde{P}} \left(\frac{d^i (U(t-\tau_0) - \tilde{U}(t-\tau_0))}{dt^i} \right)$$

$$+ \sum_{j=0}^{n-1} \left. \frac{\partial F(.)}{\partial\left(\dfrac{d^j Y(t)}{dt^j} \right)} \right|_{\tilde{P}} \left(\frac{d^j (Y(t-\tau_0) - \tilde{Y}(t-\tau_0))}{dt^j} \right) \qquad [1.4]$$

Hypothesis (e) also entails that the initial conditions of small variations $u(t)$ and $y(t)$ yielded by [1.1] are null, this being due to the additive property in the space of small variations.

1.1.3. *Dynamic model: an automation perspective*

From the automation perspective, a dynamic model is a new mathematical representation of [1.4], whose algebraic structure can be directly treated by tools available in automation. It is the case of Matlab® [ATH 13]. The two types of dynamic models commonly used are the transfer function and the state model.

1.2. Transfer functions

1.2.1. *Existence conditions*

The existence conditions of the transfer function of a dynamic process from [1.4] are dictated by hypothesis (d) defined in section 1.1.1. In other words, the parameters of [1.4] are necessarily constant.

1.2.2. *Construction*

Introducing the notations of small variations in [1.4] yields:

$$
\frac{d^{n} y(t)}{dt^{n}} = \sum_{i=0}^{m} \left(\left. \frac{\partial F(.)}{\partial \left(\frac{d^{i} U(t-\tau_{0})}{dt^{i}} \right)} \right|_{\tilde{P}} \left(\frac{d^{i} \left(u(t-\tau_{0}) \right)}{dt^{i}} \right) \right)
$$

$$
+ \sum_{j=0}^{n-1} \left(\left. \frac{\partial F(.)}{\partial \left(\frac{d^{j} Y(t)}{dt^{j}} \right)} \right|_{\tilde{P}} \frac{d^{j} \left(u(t-\tau_{0}) \right)}{dt^{j}} \right)
$$

[1.5]

The application of Laplace transform to [1.5] yields:

$$
s^{n} Y(s) = \sum_{i=0}^{m} \left(\left. \frac{\partial F(.)}{\partial \left(\frac{d^{i} U(t-\tau_{0})}{dt^{i}} \right)} \right|_{\tilde{P}} s^{i} \right) U(s) e^{-\tau_{0} s}
$$

$$
+ \sum_{j=0}^{n-1} \left(\left. \frac{\partial F(.)}{\partial \left(\frac{d^{j} Y(t)}{dt^{j}} \right)} \right|_{\tilde{P}} s^{j} \right) Y(s)
$$

[1.6]

Then the factorization of terms common to U(s) and Y(s) in [1.6] leads to relation [1.7]:

$$
\left(s^n - \sum_{j=0}^{n-1} \left(\left.\frac{\partial F\,(.)}{\partial\left(\dfrac{d^{\,j}\,Y(t)}{dt^{\,j}}\right)}\right|_{\tilde{P}}\right) s^{\,j}\right) Y(s) = \sum_{i=0}^{m} \left(\left.\frac{\partial F\,(.)}{\partial\left(\dfrac{d^{\,i}\,U(t-\tau_0)}{dt^{\,i}}\right)}\right|_{\tilde{P}}\right) s^{\,i}\,U(s)\,e^{-\tau_0\,s} \qquad [1.7]
$$

Thus, in the frequency domain, the linear structure obtained for the small variations in the vicinity of the rated point can be written:

$$
Y(s) = \frac{\displaystyle\sum_{i=0}^{m} \left(\left.\frac{\partial F\,(.)}{\partial\left(\dfrac{d^{\,i}\,U(t-\tau_0)}{dt^{\,i}}\right)}\right|_{\tilde{P}}\right) s^{\,i}}{\displaystyle s^n - \sum_{j=0}^{n-1} \left(\left.\frac{\partial F\,(.)}{\partial\left(\dfrac{d^{\,j}\,Y(t)}{dt^{\,j}}\right)}\right|_{\tilde{P}}\right) s^{\,j}}\; U(s)\,e^{-\tau_0\,s} \qquad [1.8]
$$

Considering that:

$$
bi = \left.\frac{\partial F\,(.)}{\partial\left(\dfrac{d^{\,i}\,U(t-\tau_0)}{dt^{\,i}}\right)}\right|_{\tilde{P}}\;,\quad aj = -\left.\frac{\partial F\,(.)}{\partial\left(\dfrac{d^{\,j}\,Y(t)}{dt^{\,j}}\right)}\right|_{\tilde{P}} \qquad [1.9]
$$

the expression of the transfer function deduced from [1.9] can be written as:

$$
G_c\,(s) = \frac{Y(s)}{U(s)} \qquad [1.10]
$$

with $m \leq n$ (feasibility condition).

1.2.3. *General structure of a transfer function*

The general structure of a transfer function [1.10] of a dynamic process, which is deduced from [1.8] and [1.9], is written as:

$$G_c(s) = \frac{Y(s)}{U(s)} = \frac{b_m s^m + b_{m-1} s^{m-1} + \ldots + b_1 s + b_0^c}{s^n + a_{n-1} s^{n-1} + \ldots + a_1 s + a_0} e^{-\tau_0 s} \qquad [1.11]$$

1.2.4. *Tools for the analysis of the properties of transfer functions*

The main specialized tools for the analysis of properties of transfer functions are:

– step response diagrams, for the measurement of static gain, critical times (rise, response), overshoot, accuracy, etc.;

– Bode gain and phase diagrams, for the observation and estimation of static gain, cut-off frequencies, resonance frequencies and gain, bandwidth, etc.;

– Nyquist plot, for the observation and estimation of the gain margin (gain for which the phase is equal to $-\pi$), phase margin (phase for which the gain is equal to unity), resonance gain, etc.

These tools and many others are at present integrated into automatic CAD (Computer-Aided Design) tool ranges, such as Sisotool, LTIview and Matlab/ Simulink, in order to reduce the computer-aided design and simulation efforts of automatic feedback control systems.

1.2.5. *First- and second-order transfer functions*

First- and second-order transfer functions have great practical value. Indeed, their characteristic properties are analytically known. Moreover, they can be combined for the synthesis of transfer functions of order higher than 2.

A first-order (without zero) transfer function can be written as:

$$G_c(s) = \frac{Y(s)}{U(s)} = \frac{K_s}{1 + \tau s} \qquad [1.12]$$

with:

– K_s: static gain;

– τ: time constant.

Therefore, the response $y(t)$ of [1.12] to an input step signal $U(s) = E_0/s$, obtained from the inverse Laplace transform of $Y(s) = G_c(s)\,U(s)$, can be written as:

$$y(t) = \begin{cases} 0 \text{ if } t < \tau_0 \\[2mm] K_s\,E_0\left(1 - e^{-\frac{t-\tau_0}{\tau}}\right) \text{ if } t \geq \tau_0 \end{cases}$$

[1.13]

For a second-order system, it can be written:

$$G_c(s) = \frac{Y(s)}{U(s)} = \frac{K_s\,\omega_n^2}{s^2 + 2\xi\omega_n s + \omega_n^2}$$

[1.14]

with:

– K_s: static gain;

– ω_n : natural angular frequency;

– ξ : damping coefficient.

In this case, the inverse Laplace transform of $Y(s)$ leads to equation [1.15], $y(t)$ for a step input $U(s) = E_0/s$ [KAT 90]:

$$\begin{cases} \xi < 1: \quad y(t) = K_s\,E_0 \\[2mm] \quad \left(1 - \dfrac{e^{-\xi\omega_n(t-\tau_0)}}{\sqrt{1-\xi^2}}\,\sin\left(\omega_n\sqrt{1-\xi^2}\,(t-\tau_0) + \tan^{-1}\left(\dfrac{\sqrt{1-\xi^2}}{\xi}\right)\right)\right) \\[6mm] \xi = 1: \quad y(t) = 1 - e^{-\omega_n t}(1 + \omega_n t) \\[2mm] \xi > 1: \quad y(t) = K_s\,E_0 \\[2mm] \quad \left(1 + \dfrac{\omega_n}{2\sqrt{\xi^2-1}}\left(\dfrac{e^{-\left(\xi\omega_n + \omega_n\sqrt{\xi^2-1}\right)t}}{\xi\omega_n + \omega_n\sqrt{\xi^2-1}} - \dfrac{e^{-\left(\xi\omega_n - \omega_n\sqrt{\xi^2-1}\right)t}}{\xi\omega_n - \omega_n\sqrt{\xi^2-1}}\right)\right) \end{cases}$$

[1.15]

Figure 1.2 presents the examples of graphic profiles of responses to a step E_0 (with $y(\infty) = K_s\,E_0 = 1$) of simple dynamic systems. Then Figure 1.3 presents the corresponding Bode diagrams.

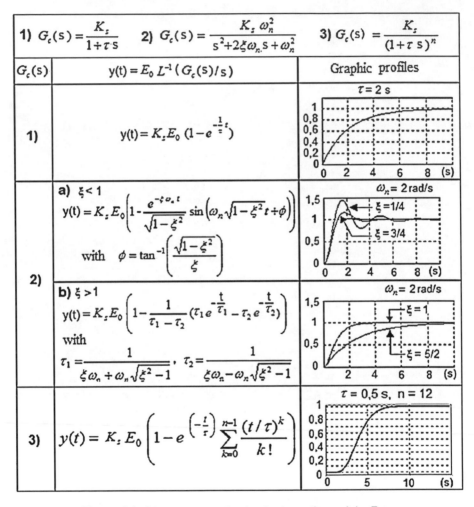

1) $G_c(s) = \dfrac{K_s}{1+\tau s}$	2) $G_c(s) = \dfrac{K_s\,\omega_n^2}{s^2 + 2\xi\omega_n s + \omega_n^2}$		3) $G_c(s) = \dfrac{K_s}{(1+\tau s)^n}$
$G_c(s)$	$y(t) = E_0\,L^{-1}(G_c(s)/s)$		Graphic profiles
1)	$y(t) = K_s E_0\left(1 - e^{-\frac{1}{\tau}t}\right)$		
2)	a) $\xi < 1$ $y(t) = K_s E_0\left[1 - \dfrac{e^{-\xi\omega_n t}}{\sqrt{1-\xi^2}}\sin\left(\omega_n\sqrt{1-\xi^2}\,t + \phi\right)\right]$ with $\phi = \tan^{-1}\left(\dfrac{\sqrt{1-\xi^2}}{\xi}\right)$		
	b) $\xi > 1$ $y(t) = K_s E_0\left[1 - \dfrac{1}{\tau_1 - \tau_2}\left(\tau_1 e^{-\frac{t}{\tau_1}} - \tau_2 e^{-\frac{t}{\tau_2}}\right)\right]$ with $\tau_1 = \dfrac{1}{\xi\omega_n + \omega_n\sqrt{\xi^2-1}}$, $\tau_2 = \dfrac{1}{\xi\omega_n - \omega_n\sqrt{\xi^2-1}}$		
3)	$y(t) = K_s E_0\left(1 - e^{\left(-\frac{t}{\tau}\right)}\sum_{k=0}^{n-1}\dfrac{(t/\tau)^k}{k!}\right)$		

Figure 1.2. *Step response to simple dynamic models. For a color version of this figure, see www.iste.co.uk/mbihi/automation.zip*

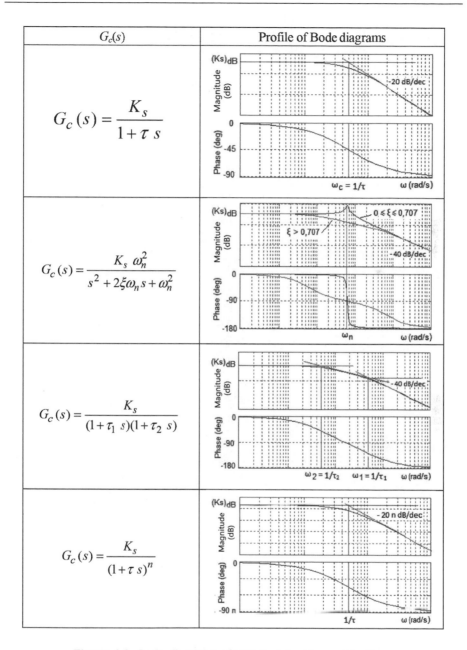

$G_c(s)$	Profile of Bode diagrams
$$G_c(s) = \dfrac{K_s}{1 + \tau\, s}$$	
$$G_c(s) = \dfrac{K_s\, \omega_n^2}{s^2 + 2\xi\omega_n s + \omega_n^2}$$	
$$G_c(s) = \dfrac{K_s}{(1 + \tau_1\, s)(1 + \tau_2\, s)}$$	
$$G_c(s) = \dfrac{K_s}{(1 + \tau\, s)^n}$$	

Figure 1.3. *Bode diagrams of simple dynamic models. For a color version of this figure, see www.iste.co.uk/mbihi/automation.zip*

Moreover, Table 1.1 summarizes the basic characteristic properties that result in each case.

Finally, the damped model of n identical poles (without zero) can be written in the following form:

$$G_c(s) = \frac{Y(s)}{E_0(s)} = \frac{K_s}{(1+\tau s)^n} \qquad [1.16]$$

It is important to note that, in experimental modeling, the basis of well-known graphic profiles, summarized in Figure 1.2, is an important source of inspiration when choosing an appropriate structure of representation of a real dynamic process to be modeled. This important remark will be revisited in chapter 2.

Properties	First-order process	Second-order process
Static gain	Ks	Ks
Bandwidth (cut-off frequency)	$f_b = \dfrac{1}{2\pi\tau}$	$f_b = \dfrac{\omega_n}{2\pi}\sqrt{1-2\xi^2 + \sqrt{4\xi^4 - 4\xi^2 + 2}}$
Overshoot	–	$\log(d) = -\dfrac{\xi\pi}{\sqrt{1-\xi^2}}$ if $\xi < 1$
Rise time	–	$T_m = \dfrac{\pi}{\omega_n\sqrt{1-\xi^2}}$ if $\xi < 1$
Response time at r %	$Tr = \tau\log\left(\dfrac{100}{100-r}\right)$	$T_r(\%) = \dfrac{\log\left(\dfrac{100}{r}\right)}{\xi\omega_n}$
Gain margin	$g_m = +\infty$	$g_m = +\infty$
Phase margin	$+90°$	–

Table 1.1. *Basic properties of dynamic processes of first and second orders*

1.3. State models

1.3.1. *Definition*

The state $X(t)$ of a dynamic process designates a quantity of information that is sufficient to predict at each instant t its future behavior. Figure 1.4 presents the variables of a dynamic process described in the state space.

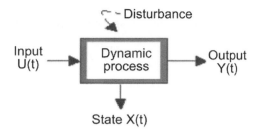

Figure 1.4. *Variables of a dynamic process in the state space*

In fact, the state model of a dynamic process corresponds to a new representation of [1.2] in a state space χ. A simple technique for building a state model from [1.2] involves drawing up an operational scheme, then making the appropriate choice of state variables, in order to write the state equations of the new model. It can already be anticipated at this stage that, based on [1.2], it is possible to build an infinity of state model representations of a dynamic process.

1.3.2. *Illustrative example*

Let us consider, without any loss of generality, a simplified case of [1.2], given by [1.17]:

$$\frac{d^n Y(t)}{dt^n} = F\left(U(t-\tau_0), Y(t), \frac{dY(t)}{dt}, \dots, \frac{d^{n-1}Y(t)}{dt^{n-1}} \right)$$ [1.17]

In these conditions, Figure 1.5 represents the operational calculus scheme of [1.17], which is obtained by means of simple algebraic operators (integrators, adders, etc.). For the sake of clarity, the notation $Y^{(k)}(t) = d^k Y(t) / dt^k k = 1, 2, \dots, n$ has been adopted in this figure.

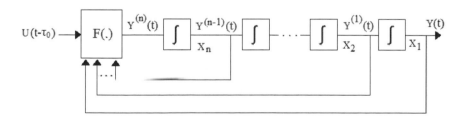

Figure 1.5. *Operational calculus scheme for a dynamic model*

Let $X_1(t)$, $X_2(t)$, ..., $X_e(t)$ be the choice of state variables indicated in this scheme and let us consider $X(t) = [X_1(t) \ X_2(t) \ ... \ X_e(t)]^T$. In these conditions, a new representation of [1.17] from Figure 1.5 is given by [1.18]:

$$
\left\{
\begin{aligned}
\frac{dX(t)}{dt} &= \begin{bmatrix} \dfrac{dX_1(t)}{dt} \\[2mm] \dfrac{dX_2(t)}{dt} \\ ... \\[2mm] \dfrac{dX_n(t)}{dt} \end{bmatrix} = \begin{bmatrix} X_2(t) \\ X_3(t) \\ ... \\ F(X(t), U(t-\tau_0), t) \end{bmatrix} \quad \text{(a)} \\
Y(t) &= X_1(t) \quad\quad\quad\quad\quad\quad\quad\quad\quad\quad \text{(b)}
\end{aligned}
\right.
\qquad [1.18]
$$

At this stage, it is therefore important to note that the choice of state variables for a dynamic process is not unique, and that some chosen states may be devoid of physical sense. Moreover, the elaboration of nonlinear state model [1.18] from [1.17] does not require linearity and time-invariance hypotheses.

1.3.3. *General structure of the state model*

The general structure of the state model of a univariate and time-invariant dynamic system can be written as:

$$
\left\{
\begin{aligned}
\frac{dX(t)}{dt} &= f(X(t), U(t-\tau_0), t) \\
Y(t) &= h(X(t), U(t-\tau_0), t)
\end{aligned}
\right.
\qquad [1.19]
$$

with:

- $X(t)$: state variable (dimension n);

- $U(t)$: scalar command quantity;

- $Y(t)$: scalar output quantity (dimension p);

- $f(.)$: vector function (generally nonlinear);

- $h(.)$: scalar function (generally nonlinear).

Thus, in contrast to the dynamic models described by transfer functions, state representations are a less restrictive approach to modeling.

Indeed, modeling in state space facilitates the study of:

– a wide variety of types of processes: univariate or multivariable, linear or nonlinear, time-variant or time-invariant, deterministic or stochastic;

– changes in state representation, with the purpose of elaborating canonical state models that are easier to handle and to analyze;

– characteristic properties of stability, controllability, stabilizability, observability and detectability;

– advanced structures of controllers.

It is nevertheless worth mentioning that the practical use in real time of a state model requires real state sensors or state observers otherwise.

1.4. Linear state models with constant parameters

There is great practical interest in linear state models with constant parameters. Indeed, the study of more complex state models requires knowledge of their properties.

1.4.1. Linearization-based construction

A linear state model can be elaborated by applying Taylor series expansion to [1.19] in the vicinity of an operating point $\tilde{P} = (\tilde{U}, \tilde{X}, \tilde{Y})$. Indeed, given $u(t)$, $x(t)$ and $y(t)$, the corresponding small variations in $U(t)$, $X(t)$ and $Y(t)$, respectively, around the operating point, defined by [1.20]:

$$\begin{cases} x(t) = X(t) - \tilde{X}(t) \\ u(t) = U(t) - \tilde{U}(t) \\ y(t) = Y(t) - \tilde{Y}(t) \end{cases} \qquad [1.20]$$

then the Taylor series expansion of [1.1] of [1.19] in the constant parameter hypothesis leads to [1.21], and then to [1.22]:

$$\begin{cases} \dfrac{dX(t)}{dt} = f(X, \tilde{U}) + \left(\dfrac{\partial f(.)}{\partial X(t)}\right)_{\tilde{P}} (X(t) - \tilde{X}) + \left(\dfrac{\partial f(.)}{\partial U(t-\tau_0)}\right)_{\tilde{P}} (U(t-\tau_0) - \tilde{U}) \\[4mm] Y(t) = h(\tilde{X}, \tilde{U}) + \left(\dfrac{\partial h(.)}{\partial X(t)}\right)_{\tilde{P}} (X(t) - \tilde{X}) + \left(\dfrac{\partial h(.)}{\partial U(t-\tau_0)}\right)_{\tilde{P}} (U(t-\tau_0) - \tilde{U}) \end{cases} \qquad [1.21]$$

$$\begin{cases} \dfrac{dX(t)}{dt} - f(\tilde{X},\tilde{U}) = \left(\dfrac{\partial f(.)}{\partial X(t)}\right)_{\tilde{P}} (X(t)-\tilde{X}) + \left(\dfrac{\partial f(.)}{\partial U(t-\tau_0)}\right)_{\tilde{P}} (U(t-\tau_0)-\tilde{U}) \\[4mm] Y(t) - h(\tilde{X},\tilde{U}) = \left(\dfrac{\partial h(.)}{\partial X(t)}\right)_{\tilde{P}} (X(t)-\tilde{X}) + \left(\dfrac{\partial h(.)}{\partial U(t-\tau_0)}\right)_{\tilde{P}} (U(t-\tau_0)-\tilde{U}) \end{cases} \quad [1.22]$$

Since the operating point $\tilde{P}$ is necessarily a solution of [1.23]:

$$\begin{cases} \dfrac{d\tilde{X}(t)}{dt} = f(\tilde{X},\tilde{U}) \\[4mm] \tilde{Y}(t) = h(\tilde{X},\tilde{U}) \end{cases} \quad [1.23]$$

then the insertion in [1.22] of the terms on the left of [1.23] yields [1.24]:

$$\begin{cases} \dfrac{dX(t)}{dt} - \dfrac{d\tilde{X}(t)}{dt} = \left(\dfrac{\partial f(.)}{\partial X(t)}\right)_{\tilde{P}(t)} (X(t)-\tilde{X}) + \left(\dfrac{\partial f(.)}{\partial U(t-\tau_0)}\right)_{\tilde{P}(t)} (U(t-\tau_0)-\tilde{U}) \\[4mm] Y(t) - \tilde{Y}(t)) = \left(\dfrac{\partial h(.)}{\partial X(t)}\right)_{\tilde{P}(t)} (X(t)-\tilde{X}) + \left(\dfrac{\partial h(.)}{\partial U(t-\tau_0)}\right)_{\tilde{P}(t)} (U(t-\tau_0)-\tilde{U}) \end{cases} \quad [1.24]$$

1.4.2. *Structure of a linear state model with constant parameters*

A linear state model with constant parameters, obtained by inserting in [1.24] the small variations defined by [1.20], can be written as:

$$\begin{cases} \dfrac{dx(t)}{dt} = \left(\dfrac{\partial f(.)}{\partial X(t)}\right)_{\tilde{P}} x(t) + \left(\dfrac{\partial f(.)}{\partial U(t)}\right)_{\tilde{P}} u(t-\tau_0) \\[4mm] y = \left(\dfrac{\partial h(.)}{\partial X(t)}\right)_{\tilde{P}} x(t) + \left(\dfrac{\partial h(.)}{\partial U(t)}\right)_{\tilde{P}} u(t-\tau_0) \end{cases} \quad [1.25]$$

Finally, considering that:

$$\begin{cases} A_c = \left(\dfrac{\partial f(.)}{\partial X(t)}\right)_{\tilde{P}}, \; B_c = \left(\dfrac{\partial f(.)}{\partial U(t)}\right)_{\tilde{P}} \\[4mm] C_c = \left(\dfrac{\partial h(.)}{\partial X(t)}\right)_{\tilde{P}}, \; D_c = \left(\dfrac{\partial h(.)}{\partial U(t)}\right)_{\tilde{P}} \end{cases} \quad [1.26]$$

then the linear state model of a dynamic process with constant parameters is given by [1.27]:

$$\begin{cases} \dfrac{dx(t)}{dt} = A_c\, x(t) + B_c\, u(t - \tau_0) \\[2mm] y = C_c\, x(t) + D_c u(t - \tau_0) \end{cases} \qquad [1.27]$$

The parameters of [1.27] have the following significance:

– A_c: state matrix of order n x n;

– B_c: input coupling gain (column vector of order n x 1);

– C_c: output coupling gain (line vector of order 1 x n);

– D_c: direct input to output transfer gain (scalar).

Moreover, the descriptive block diagram of a state model described by [1.27] is represented in Figure 1.6.

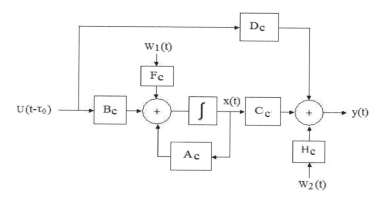

Figure 1.6. *Block diagram of a linear state model with constant parameters*

At this point, it is important to mention that the application of Laplace transform to [1.27], followed by the elimination of X(s) between the state and output equations, then by the factorization of terms in U(s) and Y(s), leads to a transfer function given by [1.28]:

$$G_c(s) = \frac{Y(s)}{U(s)} = \left(C_c \left(s\, I_n - A_c \right)^{-1} B_c + D_c \right) e^{-\tau_0 s} \qquad [1.28]$$

Thus, it becomes clear that the transfer function of a linear dynamic process with constant parameters represents the controllable and observable part of that process. In these conditions, the numerator and the denominator of the rational part of [1.28] should nevertheless have no common roots.

1.4.3. Properties of a model without pure input delay ($\tau_0 = 0$)

The basic properties of [1.27] with ($\tau_0 = 0$) are:

– stability;

– controllability;

– stabilizability;

– observability;

– detectability.

An in-depth study of these properties is explained in detail in the theory of linear dynamic systems [CHE 84].

1.4.3.1. Stability

In the internal sense, stability designates the ability of a dynamic system to return to the equilibrium state after a transient disturbance.

The stability test of [1.27] is positive if all the eigenvalues of A_c, which coincide with the roots of the characteristic polynomial, have negative real parts. Otherwise, the dynamic process model is not stable.

1.4.3.2. Controllability

Controllability designates the property of existence of a command $U(t)$ allowing [1.27] to evolve in a finite time from an initial state $x(t_0)$ to a final state $x(t_f)$.

The controllability test of [1.27] is positive if one of the following equivalent conditions is satisfied:

– rank of the controllability matrix:

$$M_C = \begin{bmatrix} B_c & A_c B_c & A_c^2 B_c & \cdots & A_c^{n-1} B_c \end{bmatrix}$$

[1.29]

is equal to n;

– For any eigenvalue λ of A_c, the rank of the associated matrix:

$$M_{O\lambda} = \begin{bmatrix} \lambda\, I_n - A_c & B_c \end{bmatrix} \qquad [1.30]$$

is equal to n.

Otherwise, [1.27] is uncontrollable.

1.4.3.3. *Stabilizability*

A dynamic model is stabilizable if it is not controllable and if all uncontrollable eigenvalues of A_c are stable (positive real part).

1.4.3.4. *Observability*

Observability designates the property of reconstruction in finite time of the state $x(t_0)$ from any reachable state $x(t_a)$, knowing the command $U(t)$ that has generated the passage of [1.27] from the initial state $x(t_0)$ to $x(t_a)$.

The observability test of [1.27] is positive if one of the following equivalent conditions is met:

– Rank of the observability matrix:

$$M_O = \begin{bmatrix} C_c \\ C_c A_c \\ C_c A_c^2 \\ \cdots \\ C_c A_c^{n-1} \end{bmatrix} \qquad [1.31]$$

is equal to n;

– For any eigenvalue λ of A_c, the rank of the associated matrix:

$$M_{O\lambda} = \begin{bmatrix} \lambda\, I_n - A_c \\ C_c \end{bmatrix} \qquad [1.32]$$

is equal to n.

Otherwise, [1.27] is not observable.

1.4.3.5. *Detectability*

A dynamic model is detectable if it is not observable and if all unobservable eigenvalues are stable (positive).

1.5. Similarity transformation

The similarity transformation of a state model defined by [1.33]:

$$\begin{cases} \dfrac{dx(t)}{dt} = A_c \, x(t) + B_c \, u(t - \tau_0) \\ y = C_c \, x(t) + D_c u(t - \tau_0) \end{cases} \tag{1.33}$$

enables the creation of a new state representation equivalent to [1.33] by means of a regular matrix P of linear transformation $z(t) = Px(t)$, where $z(t)$ becomes the new state vector considered.

Thus, knowing that $x(t) = P^{-1}(t) \, z(t)$, after arrangement and simplification of terms the state model [1.33] becomes:

$$\begin{cases} \dfrac{dz(t)}{dt} = PA_c P^{-1} \, z(t) + P \, B_c \, u(t - \tau_0) \\ y = C_c \, P^{-1} x(t) + D_c u(t - \tau_0) \end{cases} \tag{1.34}$$

Considering $\tilde{A}_c = PA_c P^{-1}, \tilde{B}_c = P \, B_c, \tilde{F}_c = P \, F_c, \tilde{C}_c = C_c \, P^{-1}$, then [1.34] becomes:

$$\begin{cases} \dfrac{dz(t)}{dt} = \tilde{A}_c z(t) + \tilde{B}_c \, u(t - \tau_0) \\ y = \tilde{C}_c \, x(t) + D_c u(t - \tau_0) \end{cases} \tag{1.35}$$

Thus, [1.33] and [1.35] are similar state representations. Moreover, among all possible similarity transformations, the most interesting in practice are those that lead to canonical structures.

Indeed, canonical structures are easier to treat and analyze. It is, for example, the case of Jordan canonical structures, for which the columns of matrix $Q = P^{-1}$ are formed of generalized eigenvectors in Jordan form associated with the eigenvalues of matrix A_c.

1.6. Exercises and solutions

Exercise 1.1.

A dynamic process, with $U(t)$ as input quantity and $Y(t)$ as output quantity, is modeled by the following differential equation:

$$\frac{dY(t)}{dt} = \sin\left(Y(t)\right) + 2\,U(t - \tau_0)$$

with $\tau_0 > 0$.

1) What does the parameter τ_0 represent?

2) What are the structural properties of this dynamic system?

3) Prove that a nominal profile of the said dynamic system is given by:

$$\tilde{Y}(t) = 100\,\pi, \quad \frac{d\tilde{Y}(t)}{dt} = 0 \text{ and } \tilde{U}(t - \tau_0) = -\frac{\sin(100\,\pi)}{2}$$

4) Find the law of linear approximation around this nominal profile as a function of small variations $y(t)$, $u(t)$ of the quantities $Y(t)$ and $U(t)$, respectively.

Solution – Exercise 1.1.

The given differential equation can be written as:

$$\frac{dY(t)}{dt} = \sin\left(Y(t)\right) + 2\,U(t - \tau_0)$$

1) Parameter τ_0 represents the pure input delay $u(t)$.

2) Structural properties: this dynamic process is:

- deterministic;

- univariate;

- with pure input delay;

- with constant parameters;

- nonlinear.

3) Since $\tilde{Y}(t) = 100\,\pi$, $\dfrac{d\tilde{Y}(t)}{dt} = 0$, $\tilde{U}(t - \tau_0) = -\dfrac{\sin(100\,\pi)}{2}$, it is then sufficient to verify that the profile thus given is a particular solution of the proposed differential equation. It is indeed easy to verify that:

$$\sin\left(\tilde{Y}(t)\right) + 2\,\tilde{U}(t - \tau_0) = s\,\mathrm{in}(100\,\pi) - 2\,\frac{\sin(100\,\pi)}{2} = 0 = \frac{d\tilde{Y}(t)}{dt}$$

Therefore, the given nominal profile is a solution of the proposed differential equation.

4) Law of linear approximation:

Let u and y be the respective variations of $U(t)$ and $Y(t)$ around the nominal profile:

$$\frac{dy(t)}{dt} = \left.\frac{\partial \sin\left(Y(t)\right)}{\partial Y(t)}\right|_{\tilde{P}(t)} y(t) + 2\left.\frac{\partial U(t - \tau_0)}{\partial U(t - \tau_0)}\right|_{\tilde{P}(t)} u(t - \tau_0)$$

$$= \cos\left(\tilde{Y}(t)\right) y(t) + 2\,u(t - \tau_0)$$

$$= \cos(100\pi)y(t) + 2u(t - \tau_0) = y(t) + 2u(t - \tau_0)$$

Exercise 1.2.

The response $y(t)$ of a dynamic operator with constant parameter(s), under a Dirac unit impulse $\delta(t)$, applied at instant $t_0 = 0$, corresponds to Figure 1.7:

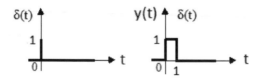

Figure 1.7. *Response of a dynamic system with input δ(t)*

It should be recalled that $\delta(t) = 1$, if $t = 0$, and $\delta(t) = 0$ otherwise.

1) What is the value of the input dead time?

2) Find the expression of $y(t)$.

3) Find the transfer function of the system.

4) Represent the response of the same system when the same impulse is applied again at instant $t_2 = 4$ s.

Solution – Exercise 1.2.

1) The value of the input dead time is $\tau_0 = 0$ s.

2) Expression of $y(t)$:

$y(t) = u(t) - u(t - 1)$, where $u(t)$ designates the unit step function.

3) Transfer function B(s) of the system:

Knowing that function B(s) corresponds to the Laplace transform of the pulse response, it can be written:

$$B(s) = L(y(t)) = L(u(t) - u(t - 1)) = 1/s - e^{-2s}/s = (1 - e^{-s})/s$$

4) Response when the same impulse is applied once again after 4 s: starting from the instant 4 s, the profile of $y(t)$ represented in Figure 1.8 is unchanged, since the system is time invariant.

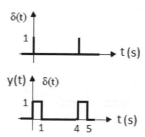

Figure 1.8. *Profile of y(t)*

Exercise 1.3.

A dynamic system is described by the differential equation:

$$\frac{d^3Y(t)}{dt^3} - \frac{d^2Y(t)}{dt^2} - 2\frac{dY(t)}{dt} - 4\,Y(t) = U(t-2)$$

with:

  – U(t): input quantity;

  – Y(t): output quantity.

1) What are the structural properties of this dynamic system?

2) Establish the corresponding operational calculus scheme.

3) Given the state variables $X_1(t) = Y(t)$, $X_2(t) = Y^{(1)}(t)$ and $X_3(t) = Y^{(2)}(t)$, find the state model of the system.

Solution – Exercise 1.3.

The given differential equation can be written as:

$$\frac{d^3 Y(t)}{dt^3} - \frac{d^2 Y(t)}{dt^2} - 2\frac{dY(t)}{dt} - 4\, Y(t) = U(t-2)$$

1) Structural properties of this dynamic system:

  - univariate;

  - linear;

  - with constant parameters;

  - deterministic.

2) Operational calculus scheme (see Figure 1.9). For the sake of clarity, the relation $Y^{(k)}(t) = d^k Y / dt^k$ has been written for $k = 1, 2$ and 3.

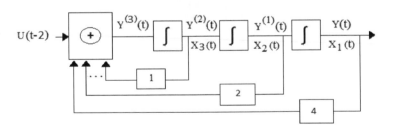

Figure 1.9. *Operational calculus scheme*

3) System state model with state variables $X_1(t) = Y(t)$, $X_2(t) = Y^{(1)}(t)$ and $X_3(t) = Y^{(2)}(t)$:

Based on the scheme, the following relations can be written:

$$\frac{dX_1(t)}{dt} = X_2(t), \quad \frac{dX_2(t)}{dt} = X_3(t),$$

$$\frac{dX_3(t)}{dt} = X_3(t) + 2X_2(t) + 4X_1(t) + U(t-2)$$

Therefore:

$$\frac{dX(t)}{dt} = \begin{bmatrix} \dfrac{dX_1(t)}{dt} \\ \dfrac{dX_2((t)}{dt} \\ \dfrac{dX_3(t)}{dt} \end{bmatrix} = \begin{bmatrix} 0 & 1 & 0 \\ 0 & 0 & 1 \\ 4 & 2 & 1 \end{bmatrix} \begin{bmatrix} X_1(t) \\ X_2(t) \\ X_3(t) \end{bmatrix} + \begin{bmatrix} 0 \\ 0 \\ 1 \end{bmatrix} U(t-2)$$

Exercise 1.4.

A simple pendulum schematized in Figure 1.10 is subjected to a motor torque $C_m(t)$.

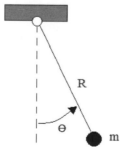

Figure 1.10. Schematic representation of a simple pendulum

Parameters R and m denote the length and the estimated point mass, respectively, K_f and g being the friction coefficient and the gravitational acceleration, respectively.

Considering $X = \Theta$ (motion angle) as an angular position variable, the dynamic behavior of this pendulum is given in these conditions by the following differential equation:

$$m R^2 \frac{dX^2 (t)}{dt^2} + K_f \frac{dX(t)}{dt} + m R g \sin(X(t)) = C_m(t)$$

1) What are the structural properties of this differential equation?

2) Using the small variations around the rated operating point defined by the respective quantities $\tilde{X}^{(2)} = 0$, $\tilde{X}^{(1)} = 0$, $\tilde{X} = \pi/4$ and $\tilde{C}_m = (m\, g\, R)\sqrt{2}/2$, verify that this rated operating point belongs to the trajectory of the angular motion of this pendulum.

3) Find the equivalent linear equation in the vicinity of the rated point.

4) Calculate the expression of the transfer function corresponding to the output $Y(t) = X(t)$.

5) Find the expression of the static gain K_s of this pendulum.

Solution – Exercise 1.4.

$$m R^2 X^{(2)}(t) + K_f X^{(1)}(t)$$
$$+ m R g \sin(X(t)) = C_m(t)$$

1) Structural properties of this differential equation:

– univariate;

– nonlinear;

– time-invariant;

– deterministic.

2) Verification of the rated operating point defined by the respective quantities $\tilde{X}^{(2)} = 0$, $\tilde{X}^{(1)} = 0$, $\tilde{X} = \pi/4$ and $\tilde{C}_m = (m\, g\, R)\sqrt{2}/2$.

Indeed, the following relation can be written:

$$m R^2 \underbrace{\tilde{X}^{(2)}(t)}_{0} + K_f \underbrace{\tilde{X}^{(1)}(t)}_{0} + m R g \sin(\tilde{X}(t)) = mgR \underbrace{\sin(\pi/4)}_{\frac{\sqrt{2}}{2}} = \tilde{C}_m(t)$$

3) The dynamic equation of the system can be written in the form:

$$X^{(2)}(t) = -\frac{K_f}{mR^2} X^{(1)}(t) - \frac{g}{R} \sin(X(t)) + \frac{C_m(t)}{mR^2} = F(X^{(1)}(t), X(t), C_m(t))$$

Therefore:

$$\left.\frac{\partial F(.)}{\partial X^{(j)}(t)}\right|_{\tilde{p}} = -\frac{K_f}{m R^2}$$

$$\left.\frac{\partial F(.)}{\partial X(t)}\right|_{\tilde{p}} = -\frac{g}{R} \cos(\tilde{X}(t)) = 0$$

$$\left.\frac{\partial F(.)}{\partial C_m(t)}\right|_{\tilde{p}} = \frac{1}{m R^2}$$

Therefore:

$$x^{(2)}(t) = -\frac{K_f}{mR^2} x^{(1)}(t) - \frac{g}{R} \cos(\tilde{X}(t))\, x(t) + \frac{C_m(t)}{mR^2}$$

Then:

$$x^{(2)}(t) = -\frac{K_f}{mR^2} x^{(1)}(t) - \frac{g}{R}\frac{\sqrt{2}}{2} x(t) + \frac{C_m(t)}{mR^2}$$

4) Expression of the transfer function corresponding to $Y(t) = X(t)$: by applying Laplace transform, we obtain:

$$G_c(s) = \frac{Y(s)}{C_m(s)} = \frac{1/(m R^2)}{s^2 + \dfrac{K_f}{mR^2} s + \dfrac{\sqrt{2}}{2}\dfrac{g}{R}}$$

5) Expression of static gain:

$$K_S = G_c(0) = \frac{1/(m R^2)}{\dfrac{\sqrt{2}}{2}\dfrac{g}{R}} = \frac{2}{\sqrt{2}}\left(\frac{1}{g\, m\, R}\right)$$

Exercise 1.5.

Let us consider a robotic axis represented in Figure 1.11. The motor torque F(t) of the actuator drives the moving arm *through* an elastic transmission connection.

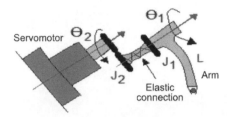

Figure 1.11. *Schematic representation of a robotic axis*

The kinematic equations of motion of this robotic axis, as a result of the application of Lagrange laws, are considered to have the following form:

$$
\begin{cases}
\dfrac{d\theta_1^2(t)}{dt^2} = -\dfrac{m}{J_1} g\, L \sin(\theta_1(t)) - \dfrac{K}{J_1}((\theta_1(t) - \theta_2(t))) \\[3mm]
\dfrac{d\theta_2^2(t)}{dt^2} = \dfrac{K}{J_2}((\theta_1(t) - \theta_2(t))) + \dfrac{F(t)}{J_2}
\end{cases}
$$

with:

- L: length of the driven arm;

- m: estimated point mass of the driven arm;

- K: stiffness coefficient of the elastic connection;

- g: gravitational acceleration;

- J_1: moment of inertia of the actuator shaft;

- J_2: moment of inertia of the arm.

1) Represent the operational calculus scheme of this dynamic system.

2) Let us consider the state variables $X_1(t) = \theta_1(t)$, $X_2(t) = \dfrac{\theta_1(t)}{dt}$, $X_3(t) = \theta_2(t)$, $X_4(t) = \dfrac{d\theta_2(t)}{dt}$. Find the corresponding nonlinear state model.

3) Find the equivalent linear state model around a rated point $\tilde{P} = [\tilde{X}_1 = 0 \ \tilde{X}_2$ $\tilde{X}_3 \ \tilde{X}_4 \ \tilde{F}]^T$.

Solution – Exercise 1.5.

The kinematic equations of motion of the robotic axis are:

$$\begin{cases} \theta_1^{(2)}(t) = -\dfrac{m}{J_1} g \, L \, \sin(\theta_1(t)) - \dfrac{K}{J_1}((\theta_1(t) - \theta_2(t)) \\ \theta_2^{(2)}(t) = \dfrac{K}{J_2}((\theta_1(t) - \theta_2(t)) + \dfrac{F(t)}{J_2} \end{cases}$$

1) The operational calculus scheme of the robot corresponds to Figure 1.12.

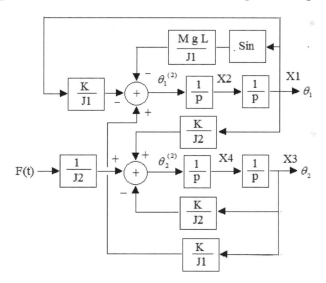

Figure 1.12. *Operational calculus scheme of the robot*

2) Let us consider the state variables:

$$X_1(t) = \theta_1(t), \quad X_2(t) = \theta_1^{(1)}(t), \quad X_3(t) = \theta_2(t), \quad X_4(t) = \theta_2^{(1)}(t).$$

The nonlinear state model is written as:

$$\begin{cases} \dfrac{dX1}{dt} = X2 \\[2mm] \dfrac{dX2}{dt} = -\dfrac{m}{J_1}\, g\, L\, \sin(X1) - \dfrac{K}{J_1}(X1 - X3) \\[2mm] \dfrac{dX3}{dt} = X4 \\[2mm] \dfrac{dX4(t)}{dt} = \dfrac{K}{J_2}(X1 - X3) + \dfrac{1}{J_2}F(t) \end{cases}$$

3) Find the equivalent linear state model around the rated point $\tilde{P} = [\, \tilde{X}_1\ \tilde{X}_2\ \tilde{X}_3\ \tilde{X}_4\ \tilde{F}\,]^{\mathrm{T}}$. The equivalent linear model around the point $\tilde{P}$ is written as follows, as a function of small variations x_1, x_2, x_3, x_4 and f:

$$\begin{cases} \dfrac{dx1}{dt} = x2 \\[2mm] \dfrac{dx2}{dt} = -\left(\dfrac{m\, g\, L + K}{J_1}\right) x1 + \dfrac{K}{J_1} x3 \\[2mm] \dfrac{dX3}{dt} = x4 \\[2mm] \dfrac{dX4(t)}{dt} = \dfrac{K}{J_2}(x1 - x3) + \dfrac{1}{J_2} f(t) \end{cases}$$

Exercise 1.6.

List the hypotheses required for the construction of a dynamic model of LTI type.

Solution – Exercise 1.6.

List of hypotheses required for the construction of an LTI model of a dynamic process:

– rated profile $\tilde{P}(t)$ is a fixed point $\tilde{P}$;

– linear profile in the vicinity of the rated point $\tilde{P}$;

– time-invariant process;

– null initial conditions for small variations.

Exercise 1.7.

A deterministic LTI dynamic process with input delay admits $u(t)$, $x(t)$ and $y(t)$ as input, state and output variables, respectively. It can be modeled by a transfer function or by a state model.

1) Write the general expression of this transfer function.

2) Write the general expression of this state model.

3) List the weaknesses of an open-loop control law of this process.

Solution – Exercise 1.7.

1) General structure and interpretation of the transfer function:

$$G_c(s) = \frac{Y(s)}{U(s)} = \frac{b_m s^m + b_{m-1} s^{m-1} + ... + b_1 s + b_0}{s^n + a_{n-1} s^{n-1} + ... + a_1 s + a_0} \, e^{-\tau_0 s}$$

$G_c(s)$ represents the Laplace transform of the pulse response.

2) General structure and interpretation of the state model:

$$\begin{cases} \dfrac{dx(t)}{dt} = A_c \, x(t) + B_c \, u(t - \tau_0) \\ y = C_c \, x(t) + D_c u(t - \tau_0) \end{cases}$$

with:

 – A_c : state matrix;

 – B_c : input matrix;

 – C_c : output matrix;

 – D_c : direct input-to-output transfer matrix.

3) List of weaknesses of an open-loop control law of this process:

 - poor performances in ideal conditions (without disturbance or noise);

 - sensitivity to disturbances;

 - sensitivity to noise.

Exercise 1.8.

The transfer function $G_c(s)$ of a dynamic process can be used to find, either directly or by calculation, several intrinsic quantities of the modeled process. Which ones?

Solution – Exercise 1.8.

The intrinsic quantities of $G_c(s)$ are:

– order of the rational part;

– input delay;

– zeros;

– poles;

– static gain.

Exercise 1.9.

What are the characteristic quantities of the transfer function $G_c(s)$ of a dynamic process, which can be estimated (if they exist) from the Bode magnitude and phase diagrams?

Solution – Exercise 1.9.

The characteristic quantities of the transfer function $G_c(s)$ that can be estimated (if they exist) from Bode diagrams:

– static gain;

– order;

– resonance frequency;

– bandwidth;

– gain margin;

– phase margin.

Exercise 1.10.

Let us consider the transfer function $G_c(s) = 1000/(s^2 + 4s + 100)$.

1) Determine the static gain.

2) Determine the natural frequency ω_n and the damping coefficient ξ of $G_c(s)$.

3) Sketch the Bode diagrams of $G_c(s)$.

Solution – Exercise 1.10.

Let us consider $G_c(s) = 1000/(s^2 + 4s + 100)$.

1) Static gain: 10.

2) Natural frequency $\omega_n = 10$ rad/s and damping coefficient $\xi = 0.2$.

3) The Bode diagrams of $G_c(s)$ are represented in Figure 1.13.

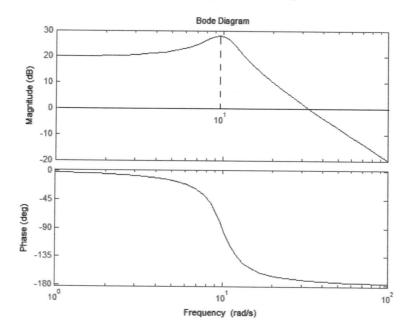

Figure 1.13. Bode diagrams of $G_c(s)$

Exercise 1.11.

The state model of a dynamic process is given by:

$$\begin{cases} \dfrac{dx_1(t)}{dt} = -2x_1(t) + x_2(t) \\ \dfrac{x_2(t)}{dt} = -x_2(t) + 10u(t) \\ y(t) = x_1(t) \end{cases}$$

with:

- u: input quantity;

- (x_1, x_2): state quantity;

- y: output quantity.

1) Deduce the characteristic matrices $\{A_c, B_c, C_c, D_c\}$ of this model.

2) Analyze the stability property.

3) Analyze the controllability property.

4) Analyze the observability property.

5) Let us consider the linear and reversible state transformation $z = P x$, with

$P = \begin{bmatrix} 3 & 1 \\ 5 & 2 \end{bmatrix}$, $x = \begin{bmatrix} x_1 & x_2 \end{bmatrix}^T$, and $z = \begin{bmatrix} z_1 & z_2 \end{bmatrix}^T$. Find the new state model associated

with z.

Solution – Exercise 1.11.

The state model of a dynamic process is given by:

$$\begin{cases} \dfrac{dx_1(t)}{dt} = -2x_1(t) + x_2(t) \\ \dfrac{x_2(t)}{dt} = -x_2(t) + 10u(t) \\ y(t) = x_1(t) \end{cases},$$

1) Characteristic matrices $\{A_c, B_c, C_c, D_c\}$ of this model are:

$$Ac = \begin{bmatrix} -2 & 1 \\ 0 & -1 \end{bmatrix}; \; Bc = \begin{bmatrix} 0 \\ 10 \end{bmatrix}; \; C_c = \begin{bmatrix} 1 & 0 \end{bmatrix}; \; D_c = 0$$

2) Stability property:

The eigenvalues (poles) $\{-2, -1\}$ of A_c are real and negative. The system is therefore stable.

3) Controllability property:

The controllability matrix $Ctr = \begin{bmatrix} 0 & 10 \\ 10 & 10 \end{bmatrix}$ is regular. The system is therefore controllable.

4) Observability property:

The observability matrix $Obs = \begin{bmatrix} 1 & 0 \\ -2 & 1 \end{bmatrix}$ is regular, the system is therefore observable.

5) Let us consider $z = P\, x$, with $P = \begin{bmatrix} 3 & 1 \\ 5 & 2 \end{bmatrix}$, $x = [x_1 \ x_2]^T$, and $z = [z_1 \ z_2]^T$.

If $A = \begin{bmatrix} -2 & 1 \\ 0 & -1 \end{bmatrix} B = \begin{bmatrix} 0 \\ 10 \end{bmatrix}, C = [1 \ 0]$, then the previous state model can be written in the form:

$$\begin{cases} \dfrac{dx(t)}{dt} = A\, x(t) + B\, u(t) \\ y(t) = C\, x(t) \end{cases}$$

Then, knowing that $x = P^{-1}\, z$, this yields $dx/dt = P^{-1}\, dz(t)/dt$ and the new state model in z is written as:

$$\begin{cases} \dfrac{dz(t)}{dt} = PAP^{-1}\, z(t) + PB\, u(t) \\ y(t) = C\, P^{-1}\, z(t) \end{cases}$$

Or:

$$\begin{cases} \dfrac{dz(t)}{dt} = \begin{bmatrix} -22 & 12 \\ -35 & 19 \end{bmatrix} z(t) + \begin{bmatrix} 10 \\ 20 \end{bmatrix} u(t) \\ y(t) = [2 \ -1]\, z(t) \end{cases}$$

Exercise 1.12.

The state model of a univariate dynamic process is given by:

$$\begin{cases} \dfrac{dx_1(t)}{dt} = -2x_1(t) + x_2(t) \\ \dfrac{x_2(t)}{dt} = -x_2(t) + 10u(t - 0,2) \end{cases},$$
$$y(t) = x_1(t)$$

with:

– u: input quantity;

– $x = \begin{bmatrix} x_1 & x_2 \end{bmatrix}^T$: state quantity;

– y: output quantity.

1) Find the equivalent transfer function $G(s)$.

2) Write the differential equation governing $u(t)$ and $y(t)$ using the identified transfer function.

Solution – Exercise 1.12.

The state model of a univariate dynamic process is given by:

$$\begin{cases} \dfrac{dx_1(t)}{dt} = -2x_1(t) + x_2(t) \\ \dfrac{x_2(t)}{dt} = -x_2(t) + 10\,u(t - 0,2) \end{cases},$$
$$y(t) = x_1(t)$$

1) Transfer function $G(s)$:

$$G(s) = C(s\,I_2 - A)^{-1} B\, e^{-0.2\,s} = \frac{10}{s^2 + 3s + 2} e^{-0.2\,s}$$

2) Differential equation governing $u(t)$ and $y(t)$ based on $G(s)$:

$$G(s) = \frac{Y(s)}{U(s)} = \frac{10}{s^2 + 3s + 2} e^{-0.2\,s},$$

therefore, $s^2\,Y(s) + 3s\,Y(s) + 2\,Y(s) = 10\,e^{-0.2\,s}\,U(s)$, then, according to Laplace transform properties, this yields:

$$\frac{dy^2(t)}{dt} + 3\frac{dy(t)}{dt} + 2\,y(t) = 10\,u(t-0.2)$$

Exercise 1.13.

Prove that the controllability and observability properties of a state model described by the matrices $\{A_c,\ B_c,\ C_c,\ D_c\}$ are invariant during a state transformation based on a regular matrix P.

Solution – Exercise 1.13.

1) Invariance of controllability:

Let P be a regular matrix of state transformation $z = Px$. In this case, the controllability matrix in the space of the state vector z is written:

$$M_c^x = \begin{bmatrix} B & AB & A^2B & \dots & A^{n-1}B \end{bmatrix} \text{ with } A = PA_cP^{-1}\ B = PB_c\ C = C\,P^{-1}.$$

Therefore:

$$M_c^z = \begin{bmatrix} PB_c & PA_cP^{-1}PB_c & \left(PA_cP^{-1}\right)^2 PB_c & \dots & \left(PA_cP^{-1}\right)^{n-1} PB_c \end{bmatrix}$$

$$= \begin{bmatrix} PB_c & PA_c\left(P^{-1}P\right)B_c & P\left(A_c\right)^2\left(P^{-1}P\right)B_c & \dots & P\left(A_c\right)^{n-1}\left(P^{-1}P\right)B_c \end{bmatrix}$$

$$= \begin{bmatrix} PB_c & PA_cB_c & PA_c^2B_c & \dots & PA_c^{n-1}B_c \end{bmatrix} = P\begin{bmatrix} B_c & A_cB_c & A_c^2B_c & \dots & A_c^{n-1}B_c \end{bmatrix}$$

$$= P\,M_c^x$$

Since P is a regular matrix, then M_z and M_c have the same rank, hence the conservation of controllability property during a similarity transformation by a regular matrix P.

2) Invariance of observability:

if $M_o^z = \begin{bmatrix} C_c \\ C_c A_c \\ C_c A_c^2 \\ ... \\ C_c A_c^{n-1} \end{bmatrix}$, then a reasoning analog to the previous one leads to:

$$M_o^z = \begin{bmatrix} C \\ C\,A \\ C\,A^2 \\ ... \\ C\,A_c^{n-1} \end{bmatrix} = \begin{bmatrix} CP^{-1} \\ C_c P^{-1} PA_c P^{-1} \\ C_c\,P^{-1} PA_c^2 P^{-1} \\ ... \\ C_c P^{-1} P\,A_c^{n-1} P^{-1} \end{bmatrix} = \begin{bmatrix} C_c \\ C_c A_c \\ C_c A_c^2 \\ ... \\ C_c A_c^{n-1} \end{bmatrix} P^{-1}.$$

Moreover, consequently, M_o^z and M_o^x have the same rank. In other words, the observability property is preserved during a similarity transformation by a regular matrix P.

Experimental Modeling
Approach of Dynamic Processes

2.1. Introduction to experimental modeling

2.1.1. *Problem statement*

In practice, frequency models and state space representations of dynamic processes, presented in Chapter 1, can be analytically elaborated on the basis of physics and energy laws (in Lagrange's sense), governing the joint time evolution of constitutive elements at various levels: material, component, part, mechanism, subsystem, equipment or process.

Nevertheless, most real dynamic processes are essentially complex, because of the lack or the insufficiency of perfect knowledge on the dynamic behavior of their constituents. Therefore, in most practical cases, the approach used in the elaboration of rigorous models of real dynamic processes is experimental, relying on data obtained from tests and measurements.

2.1.2. *Principle of experimental modeling*

Experimental modeling involves the elaboration of a rigorous dynamic model of a real process, based on data of the experimental response to tests and measurements under appropriate conditions. The model can be searched through appropriate scientific techniques, such as:

– direct calculation based on technical indicators observed on the graph of the experimental step response (Broïda method);

– Strejc method [BSA 94];

– direct calculation based on technical indicators observed on the graph of the frequency response [BON 10];

– digital processing of experimental data according to an optimization criterion, for example:

- least squares of measurement error [TRI 88];

- minimum variance of the estimation error [BAG 93];

- maximum likelihood of conditional probability density with respect to the parameter(s) of the observation error [FRA 90].

2.1.3. *Experimental modeling methodology*

The project management methodology in case of experimental modeling of a dynamic process is represented in Figure 2.1, which points out the following main stages:

– inspection of the process site;

– experimentation;

– pre-processing;

– structural choice;

– parameter estimation;

– post-processing.

2.1.3.1. *Site inspection of the real process*

During the process site inspection stage, technical data required for planning experimental resources and protocols are collected.

The technical report drawn after the inspection stage is used for:

– controlling the experimental study conditions, as follows:

- ambient temperature, undertaken risks, safety factors;

- process constituents (mechanisms and subsystems);

- input quantity (quantities): number, nature, allowable range;

- output quantity (quantities): number, nature, allowable range;

- performance indicator(s);

– plan the appropriate means to be deployed for conducting tests and measurements. These are:

- measuring instruments and special probes;

- signal generators;

- virtual instruments;

- specialized instrumentation software;

- human resources and their skill levels.

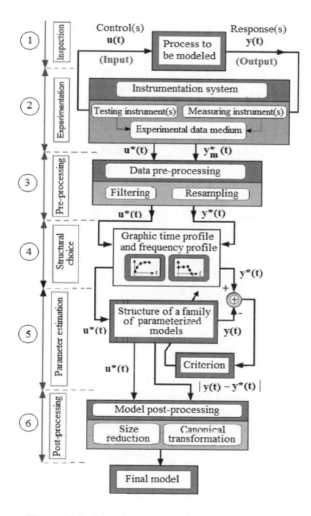

Figure 2.1. *Experimental modeling methodology*

2.1.3.2. *Experimentation*

The stage of experimentation involves exciting the real process with an appropriate test signal, then saving the response on a digital data medium. The test signal used at this stage can be: step, square, ramp, sine or arbitrary signal, depending on the instrumentation constraints and on the requirements of the algorithm to be used for optimal estimation of the searched model.

Nowadays, a virtual instrumentation system (represented in Figure 2.2) is a flexible and rapid tool that allows a real dynamic process to be subjected to automated tests and measurements. It comprises a (standard or industrial model) PC/Laptop or a PC/Tablet featuring a virtual instrumentation software application [MBI 12] and a MDAQ (Multifunction Data Acquisition) board.

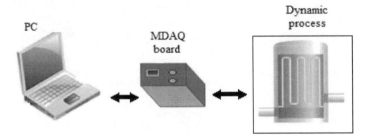

Figure 2.2. *Virtual instrumentation system*

Moreover, it is also possible to conduct remote tests on a real process by means of a remote virtual instrumentation system through the Internet, as shown in Figure 2.3.

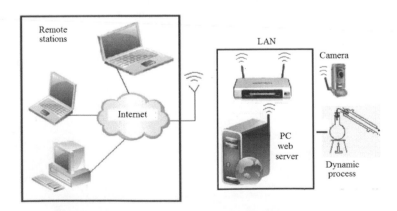

Figure 2.3. *Remote virtual instrumentation system*

In-depth technical elements on this broad topical subject, as well as a platform prototype that can be remotely operated through the Internet, are provided in a second volume related to *automation and industrial computer science*, entitled *Advanced Techniques and Control Technology and Computer-Assisted Regulation*, published by ISTE.

2.1.3.3. *Pre-processing*

Pre-processing of real-time acquired data is necessary only if, after inspection of measured data, there are undesirable effects to be eliminated by filtering (rejection of undesirable frequency ranges), by coupling (extraction of offset values) or by resampling.

2.1.3.4. *Structural choice*

In the time or frequency domain, structural choice involves observing the graphic profiles of data in order to ingeniously deduce the mathematical structure of the family of models considered admissible. For example, the ingenuity required at this stage might lead to drawing analogies between the graphic profiles of observed experimental responses and properly known profiles of responses of simple dynamic models (of order 1, 2 or higher), subjected to similar types of test signals.

2.1.3.5. *Parameter estimation*

The parameter estimation stage involves finding, within the family of retained models, the parameters of the best candidate, whose dynamic behavior generated by simulation fits best the experimental measurements, according to the optimization criterion involved and to the set precision margin.

2.1.3.6. *Post-processing*

In the post-processing stage, it is possible to reduce the order of the estimated model if the model of reduced order provides a good precision margin. In all cases, at this stage, it is important to analyze the dynamic and static performances of the retained model, in order to better assess the limits that will justify the design of a closed-loop control law.

2.1.3.7. *Analysis*

The analysis stage involves the study of fundamental properties (bandwidth, stability, rapidity, sensitivity, validity thresholds, etc.) of the optimal model elaborated on the basis of experimental data. These properties constitute a first basis of reliable technical knowledge required for the design and implementation of a strategy for the automatic control of the dynamic process being considered.

2.2. Step response-based modeling

2.2.1. *Model of order 1*

The response to a step $u(t - \tau_0)$ of magnitude E_0 of a transfer function of order 1 $G_c(s) = \dfrac{K_s}{1 + \tau s} e^{-\tau_0 \, s}$ is written:

$$y(t) = \begin{cases} 0 \ \text{if} \ t < \tau_0 \\ K_s \, E_0 \left(1 - e^{-\frac{t - \tau_0}{\tau}} \right) \ \text{if} \ t \geq \tau_0 \end{cases}$$
[2.1]

Thus, the profile of the experimental response to step E_0 of the process to be modeled is similar to that represented in Figure 2.4.

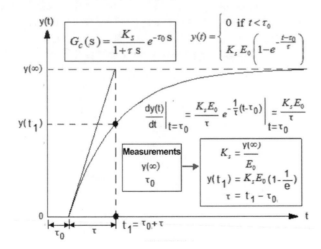

Figure 2.4. *Identification of parameters of a model of order 1 based on the response to a step u(t − τ₀) of magnitude E₀*

2.2.2. *Under-damped model of order 2 (ξ < 1)*

For an under-damped model of order 2 whose transfer function is written by:

$$G_c(s) = \frac{K_s \, \omega_n^2}{s^2 + 2\xi\omega_n s + \omega_n^2} e^{-\tau_0 s} \quad \text{with} \ \xi < 1$$
[2.2]

The theoretical response to a step E_0 is given by:

$$y(t) = K_s E_0 \left(1 - \frac{e^{-\xi \omega_n (t-\tau_0)}}{\sqrt{1-\xi^2}} \sin \left(\sqrt{1-\xi^2}\,(t-\tau_0) + \tan^{-1}\left(\frac{\sqrt{1-\xi^2}}{\xi} \right) \right) \right) \quad [2.3]$$

The graphic profile of this experimentally obtained response corresponds to Figure 2.5, which will be used as a basis for the estimation of characteristic parameters of [2.2].

Knowing that $y(\infty) = K_{si}E_0$, then the 1st peaking point of [2.3] can be obtained by solving the equation $dy(t)\,/\,ddt = 0$. This detailed solving [KAT 90] yields the following expressions of the characteristic parameters to be estimated (damping coefficient ξ, natural angular frequency and response time T_r (at r %)):

$$\begin{cases} d = e^{-\frac{\xi \pi}{\sqrt{1-\xi^2}}} \text{ hence } \xi = \dfrac{|\log(d)|}{\sqrt{\pi^2 + \log^2(d)}} \\[2em] \omega_n = \dfrac{\pi}{T_m\sqrt{1-\xi^2}}, T_r(r\%) = \dfrac{\log\left(\dfrac{100}{r}\right)}{\xi\,\omega_n} \end{cases} \quad [2.4]$$

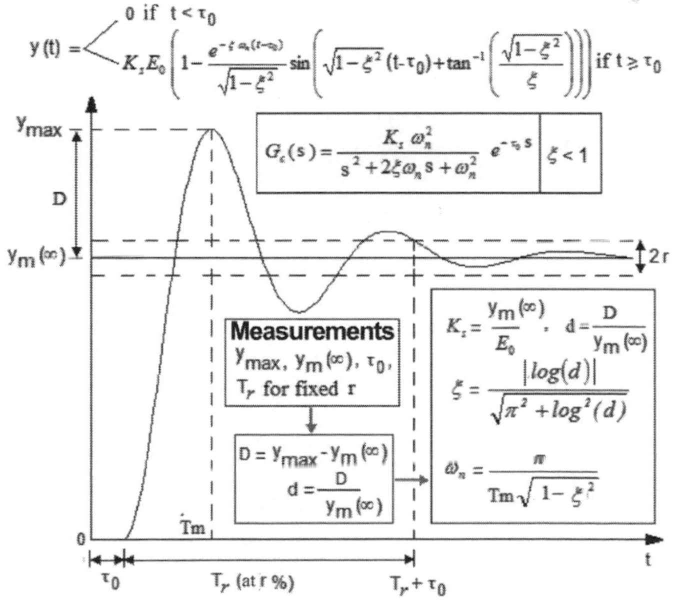

Figure 2.5. *Graphic profile of the step response of a model of order 2 (with $\xi < 1$)*

2.2.3. *Damped model of order ≥ 2 (Strejc method)*

Strejc technique is in this case an appropriate tool for elaborating $G_c(s)$ based on data measured on the experimental response to a step E_0. This technique is applicable to graphic profiles similar to those of under-damped dynamic systems. The general structure of the $G_c(s)$ model to be determined is written:

$$G(s) = \frac{Y(s)}{E_0(s)} = \frac{K_s}{(1+\tau s)^n} e^{-\tau_0 s}, \text{ with } K_s = Y(\infty)/E_0, \qquad [2.5]$$

with:

– K_s : static gain;

– τ : time constant;

– n : order;

– τ_0 : pure delay time (if applicable).

The response of [2.5] to a step E_0 is written in the form:

$$y(t) = K_s E_0 \left(1 - e^{\left(-\frac{t}{\tau}\right)} \sum_{k=0}^{n-1} \frac{(t/\tau)^k}{k!} \right) \qquad [2.6]$$

Thus, the graphic profile of the experimental response $y_m(t)$ to a step E_0 of the real process to be modeled by the Strejc model will have to be damped. In these conditions, the principle of Strejc technique for experimental modeling is represented in Figure 2.6.

The existence of inflection point P can be proved by calculating the first and second derivatives of [2.6]. Indeed, the following equations can be written:

$$y'(t) = K_s E_0 e^{\left(-\frac{t}{\tau}\right)} \frac{(t/\tau)^{n-1}}{\tau (n-1)!} \qquad [2.7]$$

$$y''(t) = K_s E_0 e^{\left(-\frac{t}{\tau}\right)} \frac{(t/\tau)^{n-2}}{\tau^2 (n-1)!} \left(n-1-\frac{t}{\tau} \right) \qquad [2.8]$$

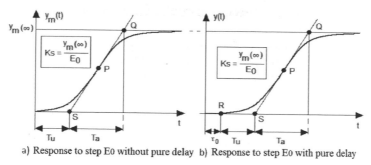

a) Response to step E0 without pure delay b) Response to step E0 with pure delay

c) Strejc table

d) Parameter estimation

Figure 2.6. *Strejc method for experimental modeling*

It can be noted that [2.8] is equal to zero only at point Q of coordinates:

$$t_1 = (n-1)\,\tau\,, \quad y(t_1) = K_s\,E_0\left(1 - e^{-(n-1)}\sum_{k=0}^{n-1}\frac{(n-1)^k}{k!}\right)$$

[2.9]

then the equation of the tangent at point Q is:

$$y_Q(t) = \frac{K_s E_0}{T_a}\,(t - T_u)$$

[2.10]

Since [2.8] and [2.10] have the same slope at point Q of abscissa t_1, the following relations can be written:

$$\left.\frac{dy(t)}{dt}\right|_{t_1} = K_s\,E_0\,e^{(-(n-1))}\frac{(n-1)^{n-1}}{\tau\,(n-1)!} = \frac{K_s\,E_0}{T_a}$$

[2.11]

Therefore, this yields:

$$\frac{T_a}{\tau} = \frac{n-1)!\,e^{(n-1)}}{(n-1)^{n-1}}$$

[2.12]

Similarly, knowing that [2.8] and [2.10] have the same ordinates at point Q, then:

$$y(t_1) = K_s\, E_0 \left(1 - e^{-(n-1)} \sum_{k=0}^{n-1} \frac{(n-1)^k}{k!}\right) = K_s\, E_0 \left((n-1)\frac{\tau}{T_a} - \frac{T_u}{T_a}\right) \qquad [2.13]$$

Therefore:

$$\frac{T_u}{T_a} = \frac{\tau}{T_a}(n-1) - 1 + e^{(n-1)} \sum_{k=0}^{n-1} \frac{(n-1)^k}{k!} \qquad [2.14]$$

Finally, knowing that the expression of τ/T_a is deduced from [2.12], this leads to:

$$\frac{T_u}{T_a} = \frac{(n-1)^{n-1}}{(n-1)!\, e^{(n-1)}} - 1 + e^{(n-1)} \left(1 + \sum_{k=1}^{n-1} \frac{(n-1)^k}{k!}\right) \qquad [2.15]$$

Relations [2.5]–[2.15] are the foundation of the Strejc method illustrated in Figure 2.6. Matlab® program "strejc.m" enables the digital generation of the first 30 lines of the Stretch table. Table 2.1 is an example of the Strejc table generated by this program.

No.	Matlab program "strejc.m"
1	clear; M = 30; % M first values
2	for n = 1:M
3	N(n) = n; Fn_1=1; n_1=n-1;
4	for i = 1:n_1 Fn_1= Fn_1*i; end
5	Fn_1 = Fn_1; Fn = Fn_1*n ; Sn=0;
6	Ta_Tau(n) = Fn_1*exp(n_1)/(n_1^n_1); Tau_Ta(n) =1/Ta_Tau(n);
7	for k = 1:n_1
8	Fk =1;
9	for i = 1:k, Fk = Fk*i; end
10	Sn = Sn + n_1^k/Fk;
11	end
12	Tu_Ta(n) = Tau_Ta(n) * n_1 -1+ (1+Sn)*exp(-n_1);
13	Tu_Tau(n) = (Tu_Ta(n)) * (Ta_Tau(n));
14	end
15	DATA = [N' Tu_Ta' Tu_Tau' Ta_Tau']

According to Figure 2.6, the operating procedure of the Strejc method is as follows:

– read $y_m(\infty)$, then calculate $K_s = y_m(\infty)/E_0$;

– read the value of τ_0 on the time axis (see Figure 2.6(b)) if it is perceptible within a sufficiently extended time scale;

– draw the tangent at inflection point P of the response $y_m(t)$. This tangent cuts the time axis at point S and the ordinate axis at point Q (see Figure 2.6(a) or 2.6(b));

– read the corresponding values of T_u and T_a and calculate $R = T_u/T_a$;

– in Strejc Table 2.1, determine the order n^* for which $R = T_u/T_a = R(n^*, 2)$. If the exact value of n^* associated with R is not in the table, consider $n^* =$ next smaller integer;

– in the Strejc table, read the value $R(n^*, 3) = T_u/\tau$ or $R(n^*, 4) = T_a/\tau$, then calculate the parameter τ by the relation $\tau = T_u/R(n^*, 3)$ or $\tau = T_u/R(n^*, 4)$.

No.	$R = \dfrac{T_u}{T_a}$	$\dfrac{T_u}{\tau}$	$\dfrac{T_a}{\tau}$	No.	$R = \dfrac{T_u}{T_a}$	$\dfrac{T_u}{\tau}$	$\dfrac{T_a}{\tau}$
1	0	0	1.0000	16	1.1046	10.7836	9.7622
2	0.1036	0.2817	2.7183	17	1.1534	11.6254	10.0789
3	0.2180	0.8055	3.6945	18	1.2009	12.4720	10.3859
4	0.3194	1.4254	4.4635	19	1.2470	13.3230	10.6841
5	0.4103	2.1002	5.1186	20	1.2919	14.1780	10.9742
6	0.4933	2.8113	5.6991	21	1.3358	15.0368	11.2568
7	0.5700	3.5489	6.2258	22	1.3786	15.8990	11.5325
8	0.7092	5.0810	7.1640	23	1.4205	16.7645	11.8017
9	0.7092	5.0810	7.1640	24	1.4615	17.6329	12.0650
10	0.7732	5.8685	7.5898	25	1.5016	18.5041	12.3226
11	0.8341	6.6673	7.9930	26	1.5410	19.3780	12.5750
12	0.8924	7.4756	8.3767	27	1.5796	20.2543	12.8224
13	0.9484	8.2924	8.7437	28	1.6175	21.1330	13.0651
14	1.0023	9.1165	9.0959	29	1.6548	22.0139	13.3034
15	1.0543	9.9471	9.4349	30	1.6914	22.8969	13.5374

Table 2.1. *Table of the first 30 lines of the Strejc table*

2.3. Frequency response-based modeling

The frequency response-based experience involves the application at process input of a sine command signal $u(t) = u_m \sin(\omega t)$, whose frequency $f = \omega/2\pi$ is variable, and to realize in steady state, for each frequency, the magnitude $y_{max}(\omega)$ and the phase $\phi(\omega)$ of the response $y(t) = y_{max} \sin(\omega t + \phi)$.

Then the transfer function $G_c(s)$ to be modeled with $s = j\omega$ is determined by means of the quantities observed on Bode diagram, which is drawn from the measurement field $\{\omega, y_{max}(\omega), \phi(\omega)\}$ in a logarithmic scale, of abscissa $\log_{10}(\omega)$ and ordinates:

$$G_{dB}(\omega) = 20 \log_{10}\left(\left|\frac{y_m(\omega)}{u_m(\omega)}\right|\right) : \quad \text{Magnitude graph} \qquad\qquad [2.16]$$

$\phi(\omega):$ Phase graph

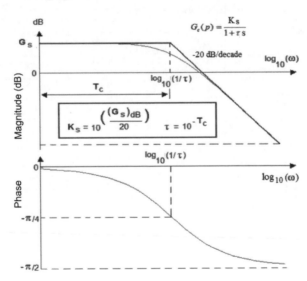

Figure 2.7. *Bode diagram of a process of order 1. For a color version of this figure, see www.iste.co.uk/mbihi/automation.zip*

The knowledge bases of Bode diagrams of simple models to be considered according to the similarity to an observed experimental profile are presented in Figure 2.7 for a process of order 1. Figures 2.8 and 2.9 show the respective cases of process of order 2, which is damped if $\xi \geq 1$, and under-damped if $\xi < 1$, where ξ is the damping coefficient.

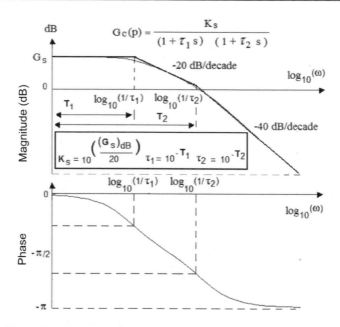

Figure 2.8. *Bode diagram of a damped process of order 2. For a color version of this figure, see www.iste.co.uk/mbihi/automation.zip*

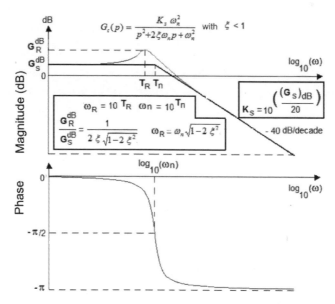

Figure 2.9. *Bode diagram of an under-damped process of order 2. For a color version of this figure, see www.iste.co.uk/mbihi/automation.zip*

2.4. Modeling based on ARMA model

2.4.1. *ARMA model*

An ARMA (*Auto Regressive Moving Average*) model is a discrete representation of a dynamic process by a linear recurrence equation. Its purpose is:

– to estimate the parameters of a process by means of identification techniques based on the optimality criterion (quadratic error, covariance matrix of the estimation error, density of conditional probability of the measurements with respect to parameters), hence the possibility of quantifying the precision of the results provided by the optimal estimator;

– to extend its use to identification problems that are nonlinear with respect to parameters;

– to analyze an experimental response obtained for a sufficiently persistent standard (square, ramp, sawtooth) or arbitrary input signal.

For a better understanding of the structure of an ARMA model, let us consider the example of a linear discrete dynamic process, described by the transfer function:

$$G(z) = \frac{Y(z)}{U(z)} = \frac{\beta_0 z^n + \beta_1 z^{n-1} + ... + \beta_{n-1} z + \beta_n}{z^n + \alpha_1 z^{n-1} + ... + \alpha_{n-1} z + \alpha_n} \qquad [2.17]$$

The n initial conditions are supposed to be null (or known, if they are not null). In these conditions, the recurrence equation associated with G(z) in discrete time for $k = n, n + 1, ..., N$ is written as:

$$\begin{aligned} y(k) = -\ & (\alpha_1 y(k-1) + \alpha_2 y(k-2) + ... + \alpha_{n-1} y(k-n+1) + a_n y(k-n)) \\ & + \beta_0 u(k) + \beta_1 u(k-1) + \beta_2 u(k-2) + ... + \beta_{n-1} u(k-n+1) + \beta_n (k-n) \end{aligned} \qquad [2.18]$$

Or in the following compact form:

$$y(k) = \underbrace{\begin{bmatrix} u(k) & u(k-1) & ... & u(k-n) & -y(k-1) & -y(k-2) & ... & -y(k-n) \end{bmatrix}}_{h^{\mathrm{T}}(k)} \begin{bmatrix} \left.\begin{matrix} \beta_0 \\ \beta_1 \\ \beta_2 \\ ... \\ \beta_n \end{matrix}\right\}\beta \\ \left.\begin{matrix} \alpha_1 \\ \alpha_2 \\ ... \\ \alpha_n \end{matrix}\right\}\alpha \end{bmatrix} \qquad [2.19]$$

Thus, each output sample $y(k)$ results from a linear combination of recent inputs and outputs, which explains the "ARMA model" designation.

NOTE ON THE DIMENSION OF THE SPACE OF PARAMETERS IN [2.19]. –

In relation [2.19], if vector β has first m parameters that are simultaneously null, they should then be omitted with their respective coefficients in $h^T(k)$ in order to reduce the dimension of the space of parameters to be identified with value $M = (2n + 1) - m$.

If $G(z) = \dfrac{Y(z)}{U(z)} = \dfrac{\beta_1}{z + \alpha_1}$, then $n = 1$ and $\beta_0 = 0$.

In this case, relation [2.19] becomes:

$$y(k) = \underbrace{[u(k-1) \quad -y_m(k-1)]}_{h^T(x(k))} \underbrace{\begin{bmatrix} \beta_1 \\ \alpha_1 \end{bmatrix}}_{\theta} \qquad [2.20]$$

Let us consider:

$$h(k) = \left[u(k)\ u(k-1)\ ...\ u(k-n)\ -y(k-1)\ -y(k-2)...-y(k-n) \right]^T$$

$$\theta = \left[\underbrace{\beta_0\ \beta_1\ \beta_2\ ...\ \beta_n}_{\text{Maximum of } n+1 \text{ parameters}}\ \alpha_1\ \alpha_2\ ...\ \alpha_n \right]^T \leftarrow M_{max} = 2n+1 \text{ parameters} \qquad [2.21]$$

Then the compact form of ARMA model [2.19] is written as follows:

$$y(k) = h^T(k)\theta \qquad [2.22]$$

with $k = n, n+1, ..., N$.

It can therefore be noted that relation [2.22] is equivalent to the model of a linear static process with respect to the vector of parameters θ.

NOTES.–

– Relation [2.22] is very useful in automation practice for the experimental modeling of certain devices (sensors/transducers, amplifiers, etc.) whose input/output characteristic is linear with respect to parameters. It is the case of a polynomial characteristic, where $h_i(u(k)) = u^i(k)$.

– When the criterion of estimation error to be minimized with respect to θ is quadratic, the problem of optimal parameter estimation of an ARMA model (of dynamic or static origin), described by [2.21] or [2.22], admits an analytical solution that will be proved in the next section. On the other hand, if the model is nonlinear with respect to θ, or if the optimization criterion considered is an arbitrary nonlinear function, the parameter estimation can only be realized by an iterative method for nonlinear optimization (Gauss–Newton, Gradient, etc.).

– Certain types of models that are nonlinear with respect to parameters can be transformed into equivalent linear models by simple change in descriptive variables. Several examples of this type of models are:

$$h(x) = K_1 e^{-K_2 x},$$
$$h(x) = e^{K_1 x_1 + K_2 x_2 + \ldots + K_n x_n}, \qquad\qquad [2.23]$$
$$h(x) = \frac{1}{a_0 + a_1 u + \ldots + a_n u^n}$$

In the first two cases, it suffices to set $Y = \log(h(x))$, then $Y = 1 / h(x)$ in the third case.

2.4.2. *Parameter estimation of an ARMA model*

The methods for parameter estimation of an ARMA model seek to determine the best parameters for which the error between measurements and the estimated response is minimum with respect to the optimization criterion. These methods generally require samples of the experimental response, obtained for a persistent input sequence (sufficiently wide frequency range). Furthermore, they rely on an optimization criterion of the model estimation error and allow the characterization of the precision of the estimated optimal parameters.

As regards the least squares method that will be considered below, the criterion function to be minimized corresponds to the variance (square of quadratic norm) of the estimation errors of the model cumulated over a horizon of N measurements. Indeed, let us consider:

– $y_m(k)$: the value of measurement at stage k for $k = 1, 2, \ldots, N - 1$;

– $y(k)$: the value corresponding to the response of the estimated value;

– $\varepsilon(h^T(k), \theta) = y_m(k) - y(k) = y_m(k) - h^T(k)\,\theta$: the estimation error at stage k.

Considering these notations, the function criterion over a horizon of N measurements is:

$$J_N(\theta) = \sum_{k=1}^{N} \left\| \varepsilon(h^T(k), \theta) \right\|^2 \quad = \sum_{k=1}^{N} \left(y_m(k) - h^T(k)\,\theta \right)^2$$

$$= \frac{1}{N} \left(\sum_{k=1}^{N} y_m^2(k) - 2\underbrace{\sum_{k=1}^{N} \left(y_m(k) \right) h^T(k)\,\theta}_{\text{since } h^T(k)\,\theta = \theta^T h(k)} + \sum_{k=1}^{N} \theta^T \overbrace{h(k)\,h^T(k)}^{\substack{N \times N \text{ symmetric matrix}}}\,\theta \right) \qquad [2.24]$$

$$= \sum_{k=1}^{N} y_m^2(k) - 2\underbrace{\sum_{k=1}^{N} \left(y_m(k) \right) h^T(k)\,\theta}_{2 \ \ Identical \ \ scalar \ \ products} + \sum_{k=1}^{N} \theta^T \underbrace{h(k)\,h^T(k)}_{N \times N \ \ matrix}\,\theta$$

Moreover:

$$\frac{\partial \left\| J_N(\theta) \right\|}{\partial \theta} = \frac{1}{N} \left(-2 \sum_{k=1}^{N} y_m(k)\,h^T(k) + \sum_{k=1}^{N} \underbrace{2\,\theta^T\,h(k)h^T(k)}_{\theta^T \left(h(k)h^T(k) + \left(h(k)h^T(k) \right)^T \right)} \right) \qquad [2.25]$$

Therefore, $\dfrac{\partial \left\| J_N(\theta) \right\|}{\partial \theta} = 0$ leads to:

$$\theta^*(N) = \left(\underbrace{\sum_{k=1}^{N} h(k)\,h^T(k)}_{\text{Sum of } N \times N \text{ matrix}} \right)^{-1} \left(\underbrace{\sum_{k=1}^{N} h(k)\,y_m(k)}_{\text{Sum of } N \times 1 \text{ vectors}} \right) \qquad [2.26]$$

Thus, considering:

$$P(N) = \sum_{k=1}^{N} h(k)\,h^T(k), \quad Y_m(N) = \sum_{k=1}^{N} h(k)\,y_m(k) \qquad [2.27]$$

Then [2.26] becomes:

$$\theta^*(N) = \left(P(N)\right)^{-1} Y_m(N) \qquad [2.28]$$

Since vectors $h(k)$ contained in P(N) depend on the input sequence $\{u(k)\}$, the existence of optimal solution [2.28] can be compromised by a non-persistent input sequence. Should that be the case, an input signal with sufficiently rich frequency range (square, ramp, triangle, sawtooth or arbitrary signal) can be used.

2.5. Matlab-aided experimental modeling

Relations [2.26] to [2.28] can be programmed in Matlab. Nevertheless, they only calculate the best estimated parameters of a transfer function in z. Therefore, the identification of the parameters of a transfer function $G_c(s)$ requires a preliminary discretization in the form $G(z)$, so that relations [2.26] to [2.28] are applicable. Moreover, the reconstruction in case of necessity of the parameters of $G_c(s)$ knowing those of $G(z)$ is generally not trivial, unless it is realized digitally by means of Matlab command " d2c".

Thus, it proves to be more rapid, in practice, to use Matlab command "tfest", which has a wider context of use. A similar command "sest" is also available in case of parameter identification of a state model.

Let us consider, for example, the data t and $y(t)$, represented numerically and graphically in Figure 2.10, resulting from the experimental response to a test signal (unit step signal) of a speed servomechanism. Furthermore, let us suppose that vectors of data t and $y(t)$ are saved in a current folder of Matlab working environment, in "t.mat" and "y.mat" formats, respectively. In these conditions, the purpose is to use the Matlab command " tfest" to identify a transfer function of the process that takes the form:

$$G_c(s) = \frac{K_s}{1+\tau s} \, e^{-\tau_0 \, s} \qquad [2.29]$$

with:

– K_s and τ: parameters to be identified;

– τ_0: fixed at 0.25 s.

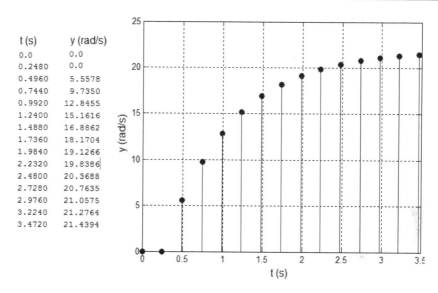

t (s)	y (rad/s)
0.0	0.0
0.2480	0.0
0.4960	5.5578
0.7440	9.7350
0.9920	12.8455
1.2400	15.1616
1.4880	16.8862
1.7360	18.1704
1.9840	19.1266
2.2320	19.8386
2.4800	20.3688
2.7280	20.7635
2.9760	21.0575
3.2240	21.2764
3.4720	21.4394

Figure 2.10. *Identification data. For a color version of this figure, see www.iste.co.uk/mbihi/automation.zip*

The following Matlab program "idprocdyn.m" allows the identification and display of the estimated model of this dynamic process of order 1.

No.	Matlab program "idprocdyn.m"		
1	% N.B.: t.mat and y.mat are in the current folder of Matlab		
2	load t ; load y ;	%	Loading of data t, y
3	T = 0.2480;	%	Sampling period
4	u = ones(length(t),1);	%	Input step
5	Data = iddata(y, u,T);	%	Creation of Object Identification
6	Np =1; Nz = 0;	%	Number of desired poles and zeros
7	IoDelay = 0.25;	%	Value of input delay, if known
8	Gc = tfest(Data,Np, Nz, IoDelay)	%	Identification of Gc(s)
9	ysim = lsim(Gc, u, t);	%	Step response of the estimated model
10	plot(te, ye,'o',t, ysim, 'k');	%	Graph of responses
11	xlabel('t(s)'); ylabel('y (rad/s)'); grid	%	Labels of axes

The execution of this Matlab code leads to the following solution:

$K_s = 2.06/1.189$, $\tau = 1/1.189$.

Figure 2.11 then shows the graphs of the experimental response with that issued from the numerical simulation of the estimated model.

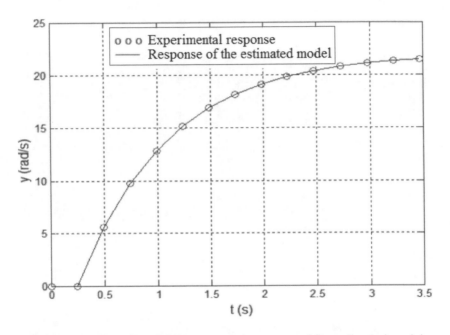

Figure 2.11. *Experimental response and response of the estimated model*

Moreover, the procedure for using command "sest" of Matlab for the identification of a state model of the process would be similar.

2.6. Exercises and solutions

Exercise 2.1.

After having consulted the methodology for the management of an experimental modeling project, list in chronological order the 10 main factors that are critical for the quality of the dynamic process model to be estimated.

Solution – Exercise 2.1.

The 10 main factors that are critical for the quality of the dynamic process model to be estimated are:

– technical characteristics of the testing instruments;

– complexity of the process to be studied;

– testing and measurement conditions (operating ranges, disturbances);

– types of test signals (step, ramp, square, triangle, sine, arbitrary);

– (analog or digital) technology of data medium;

– data representation and graphical analysis tool;

– nature of the family of models (linear, nonlinear, with or without delay);

– type of model to be estimated (transfer function, Bode diagram, etc.);

– estimation criterion (classical, least square).

– desired precision of the estimation

Exercise 2.2.

Figure 2.12 presents the graph of the response $y(t)$ to a step $E_0 = 2$ of a dynamic process of order 1.

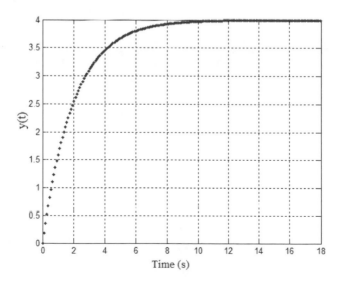

Figure 2.12. *Graph of response y(t)*

Based on this graph, estimate the static gain K_s and the time constant τ of this process, and then determine the corresponding transfer function.

Solution – Exercise 2.2.

The data that can be directly measured on the graph of the open-loop step response (see Figure 2.13) are $y(\infty)$ and τ.

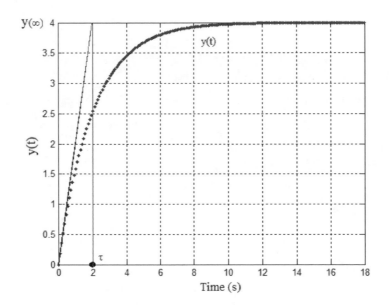

Figure 2.13. *Graph of the response to the open-loop step. For a color version of this figure, see www.iste.co.uk/mbihi/automation.zip*

The measurements conducted are used for the calculation of:

– $K_s = y(\infty) / E_0 = 4/2$ (static gain), and $\tau = 2$ s (time constant);

– $G_c(s) = Y(s)/E_0(s) = 2/(2s + 1)$.

Exercise 2.3.

Figure 2.14 presents a boost chopper controlled by duty-cycle modulation via an embedded IR2101 driver (see Figure 2.14(b)).

a) Based on the graph of the step response $x(t) = E_0 = 4\text{V}$ (see Figure 2.14(d)), estimate the static gain K_s, as well as the instant T_m and the corresponding relative value d of the first overshoot.

b) Calculate the damping factor ξ and the natural angular frequency ω_n.

c) Determine the open-loop transfer function $G(s) = V_s(s)/X(s)$.

d) Using Matlab, represent the response of the model defined by $G(s)$.

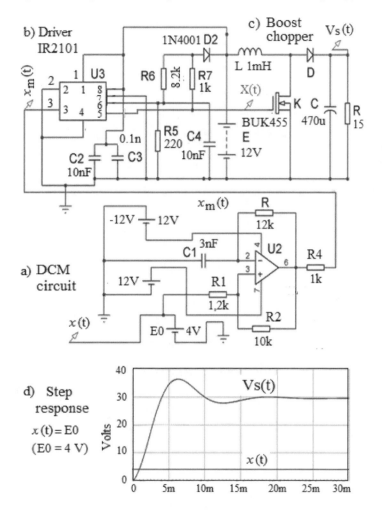

Figure 2.14. *Boost chopper controlled by DCM circuit. For a color version of this figure, see www.iste.co.uk/mbihi/automation.zip*

Solution – Exercise 2.3.

The parameters to be measured on the virtual response of Figure 2.15 are the following:

– static gain K_s;

– relative overshoot d;

– instant T_m of the first overshoot.

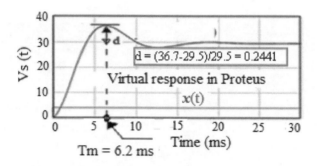

Figure 2.15. *Virtual response*

a) The measured values are:

- $K_s = V_s(\infty)/E_0 = 29.5/4 = 7.3756$;

- $d = (36.7 - 29.5)/29.5 = 0.2441$;

- $T_m = 6.2$ ms.

b) In this case, the damping factor ξ, the natural angular frequency ω_n and the transfer function $G(s) = V_s(s)/X(s)$ can be calculated as follows:

$$\begin{cases} \xi = \dfrac{\left|\log(d)\right|}{\sqrt{\pi^2 + \log^2(d)}} = 0,4095 \\ \omega_n = \dfrac{\pi}{T_m\sqrt{1-\xi^2}} = 0,5554 \; rad / s, \end{cases}$$

c) The transfer function of this Boost chopper with DCM is given by:

$$G_c(s) = \frac{V_s(s)}{E_0(s)} = \frac{K_s\,\omega_n^2}{s^2 + 2\,\xi\,\omega_n\,s + \omega_n^2} = \frac{2.275}{s^2 + 0.4549\,s + 0.3085}$$

d) Graphs of the responses to step $E_0 = 4V$:

The following lines of Matlab program serve to draw the response to the step represented in Figure 2.16:

>> s = tf('s'); E0 = 4; G=2.257*E0/(s^2+0.4549 *s + 0.3085); step(G);
>> grid; xlabel('temps(s)'); ylabel('Volts')

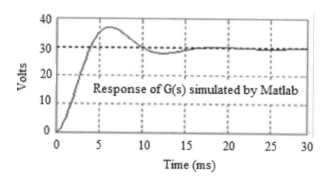

Figure 2.16. *Graph of the response to step $E_0 = 4V$*

Exercise 2.4.

A lighting system with power controllable by voltage dimmable electronic ballasts generates in the working zone a luminous flux $w(t)$ under a control voltage $u(t)$. The transfer function of this system, initially obtained experimentally, is given by:

$$G(s) = \frac{W(s)}{U(s)} = \frac{0.4914}{(1+0.035\,s)^2}\,e^{-0.005\,s}$$

a) Based on the graph of the experimental response of $G(s)$ to be drawn with Matlab, find the transfer function $G_e(s)$ of an approximate virtual model of order 1 in the Ziegler–Nichols sense. Then represent on the same Matlab figure the graph of the initial model of order 2 and of the approximate model of order 1 found.

b) Estimate the approximate model of order 1 and the graphs of the step responses.

Solution – Exercise 2.4.

a) The measurements required for the estimation of the approximate virtual model $G_e(s)$ of order 1, based on the graph of $G(s)$, are:

- $K_s = 0.4914$;

- $T_m = 0.0151$ s;

- $T_a = 0.062$ s.

b) The Matlab program for the production of graphs of $G(s)$ and $G_e(s)$ is the following:

```
>> T0=0.005; Tf = 0.4;  T=0:T0:Tf;
>> t = tf('s');  Go = exp(-0.005*s)*0.4914/((1+0.035*s)^2);  [Yo,
To] = step(Go,T);
>> Ks = 0.4914;   Tm = 0.0151;  Ta = 0.062;  s = tf('s');
>> Ge = Ks*exp(-Tm*s)*1/((Ta*s+1));  [Ye, Te] = step(Ge,T);
>> plot(T, Yo, '.',  T, Ye, 'k'); grid
```

Exercise 2.5.

The graph of the response to step $E_0 = 2V$ of a dynamic process of order 2 is represented in Figure 2.17.

a) Based on this graph, estimate the pure input delay τ_0, the static gain K_s, the relative overshoot d, the damping factor ξ and the natural angular frequency ω_n of this dynamic process.

b) Determine the corresponding transfer function $G_c(s)$.

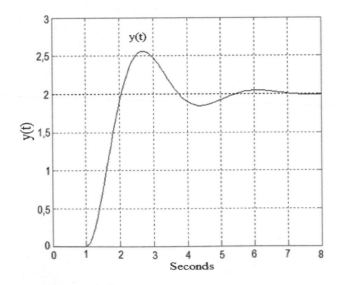

Figure 2.17. *Graph of the response to step $E_0 = 2V$*

Solution – Exercise 2.5.

The measurements D and T_m realized on the graph of the step response are presented in Figure 2.18.

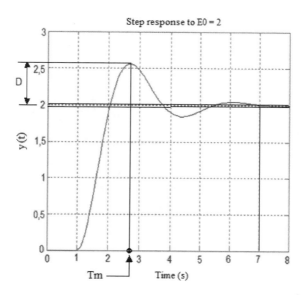

Figure 2.18. *Measurements D and T_m*

a) The measurements realized on the graph of the step response yield:

- $\tau_0 = 1$ s;

- $K_s = y(\infty)/E_0 = 2 / 2 = 1$;

- $D = 2.6 - 2 = 0.6$;

- $d = D/2 = 0.3$;

- $T_m = 2{,}75$ s, $\xi = \dfrac{\left|\log(d)\right|}{\sqrt{\pi^2 + \log^2(d)}} = 0.3579$;

- $\omega_n = \dfrac{\pi}{T_m \sqrt{1-\xi^2}} = 1.2234.$

b) $G_c(s) = \dfrac{1.4968}{s^2 + 0.8757\,s + 1.4968}\,e^{-s}$

Exercise 2.6.

Estimate the static gain K_s as well as the time constants τ_1 and τ_2 of a linear dynamic process of order 2, whose Bode diagram is represented in Figure 2.19.

Then find the corresponding transfer function $G_c(s)$.

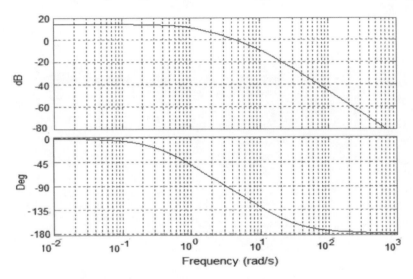

Figure 2.19. *Bode diagram of a dynamic process of order 2*

Solution – Exercise 2.6.

The measurements realized on the Bode diagram yield approximately the following (see Figure 2.20):

- $G_s = 14$ dB;
- $\omega_1 = 1$ rad/s;
- $\omega_2 = 10$ rad/s.

This leads to:

- $K_s = 10^{\,G_s/20} = 5$;
- $\tau_1 = 1 / \omega_1 = 1$;
- $\tau_2 = 1 / \omega_2 = 0.1$.

Therefore:

$$G_c(s) = \frac{Y(s)}{E_0(s)} = \frac{K_s}{(1+\tau_1 s)(1+\tau_2 s)} = \frac{5}{(1+s)(1+0.1s)} = \frac{1}{0.1\,s^2 + 1.1\,s + 1}$$

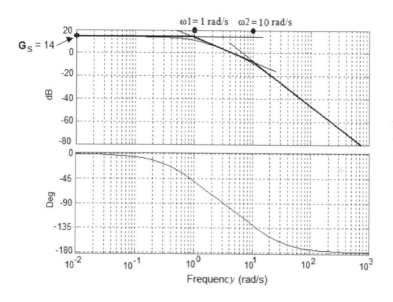

Figure 2.20. *Measurements on Bode diagram. For a color version of this figure, see www.iste.co.uk/mbihi/automation.zip*

Exercise 2.7.

Figure 2.21 represents the graph of the response $y(t)$ to a step $E_0 = 2$ of a dynamic process of order n. Using the Strejc method:

a) Estimate from this graph the static gain K_s, the order n and also the multiple time constant τ;

b) Find the corresponding transfer function $G_c(s)$.

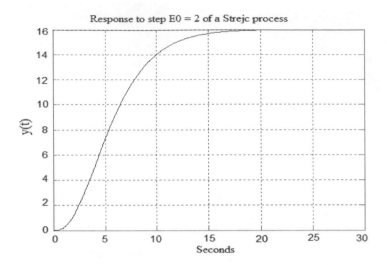

Figure 2.21. *Graph of the response y(t) to a step E₀ = 2*

Solution – Exercise 2.7.

The measurements T_u and T_a realized on the graph of the step response (see Figure 2.22) are given by:

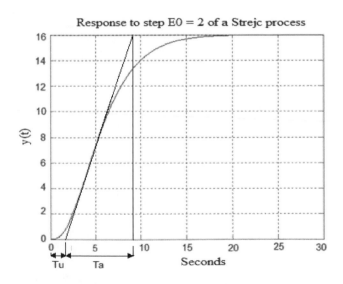

Figure 2.22. *Measurements of T_u and T_a*

a) The measurements realized on the graph of the step response yield:

- $K_s = y(\infty)/E_0 = 16/2 = 8$;

- $T_u = 1.8$ s;

- $T_a = 9$ s.

Therefore, $T_u/T_a = 0.2$ s, which yields approximately $n = 3$ in the Strejc table of parameters.

Moreover, $T_u/\tau = 0.805$; therefore, $\tau \cong T_u/0.805 = 2.236$ s.

b) $G_c(s) = \dfrac{8}{\left(1 + 2.236\ s\right)^3} = \dfrac{8}{11.8\ s^3 + 15\ s^2 + 6.708\ s + 1} = 8$

Exercise 2.8.

The experimental model for the estimation of a physical parameter β of a medium has the form $y_m(k) = \lambda + v(k)$, where $v(k)$ designates the measurement noise in stage k, with $k \in \{1, 2, 3,..., N\}$. Using the results of the least squares parameter estimation technique, prove that the best estimate $\beta*(N)$ corresponds to the average of measurements.

Solution – Exercise 2.8.

In this case where $y_m(k) = \lambda + v(k)$, $h^T(k) = 1$ for any $k = 1, 2,..., N$, and the optimal solution becomes:

$$\beta^*(N) = \frac{\sum\limits_{k=1}^{N} y_k}{N}$$

Exercise 2.9.

Let us consider a sensor whose theoretical static characteristic has the form $y = \beta_1\ x + \beta_0$, where x designates the input quantity and y the output quantity. Using the results of the least squares parameter estimation technique, calculate the best estimates $\beta_0^*(N)$ and $\beta_1^*(N)$.

Solution – Exercise 2.9.

In this case, it can be written:

$$y = \beta_1 \, x + \beta_0 = \begin{bmatrix} x & 1 \end{bmatrix} \begin{bmatrix} \beta_1 \\ \beta_0 \end{bmatrix},$$

therefore:

$$h^T(x_k) = \begin{bmatrix} x_k & 1 \end{bmatrix} \text{ and } \theta = \begin{bmatrix} \beta_1 \\ \beta_0 \end{bmatrix},$$

hence:

$$h(x_k) \, h^T(x_k) = \begin{bmatrix} x_k \\ 1 \end{bmatrix} \begin{bmatrix} x_k & 1 \end{bmatrix} = \begin{bmatrix} x_k^2 & x_k \\ x_k & 1 \end{bmatrix}$$

and

$$h(x_k) \, y_k = \begin{bmatrix} x_k \\ 1 \end{bmatrix} y_k = \begin{bmatrix} x_k \, y_k \\ y_k \end{bmatrix}$$

$$\theta_{N/N} = \frac{1}{N \sum_{k=1}^{N} x_k^2 - \left(\sum_{k=1}^{N} x_k \right)^2} \begin{bmatrix} N & -\sum_{k=1}^{N} x_k \\ -\sum_{k=1}^{N} x_k & \sum_{k=1}^{N} x_k^2 \end{bmatrix} \begin{bmatrix} \sum_{k=1}^{N} x_k \, y_k \\ \sum_{k=1}^{N} y_k \end{bmatrix}$$

Thus:

$$\beta_1^*(N) = \frac{N \sum_{k=1}^{N} x_k \, y_k - \left(\sum_{k=1}^{N} x_k \right) \left(\sum_{k=1}^{N} y_k \right)}{N \sum_{k=1}^{N} x_k^2 - \left(\sum_{k=1}^{N} x_k \right)^2}$$

$$\beta_0^*(N) = \frac{\left(\sum_{k=1}^{N} y_k \right) \left(\sum_{k=1}^{N} x_k^2 \right) - \left(\sum_{k=1}^{N} x_k \right) \left(\sum_{k=1}^{N} x_k \, y_k \right)}{N \sum_{k=1}^{N} x_k^2 - \left(\sum_{k=1}^{N} x_k \right)^2}$$

Exercise 2.10.

The methods for experimental modeling studied in this chapter have in each case advantages and drawbacks. Fill in the model Table 2.2, which allows a comparison of methods according to the mentioned criteria.

Comparison of methods for parameter identification		
Comparison criteria	Classical methods (without optimization)	Least squares method
Category of processes (dynamic or static)		
Type of model ($G_c(s)$, ARMA, etc.)		
Type of test signal		
Estimation criterion		
Algorithmic complexity		
Calculation methods		
Quality indicators		
Extension to nonlinear models		

Table 2.2. *Table for the comparison of modeling methods*

Solution – Exercise 2.10.

The comparative table of these methods is the following:

Comparison of methods for parameter identification		
Comparison criteria	Classical methods (without optimization)	Least squares method
Category of processes (dynamic or static)	Dynamic	Dynamic and static
Type of model ($G_c(s)$, ARMA, etc.)	$G_c(s)$	ARMA
Type of test signal	Step, sine	Arbitrary signal
Estimation criterion		Quadratic error
Algorithmic complexity	Low	High
Calculation methods	Direct	Programmable
Quality indicators	Empirical	Precision calculation
Possible extension to nonlinear models	No	Yes

Table 2.3. *Comparison of modeling methods*

Exercise 2.11.

Interpret the elements constituting the following Matlab command line: Gc = tfest(Data, Np, Nz, IoDelay)

Solution – Exercise 2.11.

In the following Matlab command line, Gc = tfest(Data, Np, Nz, IoDelay), the constitutive elements are:

– Data: table of identification data;

– Np: number of desired poles of the transfer function to identify;

– Nz: number of desired zeros of the transfer function to identify;

– IoDelay: pure input delay;

– Gc: returned result (identified transfer function).

Review of Analog Feedback Control Systems

3.1. Open-loop analog control

3.1.1. *Principle*

The principle of open-loop analog control of a dynamic process is illustrated in Figure 3.1, where $r(t)$ designates the desired response and $u(t)$ the direct control obtained when $r(t)$ is shaped by a conformer with characteristic $u(r)$. Thus, the open-loop control law $u(r(t))$ does not take into account the corresponding response $y(t)$ generated at the output.

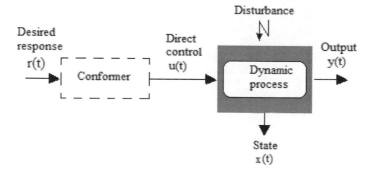

Figure 3.1. *Open-loop control of a dynamic process*

3.1.2. *Open-loop control*

In most practical cases, applying open-loop control in a real context raises serious problems, most important of which are:

– sensitivity to the effects of unknown disturbances on the effective behavior of the dynamic power process;

– sensitivity to the effects of structural and parametric uncertainties of the dynamic model used for the calculation of the predicted command;

– insufficient or weak dynamic and static performances.

In automation theory, the permanent presence of these unpredictable factors in the environment of real dynamic processes justifies the practical interest of feedback control, i.e. of regulation.

3.2. Analog control system

The principle of an analog feedback control system of a dynamic process (see Figure 3.2) involves the application of a control law $u(t)$ or $U(s)$, allowing the reduction of the possible error between desired output and generated response $y(t)$ or $Y(s)$.

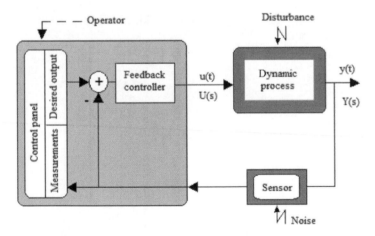

Figure 3.2. *Control principle of a dynamic process*

Several configurations of block diagrams of analog control systems are possible from Figure 3.2. Figure 3.3 corresponds to an example of a generic block diagram, where $H(s)$, $G_c(s)$, $D_c(s)$ and $H_c(s)$ are the transfer functions of conformer/sensor, controller and dynamic process, respectively. Moreover, the signals shown in Figure 3.3 are:

- Y_r: desired response;

- U: control input;

- Y: observed or desired output;

- υ: power process disturbance;

- W: measurement noise.

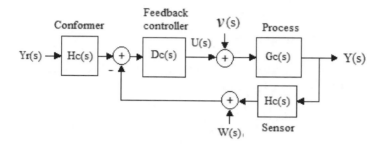

Figure 3.3. *Generic block diagram of analog control systems*

3.3. Performances of an analog control system

3.3.1. *Closed-loop transfer functions*

Considering, without loss of generality, that in Figure 3.3 $H(s) = 1$, it can be verified that in these conditions:

$$Y(s) = \frac{G_c(s)D_c(s)}{1+G_c(s)D_c(s)}U(s) + \frac{G_c(s)}{1+G_c(s)D_c(s)}V(s) - \frac{G_c(s)D_c(s)}{1+G_c(s)D_c(s)}W(s) \qquad [3.1]$$

Thus, the characteristic transfer functions of an analog control system are:

- $G_o(s) = G_c(s)D_c(s)$ (Loop gain) $\qquad\qquad$ [3.2]

- $\hat{G}_s(s) = \dfrac{1}{1+G_c(s)D_c(s)}$ (Sensitivity function) $\qquad\qquad$ [3.3]

- $F_c(p) = \dfrac{G_c(s)D_c(s)}{1+G_c(s)D_c(s)}$ (Closed-loop transfer function) $\qquad\qquad$ [3.4]

In practice, control is expected to meet the following constraints:

$- G_o(s) \gg 1$ at low frequencies, when noise is nearly absent, in order to guarantee a proper follower behavior, since $G_c(s) \to 0$ and $F_c(s) \to 1$;

$- G_o(s) \ll 1$ at high frequencies, when desired response and disturbance are nearly absent, so that noise is sufficiently damped;

$- F_c(s) = \dfrac{G_c(s)D_c(s)}{1+G_c(s)D_c(s)}$ stable (if the roots of the equation $1+G_O(s)=0$ have

negative real parts in the complex plane of variable p).

3.3.2. *Performance quantities*

The performance quantities that allow the synthesis of control laws in the frequency domain knowing the model of dynamic process are:

– Stability, which characterizes in the internal sense the property of a process to return within finite time to its initial equilibrium state after a disturbance. On the other hand, it characterizes in the input/output sense the fact that every bounded input results in a bounded output.

– Static precision, quantifiable by the error percentage, in steady state, between the desired output and the generated response.

– Rapidity, defined on the basis of time response to a control input.

– Optimality, characterized by the possibility of a control law to provide the optimal value of a functional criterion.

3.4. Simple analog controllers

Let us remember that a controller (central device of the control system in Figure 3.3) is modeled in the frequency domain by its transfer function $D_c(s)$. For modest levels of performance, the use of controllers described by simple transfer functions may be sufficient. This is the case of:

– proportional controller:

$$D_c(s) = K_c;$$ [3.5]

– phase-lead controller:

$$D_c(s) = \frac{K_c(1+\tau s)}{1+\alpha \tau s} \quad \text{with } \alpha < 1;$$ [3.6]

– phase-lag controller:

$$D_c(s) = \frac{K_c(1+\tau s)}{1+\alpha(\tau s)} \quad \text{with } \alpha > 1.$$ [3.7]

On the other hand, for higher levels of performance, PID/PIDF controllers, which will be studied in detail below, can be used.

3.5. PID/PIDF controllers

3.5.1. *Structure and role of the parameters of a PID/PIDF controller*

A simple PID controller is described by the transfer function:

$$D_c(s) = K_p + \frac{K_i}{s} + K_d\, s = K_p \left(1 + \frac{1}{T_i\, s} + T_d\, s\right)$$ [3.8]

with:

– K_p: proportional gain;

– T_i: K_p/K_i (integral time constant);

– T_d: K_d/K_p (differential time constant).

On the other hand, a PIDF (PID-Filter) is an extended variant of PID, defined by four parameters. The transfer function of the PIDF controller has the form:

$$D_c(s) = K_p + \frac{K_i}{s} + \frac{K_d\, s}{1+T_f\, s} = K_p \left(1 + \frac{1}{T_i\, s} + \frac{T_d\, s}{1+T_f\, s}\right)$$ [3.9]

It is worth noting that the rational structure of a PIDF controller defined by [3.9] is proper, unlike that of a standard PID controller [3.8]. Moreover, parameters K_p, K_i, K_d and T_f play complementary roles if they are adequately sized. Figure 3.4 presents typical examples of closed-loop step response profiles of a dynamic process modeled by $G_c(s) = \dfrac{20}{s^2+s+0.1}$, controllable by P, PI, PID and PIDF controllers, with $K_p = 0.05$; $K_i = 0.005$; $K_d = 0.035$ and $T_f = 0.25$ s.

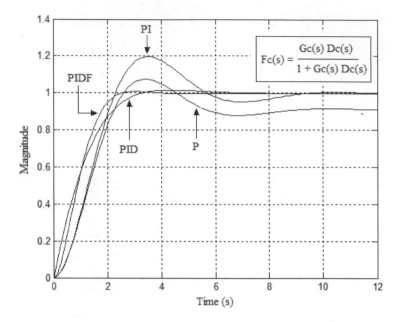

Figure 3.4. *Roles of parameters of a PIDF controller*

A visual analysis of the morphological configurations between the step responses observed in Figure 3.4 leads to the following observations:

– K_p is a stability parameter. It allows a closed-loop system under a P controller to start until reaching a permanent state that is close to the desired output profile. The generated static error may nevertheless be significant.

– K_i is a static precision parameter. It allows a closed-loop system under a PI controller to cancel the static error in steady state. Nevertheless, the integral action of K_i generates a degradation of transient performances (undesired magnitude overshoots, significant response time, etc.);

– K_d is a transient compensation parameter. It allows a closed-loop system under a PID controller to correct the possible degrading effects caused by the integral action of K_i. However, the differential action of K_d may lead to a closed-loop structure of rational and not proper type, which involves the risk of undesirable deformation of the bandwidth;

– T_f is a structural quality parameter. It allows a closed-loop system under a PIDF controller to have a proper rational structure and to offer a good bandwidth.

3.5.2. Ziegler–Nichols methods for parameter calculation

Among the published experimental techniques for determining the parameters of a PID controller, the easiest to implement are those of Ziegler–Nichols [ZIE 42]. They however rely either on the test results of the open-loop step response or on the experimental research on the closed-loop limit gain, for which the first oscillations occur.

Figure 3.5 shows (for each type of test considered) the quantities to measure on the graphic profile of the corresponding experimental response, in order to calculate the Ziegler–Nichols parameters according to the algorithmic specifications presented in Table 3.1. Let us remember that, for Figure 3.5(a), $T_a = \tau$ (time constant of the process of order 1).

Tests	Control	K_p	T_i	T_d
Profile of the open-loop step response (order 1) Figure 3.5(a)	P	$(E_0 / H) (T_a / T_m)$	–	–
	PI	$0.9(E_0 / H) (T_a / T_m)$	$3.33\ T_m$	–
	PID	$1.2(E_0 / H) (T_a / T_m)$	$2\ T_m$	$T_m / 2$
Profile of the open-loop step response (order ≥ 2) Figure 3.5(b)	P	$(E_0 / H) (T_a / T_m)$	–	–
	PI	$0.9(E_0 / H) (T_a / T_m)$	$3.33\ T_m$	–
	PID	$1.2E_0T_a / (HT_m)$	$2\ T_m$	$T_m/2$
Profile of the closed-loop oscillating response (stability limit) Figure 3.5(c)	P	$0.5\ Kosc$	–	0
	PI	$0.45\ Kosc$	$Tosc / 1.2$	0
	PID	$0.6\ Kosc$	$Tosc / 2$	$Tosc / 8$

Table 3.1. Determination of PID parameters by Ziegler–Nichols methods

3.5.3. Calculation of parameters by pole placement

The pole placement method allows the calculation of PID parameters knowing the transfer function $G_c(s)$ of an open-loop dynamic process. This method involves solving the system of equations resulting from the comparison of a desired closed-loop characteristic polynomial $P(\lambda)$ and a characteristic polynomial given by the equation $1 + D_c(s)\, G_c(s) = 0$.

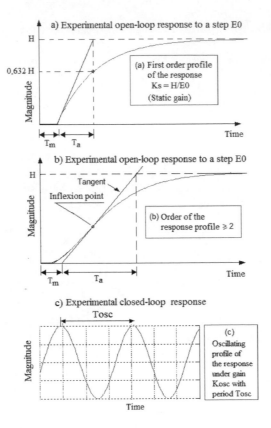

Figure 3.5. *Open-loop response of the test to step E_0. For a color version of this figure, see www.iste.co.uk/mbihi/automation.zip*

For example, let us consider the following case:

$$G_c(s) = \frac{K}{s\ (1+\tau\ s)}$$

$$D_c(s) = K_p + \frac{K_i}{s} + K_d s$$

[3.10]

In this case, it can be verified that:

$$F_c(s) = \frac{G_c(s)D_c(s)}{1+G_c(s)D_c(s)} = \frac{K\ (K_i + K_p\ s)}{\tau\ s^3 + (1+K_d\ K)\ s^2 + K\ K_p\ s + K\ K_i}$$

[3.11]

or:

$$F_c(s) = \frac{K\,K_p}{\tau} \cdot \frac{\left(s + \dfrac{K_i}{K_p}\right)}{s^3 + \dfrac{(1 + K_d\,K)}{\tau}s^2 + \dfrac{K\,K_p}{\tau}s + \dfrac{K\,K_i}{\tau}}$$

[3.12]

Therefore, if p_1, p_2 and p_3 are desired closed-loop poles that are considered known, then the searched parameters can be found by solving the equation:

$$s^3 + \frac{(1 + K_d\,K)}{\tau}s^2 + \frac{K\,K_p}{\tau}s + \frac{K}{\tau} = (s - p_1)(s - p_2)(s - p_3)$$

$$= s^3 - (p_1 + p_2 + p_3)s^2 + (p_1 p_2 + p_1 p_3 + p_2\, p_3)s - p_1 p_2\, p_3$$

[3.13]

The equalization of coefficients of the same degree on each side of the equality leads to the following solution:

$$Kp = (p_1 p_2 + p_1 p_3 + p_2\, p_3)\frac{\tau}{K}$$

$$K_d = -\frac{1 + (p_1 + p_2 + p_3)\,\tau}{K}$$

$$K_i = -p_1 p_2\, p_3\, \frac{\tau}{K}$$

[3.14]

3.5.4. *Direct calculation of optimal PID parameters*

Most methods for the direct calculation of optimal PID parameters rely on the functional criteria of error between desired response and output. Examples of criteria are as follows [OGA 90, TAV 03]:

– IAE = $\int_0^\infty |e(t)|\, dt$ (*Integral Absolute Error*)   [3.15]

– ITAE = $\int_0^\infty t\,|e(t)|\, dt$ (*Integral Time Absolute Error*)   [3.16]

– ISE – $\int_0^\infty e^2(t)\, dt$ (*Integral Square Error*)   [3.17]

– ITSE = $\int_0^\infty t\, e^2(t)\, dt$ (*Integral Time Square Error*)   [3.18]

– ISTE = $\int_0^\infty (t\, e)^2 (t)\, dt$ (*Integral Square Time Error*)   [3.19]

Literature mentions various types of optimization algorithms, whose results are published as tables, which allow the direct calculation of optimal parameters of a PID controller for some criteria chosen in [3.15] to [3.19]. Nevertheless, most of these tables are not readily exploitable directly, except for dynamic models of specific structure.

Table 3.2 presents an example of a table for calculating PID parameters [TAV 03] based on reduction to unitless quantities {K K_p, T_i / τ_m, T_i / τ_m}, followed by a process of numerical optimization in this new homogeneous parametric space. It is intended for open-loop dynamic models described by the following transfer function:

$$G(s) = \frac{K}{1 + \tau s} e^{-\tau_m s} \qquad\qquad [3.20]$$

Criteria	Optimal parameters		
	K_p	T_i	T_d
IAE $\int_0^\infty |e(t)| \, dt$	$\dfrac{1}{K\left(0.2 + \dfrac{\tau_m}{\tau}\right)}$	$\dfrac{\tau_m\left(0.3\dfrac{\tau_m}{\tau} + 1.2\right)}{\left(0.08 + \dfrac{\tau_m}{\tau}\right)}$	$\dfrac{\tau_m}{90\left(\dfrac{\tau_m}{\tau}\right)}$
ITAE $\int_0^\infty t\,|e(t)| \, dt$	$\dfrac{0.8}{K\left(0.1 + \dfrac{\tau_m}{\tau}\right)}$	$\tau_m\left(0.3 + \dfrac{1}{\left(\dfrac{\tau_m}{\tau}\right)}\right)$	$\dfrac{0.06\ \tau_m}{0.04 + \left(\dfrac{\tau_m}{\tau}\right)}$
ISE $\int_0^\infty e^2(t)\, dt$	$\dfrac{0.3\left(\dfrac{\tau_m}{\tau}\right) + 0,75}{K\left(0.05 + \dfrac{\tau_m}{\tau}\right)}$	$\dfrac{2.4\ \tau_m}{0.4 + \dfrac{\tau_m}{\tau}}$	$\dfrac{\tau_m}{90\left(\dfrac{\tau_m}{\tau}\right)}$

Table 3.2. *Table for the calculation of the parameters of an optimal PID controller according to IAE, ITAE and ISE optimization criteria*

Matlab® functions "iaepid.m", "itaepid.m" and "isepid.m" presented below allow the calculation of PID controller parameters according to IAE, ITAE and ISE criteria, respectively. In each case, the arguments of the function to call are:

– K: static gain;

– *Tau* ≡ τ: time constant;

– *Taud* ≡ τ_d: pure input delay;

– TF: final time.

Moreover, the returned values are:

– *KpTiTd*: vector of optimal parameters K_p, T_i, T_d;

– *Time*: time vector.

No.	"iaepid.m" function
1	function [KpTiTd, Y, Time] = iaepid(K, Tau, Taud, TF)
2	Td_T = Taud/Tau;
3	s = tf('s'); G = exp(-Taud*s)*K/(1+Tau*s);% G(p)
4	Kp = (1/K)*(1)/(Td_T+0.2);
5	Ti = Taud*(0.3*Td_T+1.2)/(Td_T+0.08); % Ti
6	Td = (Taud/90)/Td_T; % Td
7	D = Kp*(1+1/(Ti*s)+Td*s); % D(p)
8	F = feedback(series(D,G),1); % F(p)
9	KpTiTd = [Kp, Ti, Td]; % Kp; Ti, Td
10	[Y, Time] = step(F, TF); % Step response

No.	"itaepid.m" function
1	function [KpTiTd, Y, Time] = itaepid(K, Tau, Taud, TF)
2	Td_T = Taud/Tau;
3	s= tf('s'); G = exp(-Taud*s)*K/(1+Tau*s); % G(p
4	Kp = (1/K)*(0.8)/(Td_T+0.1); % Kp
5	Ti = Taud*(0.3 + 1/Td_T); % Ti
6	Td = (Taud*0.06)/(Td_T+0.04); % Td
7	D = Kp*(1+1/(Ti*s)+Td*s); % D(p)
8	F = feedback(series(D,G),1); % F(p)
9	KpTiTd = [Kp Ti Td]; % Kp; TI, Td
10	[Y, Time] = step(F,TF); % Step response

No.	"isepid.m" function
1	function [KpTiTd, Y, Time] = isepid(K, Tau, Taud, TF)
2	Td_T = Taud/Tau;
3	S = tf('s'); G = exp(-Taud*s)*K/(1+Tau*s); % G(p)
4	Kp = (1/K)*(0.3*Td_T+0.75)/(Td_T+0.05); % Kp
5	Ti = 2.4*Taud/(Td_T+0.4); % Ti
6	Td = (Taud/90)/Td_T; % Td
7	D = Kp*(1+1/(Ti*s)+Td*s); % D(p)
8	F = feedback(series(D,G),1) ; % F(p)
9	KpTiTd = [Kp, Ti, Td]; % Kp; Ti, Td
10	[Y, Temps] = step(F,TF); % Step response

As an illustration, if:

$$G_c(s) = \frac{5}{1+1.5\,s}\, e^{-s} \qquad\qquad [3.21]$$

Then the above "itaepid.m" function can be used to calculate the results presented in Figure 3.6. The detailed study leading to this figure and to other criteria will be presented in a solved exercise to be found at the end of this chapter.

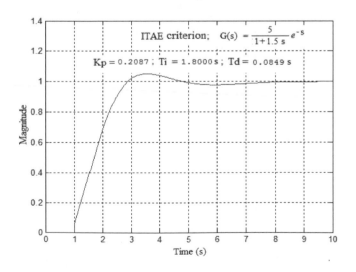

Figure 3.6. *Results of the application of ITAE criterion of Table 3.2*

3.5.5. *LQR-based indirect calculation of optimal PID parameters*

In this case, the problem of the PID controller is reformulated and solved in the space state similar to that of an LQR (*Linear Quadratic Regulator*), which is easier to solve. Then the searched parameters of the optimal PID are calculated based on those of the resulting LQR [OBR 08]. This topical subject will be examined in detail in section 3.7.

3.5.6. *Implementation of analog controllers*

The structures of simple analog controllers can be readily implemented by means of several embedded operational amplifiers and passive components (resistors and capacitors). Table 3.3 presents the electronic diagrams of simple analog P controllers, with phase-lead/lag, with PID and PIDF action, as well as the corresponding transfer functions.

Type	Electronic diagram	$D(s) = U(s)/E(s)$
P		$$-\frac{R_b}{R_a}$$
Phase-lead or lag		$$-\left(\frac{R_b}{R_a}\right)\left(\frac{1 + R_a\,C_a\,s}{1 + R_b\,C_b\,s}\right)$$ or, $$-\left(\frac{R_b}{R_a}\right)\left(1 + \frac{(R_a\,C_a - R_b\,C_b)\,s}{1 + R_b\,C_b\,s}\right)$$
PID		Serial structure $$-\left(\frac{R_b}{R_a}\right)\frac{(1 + R_a\,C_a\,s)(1 + R_b\,C_b\,s)}{R_b\,C_b\,s}$$ Parameters of the parallel structure $$K_p = -\frac{\left(R_a C_a + R_b C_b\right)}{R_a\,C_b},\quad K_i = \frac{1}{R_b C_b},$$ $$K_d = R_b C_a$$
PIDF		$$-\frac{1}{(R_a + R_s)\,C_b}\frac{(1 + R_a\,C_a\,s)\,(1 + R_b\,C_b\,s)}{p\left(1 + \frac{R_a R_s}{R_a + R_s}C_a\,s\right)}$$

Table 3.3. *Electronic diagrams and transfer functions of simple analog controllers*

As will be shown further, dynamic models of analog controllers can be easily discretized in order to be implemented by a digital processor.

Nowadays, the digital environment offers new algorithmic possibilities for implementing structures of adaptive PID/PIDF controllers, using connectionist components of artificial intelligence, based on:

– fuzzy logic [VAI 07];

– neural network [MOH 10].

3.6. Controllers described in the state space

Let us consider a deterministic dynamic process described by the following state model, assumed controllable:

$$\frac{dx(t)}{dt} = A_c\ x(t) + B_c\ u(t) \qquad\qquad [3.22]$$

with:

– A_c: $n \times n$ matrix;

– B_c: $n \times 1$ matrix.

3.6.1. *Principle and block diagram of a linear state feedback*

The principle of linear state feedback involves the determination of required values of a gain K matrix, so that the control law given by the relation:

$$u(t) = -\ K\ x(t)\ + \text{Ref} \qquad\qquad [3.23]$$

meets the considered performance criterion. The resulting structure of the linear state feedback law is described by the following relation:

$$\frac{dx(t)}{dt} = (A_c - B_c K)\ x(t) + B_c\ \text{Ref} \qquad\qquad [3.24]$$

and corresponds to the block diagram in Figure 3.7. In this case, the dynamic behavior of [3.24] is dictated by $(A_c - B_c K)$ matrix.

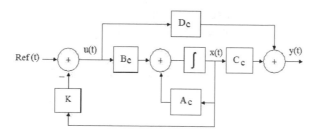

Figure 3.7. *Structure of a linear state feedback law*

3.6.2. *Techniques for calculating the state feedback gain*

Each type of state feedback controller differs from other types by the algorithmic technique used for the calculation of gain matrix K, which offers the expected closed-loop performance level.

Automation literature provides a wide variety of algorithms for the calculation of state feedback matrix K of an LTI process.

Several basic techniques for calculating the gains K of analog controllers are:

– Pole(s) placement, which involves finding vector K for which the characteristic polynomial of matrix $(A_c - B_c K)$ coincides with a fixed polynomial $P(\lambda) = \lambda^n + a_{n-1}\lambda^{n-1} + ... + a_1\lambda + a_0$. This involves finding the unknown vector $K = [K_1\ K_2\ ...\ K_n]$ by the identification of n terms of the nth-order equation:

$$\left|\lambda I_n - A_c + B_c K\right| = \lambda^n + a_{n-1}\lambda^{n-1} + ... + a_1\lambda + a_0 \qquad [3.25]$$

Under these conditions, there are two Matlab commands, namely "place" and "acker" that can be used to rapidly calculate the numerical value of gain K according to the corresponding syntaxes:

- $K = place(A_c, B_c, Vectpoles)$ % Basic algorithm

- $Kack = acker(A_c, B_c, Vectpoles)$ % Ackermann algorithm

where "VectPoles" designates the Matlab vector consisting of fixed poles.

– *Linear Quadratic Regulator* (LQR), which involves finding the gain vector $K(t)$ that minimizes or maximizes (as applicable) a functional criterion of the following form:

$$J_0 = \int_{t0}^{t1} x^T(t)Qx(t) + u^T(t)Ru(t)\ dt + \psi(x(t_1), t_1) \qquad [3.26]$$

Under the dynamic constraint described by the state model:

$$\frac{dx(t)}{dt} = A_c x + B_c u(t)$$

[3.27]

$$y(t) = C_c x(t) + D_c u(t)$$

where $Q \geq 0$, $\psi \geq 0$ and $R > 0$ are symmetric matrices.

The instantaneous solution $K(t)$ is obtained by solving the Riccati dynamic matrix equation:

$$-\frac{dS(t)}{dt} = Q + A_c^T S(t) + S(t) A_c - S(t) B_c R^{-1} B_c^T S(t):$$

[3.28]

This searched vector $K(t)$ is given by the following relations:

$$K(t) = R^{-1} B_c^T S(t)$$

[3.29]

In practice, the suboptimal solution $S(\infty) = S_\infty$ of the steady equation deduced from [3.28] is written as:

$$0 = Q + A_c^T S_\infty + S_\infty A_c - S_\infty B_c (R^{-1})^T B_c^T S_\infty$$

[3.30]

The suboptimal steady gain $K\infty = R^{-1}B^T S\infty$ obtained after solving [3.30] can be used, if needed, in many practical problems of real-time feedback control. In this case, the Matlab command "lqr" can be used to rapidly solve equation [3.30] according to the following reduced syntax:

[Kinf, Sinf] = *lqr*(A_c, B_c, Q, R) % Resolution of [3.30].

3.6.3. *Integral action state feedback*

The use of a state feedback controller allows the stabilization of a closed-loop dynamic process. In terms of precision, the state feedback effect must be reinforced by an integral action of the set point tracking error. Figure 3.8 presents the block diagram of an example of a feedback control system that uses integral action state feedback.

This system is described by the following dynamic equations:

$$\frac{dx(t)}{dt} = A_c\, x(t) + B_c\, u(t)$$

$$\frac{dx_i(t)}{dt} = y(t) - y_r = C_c\, x(t) - y_r$$

$$y(t) = C_c\, x(t)$$

[3.31]

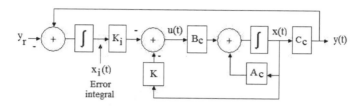

Figure 3.8. *State feedback control system with integral action*

From a matrix perspective, [3.31] can be written as:

$$\begin{bmatrix} \dfrac{dx(t)}{dt} \\ \dfrac{dx_i(t)}{dt} \end{bmatrix} = \begin{bmatrix} A_C & 0 \\ C_C & 0 \end{bmatrix}\begin{bmatrix} x(t) \\ x_i(t) \end{bmatrix} + \begin{bmatrix} B_C \\ 0 \end{bmatrix} u(t) - \begin{bmatrix} 0 \\ 1 \end{bmatrix} y_r$$

$$y(t) = \begin{bmatrix} C_C & 0 \end{bmatrix}\begin{bmatrix} x(t) \\ x_i(t) \end{bmatrix}$$

[3.32]

with:

$$u(t) = -K\, x(t) - K_i\, x_i(t) = -\begin{bmatrix} K & K_i \end{bmatrix}\begin{bmatrix} x(t) \\ x_i(t) \end{bmatrix}$$

[3.33]

This yields:

$$\begin{bmatrix} \dfrac{dx(t)}{dt} \\ \dfrac{dx_i(t)}{dt} \end{bmatrix} = \begin{bmatrix} A_c & 0 \\ C_c & 0 \end{bmatrix}\begin{bmatrix} x(t) \\ x_i(t) \end{bmatrix} - \begin{bmatrix} B_c \\ 0 \end{bmatrix}\begin{bmatrix} K & K_i \end{bmatrix}\begin{bmatrix} x(t) \\ x_i(t) \end{bmatrix} - \begin{bmatrix} 0 \\ 1 \end{bmatrix} y_r$$

$$y(t) = \begin{bmatrix} C_C & 0 \end{bmatrix}\begin{bmatrix} x(t) \\ x_i(t) \end{bmatrix}$$

[3.34]

hence the following final structure of the state feedback control system with integral action:

$$
\begin{bmatrix} \dfrac{dx(t)}{dt} \\ \dfrac{dx_i(t)}{dt} \end{bmatrix} = \begin{bmatrix} A_C - B_C K & -B_C K_i \\ C_C & 0 \end{bmatrix} \begin{bmatrix} x(t) \\ x_i(t) \end{bmatrix} - \begin{bmatrix} 0 \\ 1 \end{bmatrix} y_r
$$

$$
y(t) = \begin{bmatrix} C_C & 0 \end{bmatrix} \begin{bmatrix} x(t) \\ x_i(t) \end{bmatrix}
$$

[3.35]

For any steady feedback law, the steady states (for $t \to \infty$) can be obtained by solving the equation:

$$
\begin{bmatrix} 0 \\ 0 \end{bmatrix} = \begin{bmatrix} A_C - B_C K & -B_C K_i \\ C_C & 0 \end{bmatrix} \begin{bmatrix} x(\infty) \\ x_i(\infty) \end{bmatrix} - \begin{bmatrix} 0 \\ 1 \end{bmatrix} y_r
$$

$$
y(\infty) = \begin{bmatrix} C_C & 0 \end{bmatrix} \begin{bmatrix} x(\infty) \\ x_i(\infty) \end{bmatrix}
$$

[3.36]

Hence:

$$
\begin{bmatrix} x(\infty) \\ x_i(\infty) \end{bmatrix} = - \begin{bmatrix} A_C - B_C K & -B_c K_i \\ C_C & 0 \end{bmatrix}^{-1} \begin{bmatrix} 0 \\ 1 \end{bmatrix} y_r
$$

$$
y(\infty) = \begin{bmatrix} C_C & 0 \end{bmatrix} \begin{bmatrix} x(\infty) \\ x_i(\infty) \end{bmatrix}
$$

[3.37]

3.6.4. *State feedback with integral action and observer*

Practical implementation of the state feedback control law requires states that are accessible to measurement, which is not always the case, due to unavailability or to high costs of an appropriate instrumentation system for state measurement. The technical solution to this practical problem is a state estimator, which is an electronic device allowing full or partial reconstruction of the process state based on possible measurements.

Figure 3.9 presents the block diagram of a linear feedback control system with state estimator. Direct analysis of this diagram yields the following combined equations of the whole (state feedback and estimator):

$$\frac{dx(t)}{dt} = A_c x(t) + B_c\, u(t)$$

$$\frac{dx_i(t)}{dt} = y(t) - y_r = C_c\, x(t) - y_r \qquad\qquad [3.38]$$

$$\frac{d\hat{x}(t)}{dt} = A_c \hat{x}(t) + B_c\, u(t) + L(y(t) - \hat{y}(t))$$

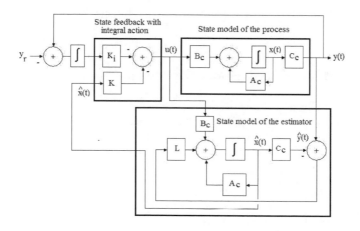

Figure 3.9. *State feedback control system with integral action and observer*

Considering that:

$$\varepsilon = x - \hat{x}(t)$$

and the following control law based on estimated state feedback under integral action:

$$u(t) = -K\,\hat{x}(t) - K_i\, x_i(t) \qquad\qquad [3.39]$$

it can be written:

$$\frac{d\varepsilon(t)}{dt} = \frac{dx(t)}{dt} - \frac{d\hat{x}(t)}{dt} = A_c \varepsilon(t) + L\, C_c\, \varepsilon(t) = (A_c + L\, C_c)\, \varepsilon(t) \qquad [3.40]$$

Therefore, the following final structure of the global system of equations is written:

$$
\begin{bmatrix} \dfrac{dx(t)}{dt} \\ \dfrac{dx_i(t)}{dt} \\ \dfrac{d\varepsilon(t)}{dt} \end{bmatrix} = \begin{bmatrix} A_c - B_c K & -B_c K_i & 0 \\ C_c & 0 & 0 \\ 0 & 0 & A_c + L\,C_c \end{bmatrix} \begin{bmatrix} x(t) \\ x_i(t) \\ \varepsilon(t) \end{bmatrix} - \begin{bmatrix} 0 \\ 1 \\ 0 \end{bmatrix} y_r \qquad [3.41]
$$

The state feedback gain [K K$_i$] and the estimation gain L can thus be determined independently.

3.6.5. *State feedback with output error compensator*

This type of situation is manifest when the feedback law has a dynamic behavior, which can consequently be described in the state space (see Figure 3.10).

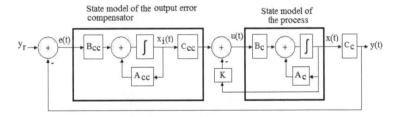

Figure 3.10. *Control system with dynamic state feedback*

Thus, the behavior of a PI controller in the state space is similar to a simple example of dynamic state feedback law, whose internal state corresponds to the integral of the output error. Smith predictor is another example of a dynamic state feedback law that is commonly used for the control of processes with time delay.

3.7. Principle of equivalence between PID and LQR controllers

The equivalence principle between PID and LQR controllers was identified a long time ago [OBR 08].

3.7.1. *Proof of the equivalence principle*

The new idea conveyed by this principle to be proven below, directly applicable to dynamic processes of order 2, is that the design of a PID controller, optimal in the sense of minimal tracking errors of the desired output, can be reduced for the same process to that of an equivalent LQR controller modeled in the state space.

Indeed, let us consider a dynamic process that admits $u(t)$ as control input and $y(t)$ as output, which is modeled by an open-loop transfer function:

$$G(s) = \frac{Y(s)}{U(s)} = \frac{K_s\,\omega_n^2}{s^2 + 2\xi\omega_n s + \omega_n^2} \qquad [3.42]$$

The objective is to equip this process with a PID controller described by:

$$D(s) = \frac{U(s)}{E(s)} = K_p + \frac{K_i}{s} + K_d\,s \qquad [3.43]$$

that minimizes, for example, the quadratic norm of the tracking error $E(s)$ of a fixed desired output.

The graphic interpretation of the PID control loop formed by [3.42] and [3.43] corresponds to Figure 3.11.

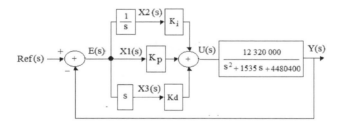

Figure 3.11. *PID control loop of a second-order process*

In order to bring the PID design problem into the space state, the following differential equation of order 2 obtained from the Laplace inverse transform of [3.42] can be used:

$$\frac{d^2 y(t)}{dt} = -2\xi\omega_n \frac{dy}{dt} - \omega_n^2\,y + K_s\,\omega_n^2\,u(t) \qquad [3.44]$$

For a control problem of Figure 3.12, let us consider, without loss of generality, that Ref $= 0$, which yields $y =$ Ref $- e = - e$. Thus, [3.44] becomes:

$$-\frac{d^2 e(t)}{dt^2} = 2\xi\omega_n \frac{de}{dt} + \omega_n^2 \, e + K_s \, \omega_n^2 \, u(t) \qquad [3.45]$$

or otherwise expressed:

$$\frac{d^2 e(t)}{dt} = -2\xi\omega_n \frac{de}{dt} - \omega_n^2 \, e - K_s \, \omega_n^2 \, u(t) \qquad [3.46]$$

State variables x_1, x_2 and x_3 indicated in Figure 3.11 are defined in the time domain by:

$$x_1 = e, \quad x_2 = \int e \, dt, \quad x_3 = \frac{de}{dt} \qquad [3.47]$$

At this stage, the relation between [3.46] and [3.47] can therefore be expressed in the form:

$$\begin{cases} \dfrac{dx_1}{dt} = \dfrac{de}{dt} = x_3, \\[2mm] \dfrac{dx_2}{dt} = e = x_1 \\[2mm] \dfrac{dx_3}{dt} = \dfrac{d^2 e}{dt^2} = -2\xi\omega_n \, x_3 - \omega_n^2 \, x_1 + K_s \, \omega_n^2 \, u(t) \end{cases} \qquad [3.48]$$

which corresponds to the following state model:

$$\begin{bmatrix} \dfrac{dx_1(t)}{dt} \\[2mm] \dfrac{dx_2(t)}{dt} \\[2mm] \dfrac{dx_3(t)}{dt} \end{bmatrix} = \begin{bmatrix} 0 & 0 & 1 \\ 1 & 0 & 0 \\ -\omega_n^2 & 0 & -2\xi\omega_n \end{bmatrix} \begin{bmatrix} x_1(t) \\ x_2(t) \\ x_3(t) \end{bmatrix} + \begin{bmatrix} 0 \\ 0 \\ K_s \, \omega_n^2 \end{bmatrix} u(t) \qquad [3.49]$$

Considering that:

$$A_c = \begin{bmatrix} 0 & 0 & 1 \\ 1 & 0 & 0 \\ -\omega_n^2 & 0 & -2\xi\omega_n \end{bmatrix} \quad B = \begin{bmatrix} 0 \\ 0 \\ K_s\,\omega_n^2 \end{bmatrix} \quad C_c = \begin{bmatrix} 1 & 0 & 0 \end{bmatrix} \quad D_c = 0 \qquad [3.50]$$

$$Q = \begin{bmatrix} q_1 & 0 & 0 \\ 0 & q_2 & 0 \\ 0 & 0 & q_3 \end{bmatrix} \quad and \quad R = r \qquad\qquad [3.51]$$

then the solution to the LQR problem over a finite time horizon, associated with [3.49], is given by:

$$u(t) = -K\,x(t) \quad with \quad K = R^{-1}\,B_c^T S \qquad\qquad [3.52]$$

where S is the solution of the Riccati equation:

$$0 = Q + A_c^T S + S\,A_c - SB_c\,R^{-1T}B_c^T S \qquad\qquad [3.53]$$

Given [3.51] and knowing that the solution to [3.53] has the form:

$$S = \begin{bmatrix} S11 & S12 & S13 \\ S21 & S22 & S23 \\ S31 & S32 & S33 \end{bmatrix} \qquad\qquad [3.54]$$

then the expression of gain K defined in [3.52] becomes:

$$u(t) = -R^{-1}B_c^T S\,x(t) = \frac{1}{r}\begin{bmatrix} 0 & 0 & K_s\omega_n^2 \end{bmatrix}\begin{bmatrix} S11 & S12 & S13 \\ S21 & S22 & S23 \\ S31 & S32 & S33 \end{bmatrix}x(t)$$

$$= \begin{bmatrix} \dfrac{K_s\omega_n^2}{r}S31 & \dfrac{K_s\omega_n^2}{r}S32 & \dfrac{K_s\omega_n^2}{r}S33 \end{bmatrix}x(t) \qquad\qquad [3.55]$$

The conclusion can therefore be drawn that the PID controller defined by [3.43] and the LQR controller given by [3.55] are structurally equivalent.

3.7.2. *Equivalence relation*

To conclude, the relation governing the equivalence principle between PID and LQR controllers results from the equality of expressions [3.43] and [3.55] in the time domain:

$$u(t) = - \underbrace{\begin{bmatrix} K1 & K2 & K3 \end{bmatrix} \begin{bmatrix} x_1(t) \\ x_2(t) \\ x_3(t) \end{bmatrix}}_{LQR} = - \underbrace{\begin{bmatrix} K_p & K_i & K_d \end{bmatrix} \begin{bmatrix} \int e(t)dt \\ e(t) \\ \dfrac{de(t)}{dt} \end{bmatrix}}_{PID} \qquad [3.56]$$

In terms of gains, the following relations are obtained:

$$\begin{cases} K_p = K_1 = \dfrac{K_s \omega_n^2}{r} S31 \\[3mm] K_i = K_2 = \dfrac{K_s \omega_n^2}{r} S32 \\[3mm] K_d = K_3 = \dfrac{K_s \omega_n^2}{r} S33 \end{cases} \qquad [3.57]$$

3.7.3. *Case study*

Figure 3.12 shows the schematic diagram of a Buck chopper under direct open-loop control via duty-cycle modulation, where:

– Ref = 2 volts;

– V_c = 15 volts;

– R_1 = 2.32 kΩ;

– R_2 = 10 kΩ;

– R = 1.2 kΩ;

– C_1 = 33 nF;

– R_4 = 1 kΩ;

– E = 12 volts;

– L = 1 mH;

– C = 220 uF;

– R_s = 2.3 Ω.

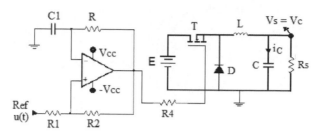

Figure 3.12. *Buck chopper with duty-cycle modulation control*

A virtual modeling-based estimation of the transfer function of this chopper based on the response to a desired response Ref = 1 volt has led to the following parameters of the equivalent model of order 2:

– Ks = 2.75 (static gain);

– ω_n = 2116.7 rad/s (natural angular frequency);

– ξ = 0.3626 (damping).

The objective is to design an optimal PID controller of this system based on solving the equivalent LQR problem.

Stage 1: Creation of the open-loop state model

Let us consider the block diagram of the PID control system in Figure 3.13, where three state variables x_1, x_2 and x_3 are fixed.

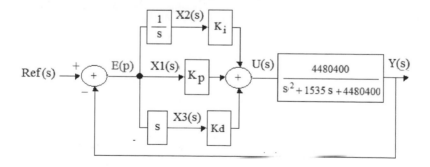

Figure 3.13. *PID control loop of a second-order process*

The resulting state model is then given by:

$$
\begin{bmatrix} \dfrac{dx_1(t)}{dt} \\[2ex] \dfrac{dx_2(t)}{dt} \\[2ex] \dfrac{dx_3(t)}{dt} \end{bmatrix} = \begin{bmatrix} 0 & 0 & 1 \\ 1 & 0 & 0 \\ -4\,480\,400 & 0 & -1535 \end{bmatrix} \begin{bmatrix} x_1(t) \\ x_2(t) \\ x_3(t) \end{bmatrix} + \begin{bmatrix} 0 \\ 0 \\ -12\,321\,000 \end{bmatrix} u(t) \qquad [3.58]
$$

Stage 2: LQR design and simulation for a desired response Ref = 6 volts.

The following "pidlqr.m" program is used for finding the optimal values of K and S by adjustment of values of Q and R = r, based on fixed initial conditions, then for simulating the trajectories of the control system by optimal PID controller equivalent to LQR.

No.	"pidlqr.m" program
1	% Stage 1 - Definition of the state model
2	Ks = 2.75; zeta = 0.3626; wn = 2116.7;
3	A = [0 0 1; 1 0 0 ; -wn^2 0 -2*zeta*wn] ;
4	B = [0 ; 0; Ks*wn^2]; C = [1 0 0];
5	% Stage 2 – LQR design
6	q1 = 0.08; q2 = 2000; q3 = 0.15e-7; r = 20; % Final values
7	Q = diag([q1, q2, q3]);
8	[K, S] = lqr(A,B,Q,r), % Calculation and display of K and S of Ric
9	Kp = K(1); Ki = K(2); Kd = K(3); % PID parameters
10	Ref = 6; % Set point quantity
11	T = 0.1e-3; Tfin = 0.3; time = 0:T:Tfin; % Time space
12	s = tf('s'); % Laplace operator
13	PIDbo = Ks*wn^2/(s^2+2*zeta*wn*s+wn^2); % Process
14	D = (Kp+Ki/s+Kd*s); % Controller
15	PIDbf = feedback(series(PIDbo,D),1); % Closed loop
16	Ypid = Ref* step(PIDbf, temps); % Step response
17	e = Ref-Ypid; % Tracking error
18	plot(temps, Ypid,'k', temps, e,'r'); % Trajectories
19	xlabel('Temps (s)'); ylabel('Amplitude (volts)')
20	axis([0, Tfin, -0.5, 6.5]); grid

The values of PID gains obtained by executing this program are:

$$\begin{cases} K_p = K_1 = 2.7154 \\ K_i = K_2 = 0.9535 \\ K_d = K_3 = 0.1347 \end{cases}$$ [3.59]

Moreover, the trajectories of the optimal control system under PID controllers thus designed and simulated are represented in Figure 3.14.

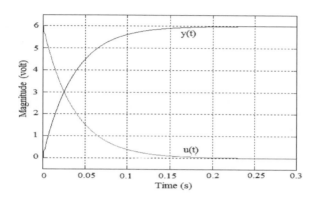

Figure 3.14. *Results of optimal control by optimal PID controller*

3.8. Exercises and solutions

Exercise 3.1.

List five structures of process control laws that can be synthesized in the frequency domain.

Solution – Exercise 3.1.

Here is a list of five structures of process control laws that can be synthesized in the frequency domain:

– proportional controller;

  phase-lead controller;

– phase-lag controller;

– PID controller;

– PIDF controller.

Exercise 3.2.

List six structures of process control laws that can be synthesized in the state space.

Solution – Exercise 3.2.

Here is a list of six structures of process control laws that can be synthesized in the state space:

- state feedback;

- state feedback with observer;

- state feedback augmented by the tracking error integral to the desired response;

- linear quadratic controller;

- linear stochastic controller;

- linear Gaussian controller.

Exercise 3.3.

A position servomechanism is modeled by the open-loop transfer function $G_c(s)$ and by the controller transfer function denoted by $D_c(s)$, with:

$$G_c(s) = \frac{K_m}{s(1+\tau s)}, \quad D_c(s) = K_p\left(1 + 1/(T_i\, s) + T_d\, s\right)$$

It is assumed that $K_m = 0.375$ and $\tau = 0.35$ s.

a) Find the expression of the closed-loop transfer function $F_c(s) = G_c(s)D_c(s) / (1 + G_c(s)D_c(s))$, then write $F_c(s)$ in the form:

$$F_c(s) = \frac{G_c(s)D_c(s)}{1 + G_c(s)D_c(s)} = \frac{a_1 s + a_0)}{s^3 + a_2 s^2 + a_1 s + a_0}$$

where a_2, a_1 and a_0 are constants to be determined depending on the parameters of $G_c(s)$ and $D_c(p)$.

b) Deduce the expressions of parameters K_p, T_i and T_d of the PID controller as a function of a_2, a_1 and a_0.

c) Knowing that the closed-loop characteristic polynomial is written as:

$$\lambda(s) = s^3 + 3.3543\ s^2 + 7.1380\ s + 0.53$$

calculate the corresponding values of parameters K_p, T_i and T_d.

d) Generate the numerical expression of $F_c(s)$, then use Matlab to draw the graph of the step response.

Solution – Exercise 3.3.

a) After expansion and arrangement of terms, the expression of $F(s)$ can be written as:

$$F_c(s) = \frac{G_c(s)D_c(s)}{1 + G_c(s)D_c(s)}$$

$$= \frac{\dfrac{K_m\ K_p}{\tau}\left(s + \dfrac{1}{T_i}\right)}{s^3 + \dfrac{1 + K_m\ T_d\ K_p}{\tau}s^2 + \dfrac{K_m\ K_p}{\tau}s + \dfrac{K_m\ K_p}{\tau\ T_i}}$$

Therefore:

$$a_2 = \frac{1 + K_m\ T_d\ K_p}{\tau}\ ;\ a_1 = \frac{K_m\ K_p}{\tau}\ ;\ a_0 = \frac{K_m\ K_p}{\tau\ T_i} = \frac{a_1}{T_i}$$

b) Expression of PID controller parameters:

$$T_i = \frac{a_1}{a_0}\ ;\ K_p = \frac{\tau}{K_m}a_1\ ;\ T_d = \frac{\tau\ a_1 - 1}{K_m\ K_p}$$

c) If $\lambda(s) = s^3 + 3.3543s^2 + 7.1380s + 0.53$, then:

- $a_2 = 3.354$;

- $a_1 = 7.1385$;

- $a_0 = 0.53$.

Therefore:

$$T_i - \frac{a_1}{a_0} - 13.9961\ s\ ;\ K_p = \frac{\tau}{K_m}a_1 = 6.6621;\ T_d = \frac{\tau\ a_1}{K_m\ K_p}\ 1 = 0.0696\ s$$

d) Graph of the step response of $F_c(s)$:

$$F(s) = \frac{G(s)D(s)}{1 + G(s)D(s)} = \frac{7.138\ s + 0.1785}{s^3 + 3.354\ s^2 + 7.385\ s + 0.785}$$

The following Matlab lines of code can be used to draw the step response represented in Figure 3.15:

>> a1= 7.1664; a2 = 3.4233; a0 = 0.1784;

>> s = tf('s'); Fc = (a1*s+a0)/(s^3+a2*s^2 + a1*s + a0); step(Fc); grid

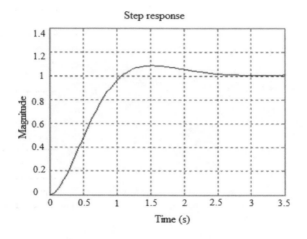

Figure 3.15. *Step response*

Exercise 3.4.

Let us consider a speed regulation system whose open-loop control voltage is $u(t)$. The transfer function of this system is given by:

$$G_c(s) = \frac{K_s}{1+\tau s} e^{-\tau_0 s}; \ K_s = 1.1; \ \tau = 0.93 \text{ s}; \ \tau_0 = 0.25 \text{ s}$$

Use Matlab to generate the closed-loop step response of this system, knowing that the parameters of the PI controller involved are:

− $K_p = 1.9$;

− $T_i = 0.57$ s.

Solution − Exercise 3.4.

$$G_c(s) = \frac{K_s}{1+\tau s} e^{-\tau_0 s}; \ K_s = 1,1; \ \tau = 0.93 s; \ \tau_0 = 0.25 \text{ s}$$

% required Matlab code

>> Ks = 1.1; Ta = 0.93; Tm = 0.25; Kp = 1.9; Ti = 0.57; Td = 0.0;

>> s = tf('s'); Gc = exp(-Tm*s)*Ks/(1+Ta*s); D = Kp+1/(Ti*s)+Td*s;

>> Fpi= feedback(series(Gc, D),1); step(Fpi); grid

The closed-loop step response corresponds to Figure 3.16.

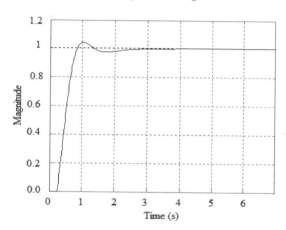

Figure 3.16. *Closed-loop step response*

Exercise 3.5.

The transfer function of a speed servomechanism is given by:

$$G(s) = \frac{K_s}{1+T_a s} e^{-T_m s}$$

with:

- $K_s = 5$;
- $T_a = 8$ s;
- $T_m = 3$ s.

a) Determine the parameters of the PI controller required by the Ziegler–Nichols technique.

b) Use Matlab to generate the graph of the closed-loop step response.

Solution - Exercise 3.5.

$$G(s) = \frac{K_s}{1+T_a\ s}\ e^{-T_m\ s}$$

with:

- $K_s = 5$;
- $T_a = 8$ s;
- $T_m = 3$ s.

a) Based on the known structure of the open-loop transfer function of the system, let us consider $K_s = 5$, $T_a = 8$ s, $T_m = 3$ s. Then the parameters of the PI controller required in the Ziegler–Nichols sense are given by:

$$K_p = 0.9\,(1/\,Ks)\,(T_a/T_m) = 0.48, \quad Ti = 3.3\,T_m = 9.9\ s$$

b) Matlab lines of code for generating the step response:

```
>> Ks = 5;  Tm = 3; Ta = 8; s = tf('s'); G = Ks*exp(-Tm*s)*1/(Ta*s+1);

>> Kp = 0.9*(1/Ks)*(Ta/Tm),  Ti = 3.3*Tm, D = Kp*(1+1/(Ti*s));

>> F=feedback(series(G,D),1), step(F); grid
```

This step response corresponds to Figure 3.17:

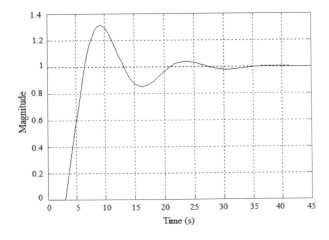

Figure 3.17. *Closed-loop step response*

Exercise 3.6.

A power lighting system generates a lighting level $w(t)$ under control voltage $u(t)$. The transfer functions $G(s)$ of the system and those of the simplified virtual model $G_e(s)$ are given, respectively, by:

$$G(s) = \frac{W(s)}{U(s)} = \frac{0.4914}{(1+0.035\,p)^2}\,e^{-0.005\,s}$$

$$G_e(s) = \frac{0.4914}{1+0.955\,s}\,e^{-0.0141\,s}$$

a) Draw the graphs of the step response of $G(s)$ and $G_e(s)$ on the same Matlab figure.

b) Based on the graph of $G_e(s)$, determine the required PID controller parameters using the Ziegler-Nichols technique.

c) Draw the graph of the closed-loop response to a lighting set point of 500 lux, in the presence of the previously determined PID controller, using the $G_e(s)$ simplified model.

d) What conclusions can be drawn?

Solution – Exercise 3.6.

The given transfer functions are:

$$G(s) = \frac{W(s)}{U(s)} = \frac{0.4914}{(1+0.035\ s)^2}\,e^{-0.005\,s}$$

$$G_e(s) = \frac{0.4914}{1+0.955\,s}\,e^{-0.0141\,s}$$

a) Approximate model of order 1 and graphs of step responses:

The following Matlab program can be used to answer the above questions, and the resulting graphs are shown in Figure 3.18.

```
>> T0=0.005; Tf= 0.4;  T=0:T0:Tf;
>> t = tf('s'); Go = exp(-0.005*s)*0.4914/((1+0.035*s)^2);
[Yo, To] = step(Go,T);
>> Ks = 0.4914;  Tm = 0.0151; Ta = 0.062;  s = tf('s');
>> Ge = Ks*exp(-Tm*s)*1/((Ta*s+1));  [Ye, Te] = step(Ge,T);
>> plot(T, Yo, '.', T, Ye, 'k'); grid
```

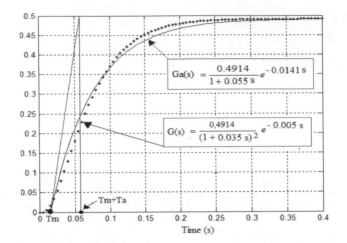

Figure 3.18. *Graphs of step responses of G(s) and G$_e$(s). For a color version of this figure, see www.iste.co.uk/mbihi/automation.zip*

b) PID parameters calculated based on the approximate model:

Let us consider:

- $K_s = 0.4914$;

- $T_a = 0.055$ s;

- $T_m = 0.0141$ s;

Then:

- $K_p = 1.2 \, (1/K_s) \, (T_a/T_m) = 2.2803$;

- $T_i = 2*T_m = 0.0302$;

- $T_d = 0.0076$.

c) Graph of responses (see Figure 3.19).

d) To conclude, the design of a PID controller of a damped system of order 2 by means of the Ziegler-Nichols method can be similar to that of an equivalent system of order 1.

A further conclusion is that it is possible that the design of a controller of a complex system comes down to that of an equivalent simplified system.

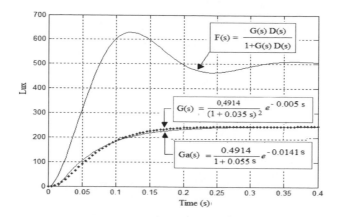

Figure 3.19. *Graphs of step responses of G(s) and Ge(s). For a color version of this figure, see www.iste.co.uk/mbihi/automation.zip*

Exercise 3.7.

a) Edit and save in a Matlab current folder the "iaepid.m", "itaepid.m" and "isepid.m" functions proposed in section 3.5.

b) Let us consider a dynamic process characterized by the following transfer function:

$$G(s) = \frac{K_s}{1+T_a s} e^{-T_m s}$$

with:

- $K_s = 5$;

- $T_a = 1.5$ s;

- $T_m = 1$ s.

Edit the following "KpTiTd.m" program, in order to test and compare "iaepid.m", "itaepid.m" and "isepid.m" functions provided in section 3.5, using the G(s) parameters below. Then draw the graphical representation of the results obtained.

No.	"KpTiTd.m" program
1	Ks = 5 ; Ta = 1.5 ; Tm = 1 ; Tfin = 10;
2	[KpTiTd_iae, y_iae, temps_iae] = iaepid(Ks, Ta, Tm, Tfin);
3	[KpTiTd_itae, y_itae, temps_itae] = itaepid(Ks, Ta, Tm, Tfin);
4	[KpTiTd_ise, y_ise, temps_ise] = isepid(Ks, Ta, Tm, Tfin);
5	plot(temps, y_ise, 'b', temps, y_iae, 'k', temps, y_itae, 'r');
6	grid; xlabel('Temps (s)');

Solution – Exercise 3.7.

$$G(s) = \frac{K_s}{1 + T_a\, s} e^{-T_m\, s}$$

with:

$- K_s = 5;$

$- T_a = 1.5$ s;

$- T_m = 1$ s.

a) Entry of functions and program.

b) Test results (see Figure 3.20):

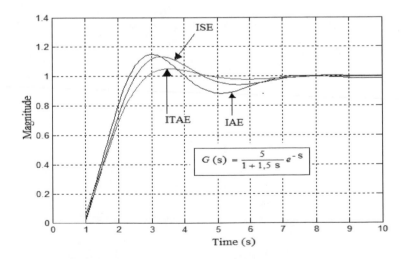

Figure 3.20. *Test results. For a color version of this figure, see www.iste.co.uk/mbihi/automation.zip*

Exercise 3.8.

What are the two most important practical constraints when implementing a state feedback control system?

Solution – Exercise 3.8.

The practical constraints when implementing a state feedback control system are:

– Controllability or stabilizability of the pair (A_c, B_c);

– Observability of the pair (A_c, C_c).

Exercise 3.9.

a) What is the role of integral feedback in a state feedback control diagram?

b) Draw the block diagram of the integral state feedback control system (Figure 3.21).

c) Analyze the stability and static precision properties of this control diagram for a desired step response $y_r = 3$, knowing that the parameters are as follows:

$$Ac = \begin{bmatrix} 1 & 0 \\ -2 & -2 \end{bmatrix}; \; Bc = \begin{bmatrix} 0 \\ 1 \end{bmatrix}; \; Cc = \begin{bmatrix} 1 & 0 \end{bmatrix}; \; K = \begin{bmatrix} 20 & 10 \end{bmatrix}; \; Ki = 20$$

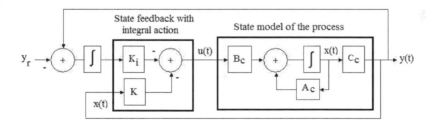

Figure 3.21. *Block diagram of integral feedback control*

Solution – Exercise 3.9.

a) Integral feedback allows the output to follow the desired response.

b) Block diagram of integral state feedback control.

c) Stability and static precision of this diagram, knowing that:

$$Ac = \begin{bmatrix} 1 & 0 \\ -2 & -2 \end{bmatrix}; Bc = \begin{bmatrix} 0 \\ 1 \end{bmatrix}; Cc = \begin{bmatrix} 1 & 0 \end{bmatrix} \begin{bmatrix} x(t) \\ x_i(t) \end{bmatrix}; \ K = [20 \ \ 10]; \ Ki = 20$$

– Stability:

The closed-loop system is described by the following equations:

$$\begin{bmatrix} \dfrac{dx(t)}{dt} \\ \dfrac{dx_i(t)}{dt} \end{bmatrix} = \begin{bmatrix} A_c - B_c K & -B_c K_i \\ C_c & 0 \end{bmatrix} \begin{bmatrix} x(t) \\ x_i(t) \end{bmatrix} - \begin{bmatrix} 0 \\ 0 \\ 1 \end{bmatrix} y_r$$

$$y(t) = \begin{bmatrix} C_c & 0 \end{bmatrix} \begin{bmatrix} x(t) \\ x_i(t) \end{bmatrix}$$

with:

$$Af = \begin{bmatrix} A_c - B_c K & -B_c K_i \\ C_c & 0 \end{bmatrix} = \begin{bmatrix} 0 & 1 & 0 \\ -22 & -12 & -20 \\ 1 & 0 & 0 \end{bmatrix}$$

The characteristic polynomial of A_f is written as:

$$p(\lambda) = \lambda^3 + 12\lambda^2 + 22\lambda + 20$$

It can be verified that one of the roots is $\lambda_1 = -10$, and the other two are $-1 \pm j$. Since all these roots (or closed-loop poles) have negative real parts, the stability condition of the closed-loop control system is met.

– Desired output tracking precision:

It is sufficient to calculate the quantity $y(\infty)$, and then compare it to the reference:

$$\begin{bmatrix} x(\infty) \\ x_i(\infty) \end{bmatrix} = -\begin{bmatrix} A_c - B_c K & -B_c K_i \\ C_c & 0 \end{bmatrix}^{-1} \begin{bmatrix} 0 \\ 0 \\ 1 \end{bmatrix} y_r = 3 \begin{bmatrix} 0 & 0 & 1 \\ 1 & 0 & 0 \\ -0,6 & -0,05 & -1., \end{bmatrix} \begin{bmatrix} 0 \\ 0 \\ 1 \end{bmatrix} = \begin{bmatrix} 3 \\ 0 \\ -3,3 \end{bmatrix}$$

$$y(\infty) = \begin{bmatrix} C_c & 0 \end{bmatrix} \begin{bmatrix} x(\infty) \\ x_i(\infty) \end{bmatrix} = \begin{bmatrix} 1 & 0 & 0 \end{bmatrix} \begin{bmatrix} 3 \\ 0 \\ 3,3 \end{bmatrix} = 3$$

As expected, it can be noted that, in steady state, the output is equal to the desired output $y_r = 3$.

Exercise 3.10.

Let us consider a servomechanism represented by the state model:

$$\frac{dx(t)}{dt} = \begin{bmatrix} 0 & 1 & 0 \\ 0 & 0 & 4,438 \\ 0 & -12 & -24 \end{bmatrix} x(t) + \begin{bmatrix} 0 \\ 0 \\ 20 \end{bmatrix} u(t)$$

Considering $A = \begin{bmatrix} 0 & 1 & 0 \\ 0 & 0 & 4,438 \\ 0 & -12 & -24 \end{bmatrix}$, $B = \begin{bmatrix} 0 \\ 0 \\ 20 \end{bmatrix}$, it can be verified that the system is controllable (rank 3 for the controllability matrix) by executing the following Matlab control lines:

>> A = [0 1 0; 0 0 4.438; 0 -12 -24];   B = [0; 0; 20];

>> Mc = $rank$(ctrb(A,B)), % Controllability matrix [A B A^2*B];

>> rg = $rank$(Mc), % Mc rank calculation

a) Find the components' values of gain $K = [k_1 \ k_2 \ k_3]$ of the state feedback $u(t) = - Kx(t) + $ Ref, knowing that the desired closed-loop characteristic polynomial has the form:

$$p_r(\lambda) = \lambda^3 + 30\lambda^2 + 162\lambda + 432$$

b) Solve a) by using Matlab commands "place" and "acker".

c) Find the state equation of the closed-loop servomechanism.

d) Use Matlab to draw the closed-loop response for Ref = 1.

Solution – Exercise 3.10.

a) Knowing that $A_f = A - BK$ with $K - [K_1 \ K_2 \ K_3]$ and that:

$$\frac{dx(t)}{dt} = \overbrace{\begin{bmatrix} 0 & 1 & 0 \\ 0 & 0 & 4,438 \\ 0 & -12 & -24 \end{bmatrix}}^{A} x(t) + \overbrace{\begin{bmatrix} 0 \\ 0 \\ 20 \end{bmatrix}}^{B} u(t)$$

Then the closed-loop characteristic polynomial under the state feedback law of gain $K = [k_1\ k_2\ k_3]$ can be written as:

$$p(\lambda, K) = det(\lambda I_3 - A_f)$$

Expansion and simplification of the terms of $p(\lambda, K)$ leads to:

$$p(\lambda, K) = p^3 + (24 + 20k_3)p^2 + (53{,}2560 + 88{,}72k_2)p + 88{,}76k_1$$

The components of K result from identifying the same degree coefficients of characteristic polynomials $p_r(\lambda)$ and $p(\lambda, K)$. This identification leads to:

- $88.76k_1 = 432$;
- $88.76k_2 + 53.2560 = 162$;
- $20k_3 + 24 = 30$.

Hence, the searched values of K:

- $K_1 = 4.8671$;
- $K_2 = 1.2251$;
- $K_3 = 0.3$.

b) Calculation of K using Matlab "place" command:

To use the "place" command, we have to know the desired closed-loop poles, which are the roots of the characteristic equation:

$$\lambda^3 + 30\lambda^2 + 162\lambda + 432 = (\lambda + 24)(\lambda^2 + 6\lambda + 18) = 0$$

These roots are:

- $\lambda_1 = -24$;
- $\lambda_2 = -3 + 3_i$;
- $\lambda_3 = -3 - 3_i$.

Matlab can then be used to calculate gain K, as follows:

>> poles = [-24 -3+3i -3-3i];

>> K = place(A, B, poles), Kack = acker(A, B, poles)

The execution of this command line yields the same results:

K = 4.8671   1.2251   0.3000

Kack = 4.8671   1.2251   0.3000

c) Closed-loop state equation:

Knowing that:

$$\frac{dx(t)}{dt} = \begin{bmatrix} 0 & 1 & 0 \\ 0 & 0 & 4,438 \\ 0 & -12 & -24 \end{bmatrix} x(t) + \begin{bmatrix} \overline{0} \\ 0 \\ 20 \end{bmatrix} u(t)$$

with $u(t) = -Kx(t) + \text{Ref}$, or expressed otherwise:

$$\frac{dx(t)}{dt} = \begin{bmatrix} 0 & 1 & 0 \\ 0 & 0 & 4,438 \\ 0 & -12 & -24 \end{bmatrix} x(t) - \begin{bmatrix} \overline{0} \\ 0 \\ 20 \end{bmatrix} \begin{bmatrix} \underset{4,8671}{K1} & \underset{1,2251}{K2} & \underset{0,3}{K3} \end{bmatrix} x(t) + \begin{bmatrix} \overline{0} \\ 0 \\ 20 \end{bmatrix} \text{Re} f$$

$$= \begin{bmatrix} 0 & 1 & 0 \\ 0 & 0 & 4.4380 \\ -20K1 & -12-20K2 & -24-20K3 \end{bmatrix} x(t) + \begin{bmatrix} \overline{0} \\ 0 \\ 20 \end{bmatrix} \text{Re} f$$

d) Closed-loop response:

The Matlab program used is as follows:

No.	The program used
1	A= [0 1 0 ; 0 0 4.438 ; 0 -12 -24] ; B = [0 ; 0 ; -20]
2	C= [1 0 0]
3	K = [4.8671 1.2251 0.3] ;
4	Af = A-B*K; Bf = B;
5	SysSS = ss(Af, Bf, C, 0); [Y,T,X] = step(SysSS),
6	plot(T, X(:,1), 'r', T, X(:,2), 'b', T, X(:,3), 'k'); grid

The graph of the response obtained is as follows:

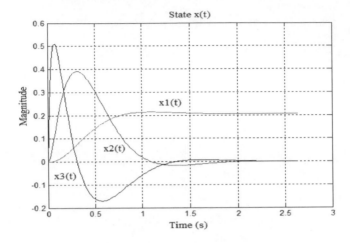

Figure 3.22. *Graph of the response obtained*

Exercise 3.11.

Let us consider a servomechanism represented by the state model:

$$\frac{dx(t)}{dt} = \begin{bmatrix} 0 & 1 & 0 & 0 \\ 0 & 0 & 4.438 & -7.396 \\ 0 & -12 & -24 & 0 \\ 0 & 0 & 0 & -1 \end{bmatrix} x(t) + \begin{bmatrix} 0 \\ 0 \\ 20 \\ 0 \end{bmatrix} u(t)$$

The following lines of Matlab can be used to verify that the system is controllable:

>> A = [0 1 0 0; 0 0 4.438 – 7.396; 0 – 12 – 24 0; 0 0 0 – 1];

>> B = [0; 0; 20; 0]; rg = rank(ctrb(A, B))

Moreover, the data required by the LQR command over an infinite time horizon are:

$$Q = \begin{bmatrix} 9 & 0 & 0 & 0 \\ 0 & 0 & 0 & 0 \\ 0 & 0 & 0 & 0 \\ 0 & 0 & 0 & 0 \end{bmatrix}, \ r = 1$$

a) Calculate gain K of LQR using the following lines of the Matlab program:

No.	Lines of program
1	A = [0 1 0 0; 0 0 4.438 -7.396; 0 -12 -24 0; 0 0 0 -1];
2	B = [0; 0; 20; 0]; C= [0 0 1 0]; rg = rank(ctrb(A,B))
3	Q = diag([9 0 0 0]), r = 1; K = lqr(A, B, Q, r)

b) Calculate the parameters of the closed-loop state model, then use Matlab to represent the state trajectories, knowing that:

$$u = - Kx + \text{Ref, with Ref} = 1.$$

No.	Lines of program
4	Af = A- B* K ; Bf = B ;
5	SysSS = ss(Af, Bf, C, 0); [Y, T, X] = step(SysSS);
6	plot(T, X(:,1), 'r', T, X(:,2), 'b', T, X(:,3), 'k'); grid

Solution – Exercise 3.11.

The known data for the synthesis of LQR commands over a finite time horizon are:

$$\frac{dx(t)}{dt} = \begin{bmatrix} 0 & 1 & 0 & 0 \\ 0 & 0 & 4.438 & -7.396 \\ 0 & -12 & -24 & 0 \\ 0 & 0 & 0 & -1 \end{bmatrix} x(t) + \begin{bmatrix} 0 \\ 0 \\ 20 \\ 0 \end{bmatrix} u(t),$$

$$Q = \begin{bmatrix} 9 & 0 & 0 & 0 \\ 0 & 0 & 0 & 0 \\ 0 & 0 & 0 & 0 \\ 0 & 0 & 0 & 0 \end{bmatrix}, \ r = 1$$

a) The execution of the following Matlab program lines:

>> A = [0   1 0   0; 0 0 4.438 -7.396; 0 -12 -24 0; 0 0 0 -1];

>> B = [0; 0; 20; 0]; rg = rank(ctrb(A,B))

>> Q = diag([9 0 0 0]), r = 1;   K = lqr(A, B, Q, r)

yields: K = [3.0000   0.8796   0.1529 – 1.8190]

b) The following lines of Matlab code calculate the full closed-loop state model, then display the optimal state trajectories (see Figure 3.23):

>> % Data A, B and Ref = 1 must be saved

>> % Data A, B and Ref = 1, must be saved

>> Af = A-B*K; Bf = B * Ref;

>> SysSS = ss(Af, Bf, [0 0 1], 0); [Y,T,X] = step(SysSS);

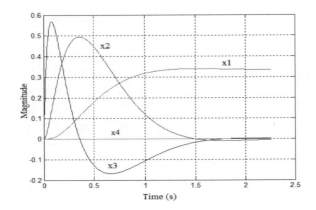

Figure 3.23. *Optimal state trajectories. For a color version of this figure, see www.iste.co.uk/mbihi/automation.zip*

Exercise 3.12.

The state model of a Buck chopper with duty-cycle modulation control is given by:

$$\begin{cases} \dfrac{dx(t)}{dt} = \begin{bmatrix} 0 & \dfrac{1}{C} \\ -C\omega_n^2 & -2\xi\omega_n \end{bmatrix} x(t) - \begin{bmatrix} 0 \\ K_s\,\omega_n^2\,C \end{bmatrix} u(t) \\ y(t) = \begin{bmatrix} 1 & 0 \end{bmatrix} x(t) \end{cases}$$

with:

– K_{si} = 2.75;

– e_n = 2116.7 rad/s;

– ξ = 0.3626.

a) Type and then test the Matlab program below, which allows the study of the optimal control problem by LRQ knowing that:

$$Q = \begin{bmatrix} 0,07 & 0 \\ 0 & 0,5 \end{bmatrix}, \quad R = 0.6$$

No.	Program lines
1	Tfin = 6e-03; wn = 2116.7; zeta = 0.3626;
2	Ks = 2.75; Cs = 220e-06;
3	A= [0 1/Cs; -Cs*wn^2 -2*zeta*wn];
4	B = [0; Ks*wn^2*Cs]; C = [1 0]; D = 0;
5	Sys = ss(A,B,C,D); [Ybo, Tbo, Xbo] = step(Sys, Tfin);
6	Q = diag([0.07 0.5]); R = 0.6; [K, S] = lqr(A,B,Q,R)

Then find the calculated state model, as well as the values of optimal gain K.

b) Complete the previous program with the one below, in order to generate on the same Matlab figure optimal open-loop and closed-loop trajectories of states in the presence of a desired output Ref = 1 volt. Then generate the figure of the obtained trajectories.

No.	Continuation of the previous program
7	Ref = 1; Af = A-B*K; Bf = B * Ref;
8	SysSS = ss(Af, Bf, [1 0], 0);
9	[Yss, Tss, Xss] = step(SysSS, Tfin);
10	plot(Tbo, Xbo, Tss, Xss); grid

Solution – Exercise 3.12.

$$\begin{cases} \dfrac{dx(t)}{dt} = \begin{bmatrix} 0 & \dfrac{1}{C} \\ -C\omega_n^2 & -2\xi\omega_n \end{bmatrix} x(t) - \begin{bmatrix} 0 \\ K_s \, \omega_n^2 \, C \end{bmatrix} u(t) \\ y(t) = \begin{bmatrix} 1 & 0 \end{bmatrix} x(t) \end{cases}$$

with:

$-K_s = 2.75$;

$-\omega_n = 2116.7$ rad/s;

$-\xi = 0.3626$;

$-Q = \begin{bmatrix} 0.07 & 0 \\ 0 & 0.5 \end{bmatrix}$, $R = 0.6$.

a) The open-loop state model is given by:

$$\begin{cases} \dfrac{dx(t)}{dt} = 10^3 \begin{bmatrix} 0 & 4.5455 \\ -0.9857 & -1.5350 \end{bmatrix} x(t) - 10^3 \begin{bmatrix} 0 \\ 2.7107 \end{bmatrix} u(t) \\ y(t) = \begin{bmatrix} 1 & 0 \end{bmatrix} x(t) \end{cases}$$

The optimal gain obtained is K = [0.1353 0.7016].

b) The execution of the complete program leads to the graphic results presented in Figure 3.24:

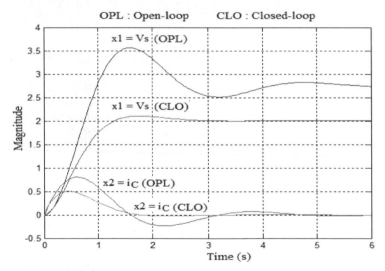

Figure 3.24. *Graphic results. For a color version of this figure, see www.iste.co.uk/mbihi/automation.zip*

Exercise 3.13.

A pulse width modulated Buck chopper with controlled voltage $u(t)$ is modeled by:

$$\frac{dx(t)}{dt} = \begin{bmatrix} 0 & 0 & 1 \\ 1 & 0 & 0 \\ -1.755 \times 10^6 & 0 & -629.8 \end{bmatrix} x(t) + \begin{bmatrix} 0 \\ 0 \\ -1.667 \times 10^6 \end{bmatrix} u(t)$$

Considering the following optimal control data over an infinite horizon:

$$Q = \begin{bmatrix} 10^{-07} & 0 & 0 \\ 0 & 10^6 & 0 \\ 0 & 0 & 10^{-9} \end{bmatrix}, \quad R = r = 1$$

a) Use the Matlab program to solve the LQR∞ problem below:

No.	Program lines
1	A= [0 0 1; 1 0 0; -1.755e6 0 -629.8]; B = [0; 0; -1.667e6];
2	sys = ss(A, B, [1 0 0],0);
3	Q = [1e-07 0 0; 0 1e6 0; 0 0 1e-9]; r = 1;
4	[KLqr, Sinf, E] = lqr(sys,Q,r);
5	Sinf, KLqr
6	Ref = 1; Af = A-B*KLqr; Bf = B; sysf = ss(Af,Bf, [1 0 0], 0);
7	[y, T, X] = step(sysf); Y = Ref - y; u = -KLqr * X';
8	plot (T, y, 'k', T, Y,'b', T, u, 'r'); grid

Then:

1) Specify the Riccati matrix S∞ obtained, as well as the corresponding gain K∞ of state feedback through LQR: $u = -K∞x(t) + Ref$;

2) Observe the graph of $y = e$, $Y = Ref$ y and of u with Ref = 1, then verify that the displayed trajectories are as predicted.

b) Complete the previous program with the one below:

No.	Continuation of the previous program
9	Ref = 1; sys = ss(A, B, C, 0); Gc = tf(sys),
10	s = tf('s'); Dc = (Kp+Ki/s+Kd*s),
11	Fpid = feedback(series(Gc,Dc),1),
12	[Ypid, Tpid] = step(Fpid); y = Ref-Ypid;
13	plot(Tpid, Ypid, Tpid,y); grid

c) Find the following results:

1) Parameters K_p, K_i, and K_d of the optimal PID controller equivalent to LQR;

2) Transfer functions $G(s)$ of the open-loop process, $D(s)$ of the optimal PID controller and closed-loop $Fpid(p)$;

3) The graphs of the output signal $ypid(t)$ and of the set point tracking error $e(t)$.

Solution – Exercise 3.13.

a) $\dfrac{dx(t)}{dt} = \begin{bmatrix} 0 & 0 & 1 \\ 1 & 0 & 0 \\ -1.755 \times 10^6 & 0 & -629.8 \end{bmatrix} x(t) + \begin{bmatrix} 0 \\ 0 \\ -1.667 \times 10^6 \end{bmatrix} u(t)$

$Q = \begin{bmatrix} 10^{-07} & 0 & 0 \\ 0 & 10^6 & 0 \\ 0 & 0 & 10^{-9} \end{bmatrix}$, $R = r = 1$

1) *After* entry and execution of the provided Matlab code lines, the following results are displayed:

$S_{Inf} = \begin{bmatrix} 7.5815e\text{-}04 & 0.9969 & 4.2501e\text{-}07 \\ 0.9969 & 1.7613e\text{+}03 & 5.9988e\text{-}04 \\ 4.2501e\text{-}07 & 5.9988e\text{-}04 & 3.7137e\text{-}10 \end{bmatrix}$,

$K_{Lqr} = [-0.7085 - 1000.0 \quad -0.0006]$

2) $K_{pid} = [-0.7085 - 1000.0 \quad -0.0006]$

The trajectories obtained for desired output Ref = 1 are represented in Figure 3.25.

b) The calculated K_{Pid} gain is:

1) $K_{Pid} = [-0.7085 \ -1000.0 \ -0.0006]$;

2) Transfer functions:

$$G_c(s) = \frac{-1.667e06}{ps + 629.8\ s + 1.755e06}$$

$$D_c(s) = \frac{-0.0006191\ s^2\ -\ 0.7085\ s-1000}{s}$$

$$Fpid(s) = \frac{1032\ s^2\ +\ 1.181e06\ s\ +\ 1.667e09}{s^3\ +\ 1662\ s^2\ +\ 2.936e06\ s\ +\ 1.667e09}$$

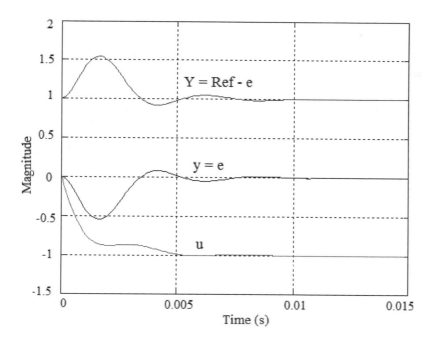

Figure 3.25. *Resulting trajectories*

3) Graphs of the signals obtained (see Figure 3.26):

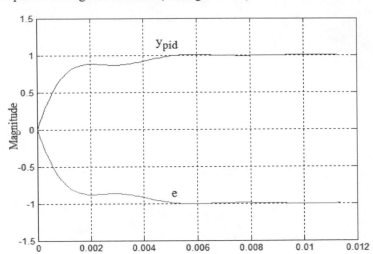

Figure 3.26. *Graph of signals obtained*

Exercise 3.14.

What are the main problems encountered when implementing analog controllers?

Solution – Exercise 3.14.

The main problems of the implementation of analog controllers are:

– significant overall dimensions;

– very costly changes in parameters and extensions;

– ageing of constituent components;

– high noise sensitivity.

PART 2

Synthesis and Computer-aided Simulation of Digital Feedback Control Systems

Synthesis of Digital Feedback Control Systems in the Frequency Domain

4.1. Synthesis methodology

The synthesis of digital feedback control systems in the frequency domain involves:

– finding the discrete transfer function G(z) of the sampled model of the dynamic process;

– using an appropriate method to find the discrete transfer function D(z) of the feedback controller;

– establishing and validating, based on simulation, the control diagram thus synthesized.

4.2. Transfer function G(z) of a dynamic process

4.2.1. *Sampled dynamic model*

A sampled dynamic model results from sampling with period T of a continuous dynamic model, equipped with an upstream digital-to-analog converter (DAC) and a downstream analog-to-digital converter (ADC). Figure 4.1 describes the methodology for the synthesis of a sampled dynamic process.

Indeed, the DAC that operates upstream of the dynamic process plays the role of a zero-order holder, whose impulse response for $0 \leq t < T$ is given by $b_0(t)$. In other words, the theoretical transfer function $B_0(s) = U(s) / U^*(s)$ of a DAC corresponds to the Laplace transform of $b_0(t)$.

Moreover, the presence upstream of the process of an ADC that acts as a sampler leads to the diagram of the sampled dynamic process, presented in Figure 4.1c, where the input and output quantities are $u^*(t)$ and $y^*(t)$, respectively.

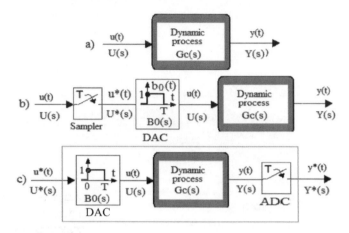

Figure 4.1. *Synthesis of a sampled dynamic model. For a color version of this figure, see www.iste.co.uk/mbihi/automation.zip*

4.2.2. Discretization of $G_c(p)$ if input delay $\tau_0 = 0$

4.2.2.1. Principle of zero-order holder

In Figure 4.1, the impulse response $b_0(t)$ of the zero-order holder operating upstream of the dynamic process model, as well as the corresponding transfer function $B_0(s)$, are given by:

$$\begin{cases} b_0(t) = \begin{cases} 1 \ if \ kT \ \le \ t \ < \ (k+1)\,T \\ 0 \ if \ \text{otherwise} \end{cases} \\ B_0(s) = \int_0^T e^{-s\,t}\,dt = -\frac{1}{s}\left[e^{-s\,t}\right]_0^T = \frac{1-e^{-s\,T}}{s} \end{cases} \qquad [4.1]$$

Knowing that $z = e^{Ts}$, the presence of the term $z^{-1} = e^{-Ts}$ in [4.1] can be noted.

4.2.2.2. Calculation of $G(z)$ based on $G_c(s)$

Considering $G_c(s) = Y(s)/U(s)$, the transfer function of the process, according to Figure 4.1(b), the following can be written as:

$$Y(s) = G_c(s)\,B_0(s)\,U*(s) \qquad [4.2]$$

or the Laplace transform $Y^*(s)$ of the sampled signal obtained by sampling of [4.2] at frequency $1/T = \omega_0 / 2\pi$ can be written as:

$$Y^*(s) = \frac{1}{T}\left(\sum_{k=-\infty}^{\infty} G_c(s+j\,k\,\omega_0)B_0(s+j\,k\,\omega_0)\,U^*(s+jk\,\omega_0)\right) \qquad\text{(a)}$$

$$= \frac{1}{T}\left(\sum_{k=-\infty}^{\infty} G_c(s+j\,k\,\omega_0)B_0(s+j\,k\,\omega_0)\,U^*(s)\right) \qquad\text{(b)}$$

$$= \frac{1}{T}\left(\sum_{k=-\infty}^{\infty} G_c(s+j\,k\,\omega_0)B_0(s+j\,k\,\omega_0)\right)U^*(s) \qquad\text{(c)}$$

$$= \underbrace{\left(G_c(s)B_0(s)\right)^*}_{G^*(s)}\;U^*(s)\; = G^*(s)\;U^*(s) \qquad\text{(d)}$$

[4.3]

The passage from [4.3a] to [4.3b] relies on the periodicity of $U^*(s)$ with period ω_0. Then, since in [4.3b] $U^*(s)$ no longer depends on the summation index k, equality [4.3c] results. Finally, the passage from [4.3c] to [4.3d] results from the periodicity of the Fourier transform of the sampled quantity $(G_c(s)B_0(s))^*$.

Applying z-transform to [4.3d] yields:

$$Z\left(Y^*(s)\right) = Z\left(G_c(s)B_0(s)\;U^*(s)\right) = Z\left(G_c(s)B_0(s)\right)\;Z\left(U^*(s)\right) \qquad [4.4]$$

Therefore:

$$Y(z) = Z\left(G_c(s)B_0(s)\right)\;U(z)$$

$$= Z\left(G_c(s)\frac{1-e^{-T\,s}}{s}\right)U(z) \qquad [4.5]$$

$$= \left(\frac{z-1}{z}\right)Z\left(\frac{G_c(s)}{s}\right)U(z)$$

Thus, the discrete transfer function of a linear process described by a continuous transfer function $G_c(s)$ is written as:

$$G(z) = \frac{Y(z)}{U(z)} = \left(\frac{z-1}{z}\right)Z\left(\frac{G_c(s)}{s}\right) \qquad [4.6]$$

One of the following two tools can be used in practice, as applicable, to calculate $G(z)$ from relation [4.6]:

– the table of z-transforms in order to obtain an analytical expression (Appendix 1 provides an example of table of z-transforms);

– Matlab® command "c2d" (Gc, T, "zoh"), which returns a numerical expression of $G(z)$.

In all cases, it is important to validate the expression of $G(z)$ obtained by simulation of the respective responses of $G_c(s)$ and $G(z)$ with the same types of inputs.

4.2.3. *Discretization of G_c(s) if input delay τ_0 # 0*

Let us consider the following transfer function $G_c(s)$:

$$G_c(s) = \frac{Y(s)}{U(s)} = G_0(s)\, e^{-\tau_0\, s} \qquad\qquad [4.7]$$

with:

$$G_0(s) = C_c(s\, I_n - A_c)^{-1} B_c + D_c = \frac{\displaystyle\sum_{j=0}^{n-1} b_j s^j}{s^n + \displaystyle\sum_{i=0}^{n-1} a_i s^i} \qquad\qquad [4.8]$$

4.2.3.1. *Discretization of G_c(s) based on the Padé transform*

4.2.3.1.1. Principle

This method first involves the substitution in [4.7] of the term $e^{-\tau_0\, s}$ by its Padé transform $[m_a\,/\,n_a]$, then the use of the step invariance method in order to discretize the new transfer function whose numerator and denominator have the orders $M = m + m_a$ and $N = n + n_a$, respectively.

4.2.3.1.2. Padé transform of the function $e^{-\tau_0\, s}$

Table 4.1 presents the first terms $[0\,/\,0]$ to $[2\,/\,3]$ of the Padé transform of function e^x, knowing that $x = -\tau_0\, s$.

For example, for a transfer function $G_c(s) = \dfrac{1}{s+1} e^{-s}$, the Padé approximant of

order [0 / 1] of $G_c(s)$ is: $G_c(s) \approx \left(\dfrac{1}{s+1}\right)\left(\dfrac{1}{1+s}\right)$. Then applying the step invariance

discretization technique, the following is obtained:

$$G(z) = \frac{z-1}{z} Z\left(\frac{1}{s(s+1)^2}\right) = \frac{z}{z-1} - \frac{z}{z-e^{-T}} - \frac{Te^{-T} z}{\left(z-e^{-T}\right)^2} \qquad [4.9]$$

m_a / n_a	$m_a = 0$	$m_a = 1$	$m_a = 2$
$n_a = 0$	1	$1+x$	$1+x+\dfrac{x^2}{2}$
$n_a = 1$	$\dfrac{1}{1-x}$	$\dfrac{1+\dfrac{x}{2}}{1-\dfrac{x}{2}}$	$\dfrac{1+\dfrac{2x}{3}+\dfrac{x^2}{6}}{1-\dfrac{x}{3}}$
$n_a = 2$	$\dfrac{1}{1-x+\dfrac{x^2}{2}}$	$\dfrac{1+\dfrac{x}{3}}{1-\dfrac{2x}{3}+\dfrac{x^2}{6}}$	$\dfrac{1+\dfrac{x}{2}+\dfrac{x^2}{12}}{1-\dfrac{x}{2}+\dfrac{x^2}{12}}$
$n_a = 3$	$\dfrac{1}{1-x+\dfrac{x^2}{2}-\dfrac{x^3}{6}}$	$\dfrac{1+\dfrac{x}{4}}{1-\dfrac{3x}{4}+\dfrac{x^2}{4}-\dfrac{x^3}{24}}$	$\dfrac{1+\dfrac{x}{4}}{1-\dfrac{3x}{4}+\dfrac{x^2}{4}-\dfrac{x^3}{24}}$

Table 4.1. *Padé approximant of e^x with $x = -T_0 p$*

4.2.3.2. *Discretization of $G_c(s)$ by z-transform*

Applying the step invariance discretization technique leads to:

$$G(z) = \left(\frac{z-1}{z}\right) Z\left(\frac{G_0(s)}{s} e^{-\tau_0 s}\right) \qquad [4.10]$$

Let us consider an integer $m \in \{1, 2, 3, \ldots\}$, so that:

$$\tau_0 = mT \qquad [4.11]$$

where T designates the discretization period. In this case, [4.10] becomes:

$$G(z) = \left(\frac{z-1}{z}\right) Z\left(\frac{G_0(s)}{s} e^{-mTs}\right) = \left(\frac{z-1}{z}\right) Z\left(\frac{G_0(s)}{s}\left(e^{Ts}\right)^{-m}\right) \quad [4.12]$$

In [4.12], $Z(.)$ represents the z-transform associated with operator $z = e^{Ts}$, while the term $\left(e^{Ts}\right)^m = z^m$ is similar to a modified z operator.

Thus, [4.12] becomes:

$$G(z) = \left(\frac{z-1}{z}\right) Z\left(\frac{G_0(s)}{s} z^{-m}\right) = z^{-m}\left(\frac{z-1}{z}\right) Z\left(\frac{G_0(s)}{s}\right) \quad [4.13]$$

It can be noted in [4.13] that the time delay effect is reflected in the frequency domain by m poles $p_1 = p_2 = \ldots = p_m = 0$. Since the transfer function $G_0(s)$ in [4.12] is rational and strictly proper, then the exact expression of the term $Z\left(\frac{G_0(s)}{s}\right)$ can be determined from a z-transforms table. If needed, it can also be numerically calculated with the Matlab command "c2d".

In practice, the values of m and T in [4.12] can be determined by identifying on the graph of hyperbolic constraint $T = \tau_0 / m$, a point (m^*, T^*) for which the value of T^* to be used for discretization is satisfactory.

4.2.3.3. *Structure of a z-transfer function*

4.2.3.3.1. Expression

The solution to the previous discretization problem indicates that the general expression of the transfer function $G(z)$ of a rational and strictly proper dynamic process has the following form:

$$G(z) = \frac{Y(z)}{U(z)} = \frac{\sum\limits_{i=1}^{n} b_i z^{n-i}}{z^n + \sum\limits_{i=1}^{n} a_i z^{n-i}} = \frac{b_1 z^{n-1} + \ldots + b_{n-1} z + b_n}{z^n + a_1 z^{n-1} + \ldots + a_{n-1} z + a_n} \quad [4.14]$$

4.2.3.3.2. Recurrence equation

The recurrence equation is a numerical series allowing the simulation in discrete time of the response of G(z) to a known input sequence. Indeed, based on [4.14], the following can be written as:

$$Y(z)(z^n + a_1 z^{n-1} + ... + a_{n-1} z + a_n) = U(z)(b_1 z^{n-1} + ... + b_{n-1} z + b_n) \qquad [4.15]$$

or still:

$$Y(z)(1 + a_1 z^{-1} + ... + a_{n-1} z^{-n(-1)} + a_n z^{-n}) = U(z)(b_1 z^{-1} + ... + b_{n-1} z^{-(n-1)} + b_n z^{-n}) \qquad [4.16]$$

Thus, the recurrence equation allowing the implementation of the frequency dynamic model [4.14], during simulation or in real time, depending on the context, is obtained by projecting relation [4.16] in discrete time space, taking into account the delay property of the z-transform. This recurrence equation is written as:

$$y(kT) \equiv y(k) = \sum_{i=1}^{n} \left(b_i u(k-i) - a_i \ y(k-i) \right), \qquad [4.17]$$

with the following initial conditions to be considered under the hypothesis of signal causality:

$$\begin{cases} y(0) = 0 \\ y(k) = \sum_{i=1}^{k} \left(b_i u(k-i) - a_i \ y(k-i) \right) \end{cases} \text{, with } k = 1, 2, ..., n-1 \qquad [4.18]$$

4.2.3.4. Properties of G(z)

The properties of a transfer function are indicators of the dynamic and static performances of the modeled process. These indicators are:

– Realizability, which expresses the non-anticipative dynamic behavior, in the sense that at each discrete instant, the output does not depend on the future of the input. The realizability test is reflected by the fact that the degree of the numerator of the transfer function in z is below that of the denominator. For example, the transfer function $H(z) = Y(z) / X(z) = (z^2 + az + b) / (z + c)$ admits at instant kT, a recurrence equation:

$$y(k) = -cy(k-1) + x(k+1) + ax(n) + bx(n-1) \qquad [4.19]$$

that depends on the future value $x(n + 1)$. It is therefore not realizable;

– Stability, which expresses the fact that the process can return to an equilibrium state after a disturbance. Knowing that $z = e^{Ts}$, the stability test reflects the fact that all the poles of the z-transfer function are contained in the disk of unit radius;

– Rapidity, which expresses the time after which the response to an input is contained in the vicinity of r % of the steady-state response;

– Precision, which expresses the margin of static error and is reflected by the steady-state error between the desired output and the response obtained. For example, if $H(z) = Y(z)/X_r(z)$, the error $\in (z)$ is defined by the relation:

$$\in (z) = Y(z) - X_r(z) = \frac{H(z)}{1 + H(z)} X_r(z) - X_r(z) = \frac{1}{1 + H(z)} X_r(z) \qquad [4.20]$$

Hence, the following expressions of position error ($\in_p$) and speed error ($\in_v$):

$$\in_p = \underset{z \to 1}{Lim} \left((z-1) \left(\frac{z}{z-1} \right) \frac{1}{1 + H(z)} \right) = \frac{1}{H(1)} \qquad [4.21]$$

$$\in_v = \underset{z \to \infty}{Lim} \left((z-1) \left(\frac{T\,z}{(z-1)^2} \right) \frac{1}{H(z)} \right) = \underset{z \to \infty}{Lim} \left(\left(\frac{T\,z}{(z-1)} \right) \frac{1}{H(z)} \right) \qquad [4.22]$$

– Robustness, which expresses the level of sensitivity of the output response in the presence of uncertain phenomena such as disturbances, noises and variations of parameters.

4.2.4. *Examples of calculation of G(z) by discretization of G_c(s)*

4.2.4.1. *Calculation of G(z) from the table of Laplace transforms*

Let us consider the transfer function:

$$G_c(s) = \frac{b}{s^2 + 2\,a\,s + b} \qquad [4.23]$$

with $b > a^2$, e.g. $a = 1$ and $b = 6$.

The problem to be solved involves the calculation and validation of the analytical expression of the corresponding z-transfer function, denoted as $G(z)$, which will be obtained by the discretization of $G_c(s)$ considering a symbolic sampling period T.

From relation [4.23], the following can be written as:

$$G(z) = \left(\frac{z-1}{z}\right) Z\left(\frac{b}{s\,(s^2 + 2\,a\,s + b)}\right) \tag{4.24}$$

Then, knowing that:

$$\frac{b}{s\,(s^2 + 2\,a\,s + b)} = \frac{1}{s} - \frac{s + 2\,a}{s^2 + 2\,a\,s + b}$$

$$= \frac{1}{s} - \frac{s + a}{s^2 + 2\,a\,s + b} - \frac{a}{s^2 + 2\,a\,s + b}$$

$$= \frac{1}{s} - \frac{s + a}{(s + a)^2 + b - a^2} - \frac{a}{(s + a)^2 + b - a^2} \tag{4.25}$$

$$= \frac{1}{s} - \frac{s + a}{(s + a)^2 + b - a^2} - \left(\frac{a}{\sqrt{b - a^2}}\right)\frac{\sqrt{b - a^2}}{(s + a)^2 + b - a^2}$$

and that $\omega_0 = \sqrt{b - a^2}$, using the table of z-transforms yields:

$$Z\left(\frac{b}{s\,(s^2 + 2\,a\,s + b)}\right) = \frac{z}{z-1} - \frac{z^2 - e^{-a\,T}\left(\cos(\omega_0 T) - \frac{a}{\omega_0}\sin(\omega_0 T)\right)z}{z^2 - 2e^{-a\,T}\cos(\omega_0 T)\,z + e^{-2\,a\,T}}$$

$$= \left(\frac{z}{z-1}\right)\left(1 - \frac{(z-1)\left(z - e^{-a\,T}\left(\cos(\omega_0 T) - \frac{a}{\omega_0}\sin(\omega_0 T)\right)\right)}{z^2 - e^{-a\,T}\left(\cos(\omega_0 T) - \frac{a}{\omega_0}\sin(\omega_0 T)\right)z}\right) \tag{4.26}$$

After reduction in the same denominator and arrangement of terms of [4.26] in decreasing power orders of z, this becomes:

$$G(z) = \frac{\left[1 - 2\,e^{-a\,T}\cos(\omega_0 T) + e^{-a\,T}\left(\cos(\omega_0 T) - \frac{a}{\omega_0}\sin(\omega_0 T)\right)\right]z}{z^2 - 2e^{-a\,T}\cos(\omega_0 T)\,z + e^{-2\,a\,T}}$$

$$+ \frac{e^{-2\,a\,T} - e^{-a\,T}\left(\cos(\omega_0 T) - \frac{a}{\omega_0}\sin(\omega_0 T)\right)}{z^2 - 2\,e^{-a\,T}\cos(\omega_0 T)\,z + e^{-2\,a\,T}} \tag{4.27}$$

In particular, if $a = 1$, $b = 6$, and $T = 0.1$ s, relation [4.27] becomes:

$$G(z) = \frac{Y(z)}{U(z)} = \frac{\beta_1 z + \beta_2}{z^2 + \alpha_1 z + \alpha_2}$$

[4.28]

$$\beta_1 = 0.2796; \; \beta_2 = 0.02615; \; \alpha_1 = -1.765; \; \alpha_2 = 0.8187$$

The recurrence equation resulting from [4.28] can be written as:

$$y(k) = -a_1 \, y(k\text{-}1) + b_1 \, u(k\text{-}1) - a_2 \, y(k\text{-}2) + b_2 \, u(k\text{-}2),$$

[4.29]

with:

– $y(0) = 0$;

– $y(1) = \beta_1 u(0)$.

Thus, the recursive treatment of [4.29] for the purpose of numerical simulation of the response to an arbitrary sequence of discrete controls can be performed with any numerical analysis tool.

The following "EquaRec.m" program can be used for calculating the first N samples of the step response to recurrence equation [4.29].

No.	"EquaRec.m" program	
1	a = 1; b = 6;	% Process parameters
2	T = 0.1;	% Sampling period
3	b1 = 0.02796; b2 = 0.02615;	% β1 and β2
4	a1 = -1.765; a2 = 0.8187;	% α1 and α2
5	u = ones(1,N);	% Step of N values
6	yk(1) = 0; yk(2) = b1 * u(1);	% Initial conditions of y(k)
7	N = 11; t(1) = 0; t(2) = T;	% Initial conditions in t(k)
8	for k = 3:N,	% Recurrence equation loop
9	t(k) = (k-1)*T ;	% Values of discrete time
10	uk = u(k) ;	% Control value s
11	byk(k) = -a1* yk(k-1) - a2 *yk(k-2) + b1 * uk + b2 * uk;	% Output
12	end	% End of loop
13	[t' u' yk']	% Display of the table of values

The numerical values resulting from the execution of the previous program are presented in Table 4.2.

k	k T	u(k)	y(k)	k	k T	u(k)	y(k)
0	0.0	1	0.0000	11	1.1	1	1.1693
1	0.1	1	0.0280	12	1.2	1	1.2162
2	0.2	1	0.1035	13	1.3	1	1.2435
3	0.3	1	0.2138	14	1.4	1	1.2531
4	0.4	1	0.3468	15	1.5	1	1.2478
5	0.5	1	0.4912	16	1.6	1	1.2306
6	0.6	1	0.6371	17	1.7	1	1.2045
7	0.7	1	0.7765	18	1.8	1	1.1726
8	0.8	1	0.9030	19	1.9	1	1.1376
9	0.9	1	1.0122	20	2.0	1	1.1020
10	1.0	1	1.1013	21	2.1	1	1.0677

Table 4.2. *Results of the numerical calculation of [4.29]*

4.2.4.2. *Use of specialized Matlab commands*

4.2.4.2.1. Commands "c2d" and "dstep" (or "dlsim")

The numerical expression of $G(z)$ knowing $G_c(s)$ can be directly calculated and processed with the following the Matlab commands:

– "c2d" (Gc, T, "zoh"): discretization of object $G_c(s)$;

– "dstep": simulation of the step response over a given time horizon;

– "dlsim": simulation of the response for an input sequence to be specified.

4.2.4.2.2. Example

The following "RepInd.m" program allows the simulation and representation of the step response of $G_c(s) = \dfrac{Y(s)}{U(s)} = \dfrac{6}{s^2 + 2\ s + 6}$, as well as the resulting one, $G(z)$ for T = 0.1 s.

No.	"RepInd.m" program	
1	a =1; b = 6;	% Process parameters
2	T = 0.1; t = 0:T:6; N = length(t);	% Time
3	Gc = tf(b, [1 2*a b]) ;	% Gc(p) = b/(p^2+2 a p + b)
4	yc = step(Gc, t);	% Step response of $G_c(s)$
5	Gz = c2d(Gc, T,'zoh')	% G(z) calculated by c2d
6	[numz , denz] = tfdata(Gz,'v')	% Parameters of G(z)
7	yz = dstep(numz, denz, length(t));	% Step response of G(z)
8	plot(t, yc, 'r'); grid; hold;	% Graph of yc
9	stem(t, yz); xlabel('Temps (s)');	% Graph of yz

Figure 4.2 shows a comparison of the graphs of step responses of $G_c(s)$ and $G(z)$. The quasi-null errors between these responses at sampling instants allow the validation of the quality of the equivalent discrete model.

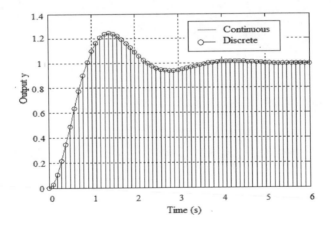

Figure 4.2. *Comparison of step responses of $G_c(s)$ and $G(z)$. For a color version of this figure, see www.iste.co.uk/mbihi/automation.zip*

4.3. Transfer function D(z): discretization method

4.3.1. *Interest of discretization*

The transfer function of an analog controller can be realized by means of basic components of analog electronics (operational amplifiers, resistors and capacitors) assembled as a printed circuit board.

On the contrary, a digital controller is in reality a software module (see Figure 4.3) that automatically calculates, at each sampling period T, the numerical compensation law $u(kT)$ of the error $e(kT) = y(kT) - yr(kT)$ between the desired output $yr(k)$ and the effective response $y(k)$ of a dynamic process. The structure of this law is a recurrence equation similar to that of a digital filter.

The discretization of the transfer function $D_c(s)$ of an analog controller is a technique used to synthesize in the discrete domain a transfer function $D(z)$, equivalent to $D_c(s)$ according to some criterion, for an implementation using programmable technology.

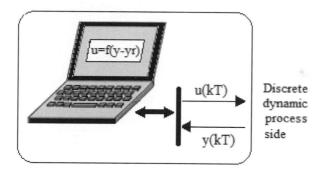

Figure 4.3. *Software nature of a digital controller law*

Two classes of methods for the discretization of transfer functions of controllers can be identified:

– invariance methods, which aim at identifying a discrete model whose response to a given type of input signal is equivalent to that of a continuous model;

– transformation methods, based on the transposition of the continuous model towards the discrete domain, according to a fixed conformal corresponding law.

4.3.2. Discretization of $D_c(s)$ by invariance methods

4.3.2.1. Impulse invariance method

This method involves three stages:

– calculation of the z-transform of $D_c(s)$ denoted as $Z(D_c(s))$. The term $Z(G_c(s))$ characterizes in the exact sense the z-transform of the impulse response of the discrete compensator, while $D_c(s)$ represents the Laplace transform of the impulse response of the analog compensator;

– determination of the constant k allowing $D_c(s)$ and $D(z)$ to have the same static gain for $s \to 0$;

– calculation of the equivalent discrete transfer function: $D(z) = kZ(D_c(s))$.

The three previous stages, relative to the calculation of $D(z)$ from $D_c(s)$, are summarized by the following relation:

$$D(z) = \left(\frac{D_c(s)|_{s \to 0}}{Z(D_c(s))|_{z \to 1}} \right) Z(D_c(s)) \qquad [4.30]$$

EXAMPLE.– For $D_c(s) = \dfrac{a}{s+a}$, the following can be written as:

$$Z(D_c(s)) = \frac{a\,z}{z - e^{-aT}} \,;\; k = \frac{D_c(s)|_{s=0}}{Z(D_c(s))|_{z=1}} = \frac{1 - e^{-aT}}{a} \qquad [4.31]$$

Therefore:

$$D(z) = \frac{\left(1 - e^{-aT}\right)z}{z - e^{-aT}} \qquad [4.32]$$

4.3.2.2. Discretization of $D_c(z)$ by step invariance

The algorithm of the step invariance method is given by:

$$D(z) = \left(\frac{z-1}{z} \right) Z\left(\frac{D_c(s)}{s} \right) \qquad [4.33]$$

EXAMPLE.– Let us consider the transfer function $D_c(s) = \dfrac{a}{s+a}$. In the presence of a zero-order holder, the following relation can be written as:

$$D(z) = \left(\frac{z-1}{z} \right) Z\left(\frac{a}{s(s+a)} \right) \qquad [4.34]$$

Using the table of z-transforms, the following can be written as:

$$D(z) = \left(\frac{z-1}{z}\right)\frac{z(1-e^{-aT})}{(z-1)(z-e^{-aT})} = \frac{(1-e^{-aT})}{(z-e^{-aT})}$$

[4.35]

4.3.3. Discretization of $D_c(s)$ by transformation methods

4.3.3.1. Discretization by the first-order Euler transformation

The transformation used corresponds in this case to the Padé approximant [1 / 0] of e^{Ts}, which corresponds to the first-order Taylor expansion of e^{Ts} or $z = 1 + T\,s$, hence the law of transformation:

$$s \rightarrow \frac{z\text{-}1}{T}$$

[4.36]

Thus, if $G_c(s)$ designates the transfer function of a continuous system, then:

$$D(z) = \left[D_c(s)\right]_{s \to \frac{z-1}{T}}$$

[4.37]

EXAMPLE.– If $D_c(s) = \dfrac{a}{s+a}$, then:

$$D(z) = \frac{a}{\dfrac{z-1}{T}+a} = \frac{aT}{Z-1+aT}$$

[4.38]

It is worth noting, for this example, that $G_c(s)$, when $s \to 0$ and $D(z)$, when $z \to 1$ have the same static gain equal to 1.

4.3.3.2. Discretization by the second-order Euler transformation

The transposition used in this case corresponds to the Padé approximant [1 / 0] of e^{Ts}, $z = \dfrac{1}{1-T\,s}$, hence the law of transformation:

$$s \rightarrow \frac{z\text{-}1}{T\,z}$$

[4.39]

Thus, if $D_c(s)$ designates the transfer function of a continuous system, then:

$$D(z) = [D_c(s)]_{s \to \frac{z-1}{Tz}} \tag{4.40}$$

EXAMPLE.– If $D_c(s) = \dfrac{a}{s+a}$, then:

$$D(z) = \frac{a}{\dfrac{z-1}{Tz} + a} = \frac{aTz}{(1+aT)z-1} \tag{4.41}$$

For this example, $D_c(z)$ for $s \to 0$ and $D(z)$ for $z \to 1$ have the same static gain.

4.3.3.3. *Discretization of $D_c(p)$ by the Tustin transformation*

The transformation used in this case corresponds to the Padé approximant $[1 / 1]$ of $z = e^{Ts}$, which yields $z = \dfrac{1 + \dfrac{T}{2} s}{1 - \dfrac{T}{2} s}$, hence the transformation:

$$s \to \left(\frac{2}{T}\right)\left(\frac{z-1}{z+1}\right) \tag{4.42}$$

Thus, if $G_c(s)$ designates the transfer function of a continuous system, then:

$$D(z) = [D_c(s)]_{s \to \left(\frac{2}{T}\right)\left(\frac{z-1}{z+1}\right)} \tag{4.43}$$

EXAMPLE.– If $D(s) = \dfrac{a}{s+a}$, then:

$$D(z) = \frac{a}{\dfrac{2}{T}\left(\dfrac{z-1}{z+1}\right) + a} = \frac{aT(z+1)}{(aT+2)z + aT - 2} \tag{4.44}$$

Let us note as well, for this example, that $G_c(s)$ and $G(z)$ have the same static gain, hence:

$$D_c(s)\big|_{s \to 0} = D(z)\big|_{z \to 1} = 1 \qquad\qquad [4.45]$$

4.3.3.4. *Discretization by the transformation of pole(s) and zero(s)*

In this case, the transformation is limited to the poles and zeros of the transfer function. Therefore, given a transfer function $D_c(s)$ with known poles and zeros, the problem to be solved is to find the transfer function $D(z)$ with the following characteristics:

– all the poles of $D(z)$ result from the transformation of poles q of $D_c(s)$ using the function e^{Tq};

– all the finite zeros of $D(z)$ result from the transformation of zeros v of $D_c(s)$ by the function e^{Tv};

– the static gain of $D(z)$ is equal to that of $D_c(p)$ or:

$$D_c(s)\big|_{s \to 0} = D(z)\big|_{z \to 1} \qquad\qquad [4.46]$$

EXAMPLE.– Let us consider the transfer function $D_c(s) = \dfrac{a}{s+a}$ characterized by:

– no zero;

– one pole at $s = -a$;

– static gain of 1.

Thus, it can be written as:

$$D(z) = \frac{K}{z - e^{-aT}} \qquad\qquad [4.47]$$

or, the following should be true:

$$D(z \to 1) = \frac{K}{1 - e^{-aT}} = D_c(s \to 0) = 1 \qquad\qquad [4.18]$$

Hence:

$$K = 1 - e^{-T} \text{ and } D(z) = \frac{1 - e^{-aT}}{z - e^{-aT}}$$ [4.49]

4.3.4. z-Transfer functions of simple controllers

Let us consider the following simple controllers:

– Phase-lead/lag, defined by the transfer function:

$$D_c(s) = \frac{K_c(1 + \tau s)}{1 + \alpha \tau s};$$ [4.50]

with $\alpha < 1$ (if phase-lead, and phase-lag if otherwise);

– PID, defined by the transfer function:

$$D_c(s) = K_p + \frac{Ki}{s} + K_d \, s = K_p \left(1 + \frac{1}{T_i \, s} + T_d \, s \right);$$ [4.51]

with:

- $T_i = K_p / K_i$;
- $T_d = K_d / K_p$.

– PIDF, defined by the transfer function:

$$D_c(s) = K_p + \frac{Ki}{s} + \frac{K_d \, s}{1 + T_f s} = K_p \left(1 + \frac{1}{T_i \, s} + \frac{T_d \, s}{1 + T_f \, s} \right);$$ [4.52]

Tables 4.3, 4.4 and 4.5 present the expressions of D(z) of common simple controllers, modeled by [4.50], [4.51] and [4.52], respectively, depending on the possible methods of discretization considered.

Methods for calculating D(z)	$$D_c(s) = \dfrac{K_c(1+\tau s)}{1+\alpha \tau s}$$
Step invariance	$$D(z) = K_c \,\dfrac{z+\alpha\,(1-e^{-\frac{T}{\alpha \tau}})-1}{\alpha\,(z-e^{-\frac{T}{\alpha \tau}})}$$
Euler transformation 1	$$D(z) = K_c \,\dfrac{(\tau\,z+T-\tau)}{\alpha\,\tau\,z+T-\alpha\,\tau}$$
Euler transformation 2	$$D(z) = K_c \,\dfrac{(\tau+T)\,z-\tau}{(T+\alpha\,\tau)\,z-\alpha\,\tau}$$
Tustin transformation	$$D(z) = K_c \,\dfrac{(T+2\,\tau)\,z+T-2\,\tau}{(T+2\,\alpha\,\tau)\,z+T-2\,\alpha\,\tau}$$
Transformation of poles and zeros	$$D(z) = K_c \,\dfrac{(1-e^{-\frac{T}{\alpha \tau}})\,(z-e^{-\frac{T}{\tau}})}{(1-e^{-\frac{T}{\tau}})\,(z-e^{-\frac{T}{\alpha \tau}})}$$

Table 4.3. D(z) for phase-lead/lag controller

Calculation methods	$$D_c(s) = K_p\left(1+\dfrac{1}{T_i\,s}+T_d\,s\right)$$
Direct linear transformation	$$D(z) = Kp\,\dfrac{\dfrac{T_d}{T}z^2+\left(1-2\dfrac{T_d}{T}\right)z+\dfrac{T}{T_i}+\dfrac{T_d}{T}-1}{z-1}$$
Inverse linear transformation	$$D(z) = K_p\,\dfrac{\left(1+\dfrac{T}{T_i}+\dfrac{T_d}{T}\right)z^2-(1+2\dfrac{T_d}{T})z+\dfrac{T_d}{T}}{z^2-z}$$
Tustin transformation	$$D(z) = K_p\,\dfrac{\left(\dfrac{T}{2\,T_i}+2\dfrac{T_d}{T}+1\right)z^2+(\dfrac{T}{T_i}-4\dfrac{T_d}{T})\,z+\dfrac{T}{2\,T_i}+2\dfrac{T_d}{T}-1}{z^2-1}$$

Table 4.4. D(z) for PID controller

4.3.5. *General structure of D(z) and recurrence equation*

The discretization examples presented in Tables 4.3, 4.4 and 4.5 indicate that the general structure of D(z) can be written in the form:

$$D(z) = \frac{U(z)}{E(z)} = \frac{\sum_{j=0}^{m} \beta_j z^{m-j}}{z^m + \sum_{i=1}^{m} \alpha_i z^{n-i}} = \frac{\beta_0 z^m + \beta_1 z^{m-1} + ... + \beta_{m-1} z + \beta_m}{z^m + \alpha_1 z^{m-1} + ... + \alpha_{m-1} z + \alpha_m} \qquad [4.53]$$

The following can therefore be written as:

$$U(z)\,(z^m + \alpha_1 z^{m-1} + ... + \alpha_{m-1} z + \alpha_m) = E(z)\,(\beta_0 z^m + \beta_1 z^{m-1} + ... + \beta_{m-1} z + \beta_m) \quad [4.54]$$

or expressed differently:

$$\begin{aligned}
&U(z)\,(1 + \alpha_1 z^{-1} + ... + \alpha_{m-1} z^{-(m-1)} + \alpha_m z^{-m}) \\
&= E(z)\,(\beta_0 + \beta_1 z^{-1} + ... + \beta_{m-1} z^{-(m-1)} + \beta_m z^m)
\end{aligned} \qquad [4.55]$$

Thus, the resulting recurrence equation for real-time programming is obtained by direct transposition of [4.55] in discrete time, thanks to the delay properties of the z-transform. This direct transposition leads to:

$$\begin{aligned}
u(k) = &-\alpha_1 u(k-1) - \alpha_2 u(k-2) - ... - \alpha_{m-1} u(k-(m-1)) - \alpha_m u(k-m) \\
&+ \beta_0 e(k) + \beta_1\, e(k-1) + \beta_2 e(k-2) + ... + \beta_{m-1} e(k-(m-1)) + \beta_m e(k-m)
\end{aligned} \qquad [4.56]$$

Hence, the compact notation:

$$u(k) = \beta_0 e(k) + \sum_{i=1}^{m} \left(-\alpha_i u(k-i) + \beta_i\, e(k-i)\right) \qquad [4.57]$$

with the initial conditions:

$$\begin{cases}
u(0) = \beta_0 e(0) \\
u(k) = \beta_0 e(k) + \sum_{i=1}^{k} \left(\beta_i e(k-i) - \alpha_i\, u(k-i)\right),
\end{cases} \text{with } k = 1, 2, ..., m-1 \qquad [4.58]$$

Methods for calculating D(z)	$D_c(s) = K_p \left(1 + \dfrac{1}{T_i\,s} + \dfrac{T_d\,s}{1+T_f\,s} \right)$
Euler 1	$D(z) = \dfrac{K_p \left(a_0 z^2 + a_1 z + a_2 \right)}{T_i(z-1)\,(T_f z + T - T_f)}$ with $\begin{cases} a_0 = T_i T_f + T_d T_i \\ a_1 = T_i(T - T_f) + (T - T_i)\,T_f - 2T_d T_i \\ a_2 = (T - T_i)\,(T - T_f) + T_d T_i \end{cases}$
Euler 2	$D(z) = \dfrac{K_p \left(a_0 z^2 + a_1 z + a_2 \right)}{T_i(z-1)\left((T - T_f)z - T_f \right)}$ with $\begin{cases} a_0 = (T + T_i)\,(T + T_f) + T_d T_i \\ a_1 = T_f(T + T) + (T + T_f)\,T_i + 2T_d T_i \\ a_2 = T_i T_f + T_d T_i \end{cases}$
Tustin method	$D(z) = \dfrac{K_p \left(a_0 z^2 + a_1 z + a_2 \right)}{2\,T_i(z-1)\left((T + 2T_f)z + T - 2T_f \right)}$ with $\begin{cases} a_0 = (T + 2T_i)\,(T + 2T_f) + 4T_d T_i \\ a_1 = 2T^2 - 8T_i(T_f + T_d) \\ a_2 = (T - 2T_i)\,(T - 2T_f) + 4T_d T_i \end{cases}$

Table 4.5. *D(z) for PIDF controller*

4.3.6. *Discretization of transfer functions with Matlab*

The numerical expression of $D(z)$ can also be directly calculated from $D_c(s)$ using the Matlab command "c2d" (Gc, T, "zoh"). In this case, the optional argument to be specified as third argument depending on the desired discretization technique can be substituted by:

– "impulse" (impulse invariance);

– "zoh" (step invariance by zero-order holder);

– "Tustin" (Tustin);

– "matched" (poles-zeros).

4.4. Transfer function D(z): model method

4.4.1. *Principle of the model method*

Let us consider:

– G(z) the transfer function in z of a dynamic process;

– F(z) the desired closed-loop transfer function.

The model approach involves finding D(z), so that:

$$F(z) = \frac{Y(z)}{R\,ef(z)} = \frac{D(z)\,G(z)}{1 + D(z)\,G(z)} \qquad [4.59]$$

Under these conditions, the unknown D(z), found from [4.59], can be written as:

$$D(z) = \frac{F(z)}{G(z)\,(1 - F(z))} \qquad [4.60]$$

4.4.2. *Examples of direct design of digital controllers*

4.4.2.1. *Example 1*

The z-transfer function of a dynamic process is given by:

$$G(z) = \frac{0.3678\,z + 0.2644}{z^2 - 1.3678z + 0.3678} \qquad [4.61]$$

while the desired closed-loop one is written as:

$$F(z) = \frac{0.3678\,z + 0.2644}{z^2 - z + 0.6322} \qquad [4.62]$$

Using [4.3] and [4.4] in [4.2], it can be verified that:

$$D(z) = \left(\overbrace{\frac{z^2 - 1.3678z + 0.3678}{0.3678\,z + 0.2644}}^{1/G(z)} \right) \left(\overbrace{\frac{0.3678\,z + 0.2644}{z^2 - 1.3678\,z + 0.3678}}^{F(z)/(1-F(z))} \right) = 1 \qquad [4.63]$$

It can be noted that [4.63] corresponds to a digital proportional controller.

4.4.2.2. *Example 2*

Let us consider a dynamic process whose transfer function in z is written as:

$$G(z) = \frac{1 - e^{-aT}}{z - e^{-aT}} \qquad [4.64]$$

Then, the closed-loop transfer function to be obtained is:

$$F(z) = \frac{1 + K(1 - e^{-aT}) - e^{-aT}}{z + K(1 - e^{-aT}) - e^{-aT}} \qquad [4.65]$$

where K is a constant, allowing the stabilization of F(z). It is clear that the static gain of F(z) for $z = 1$ is equal to 1.

Using [4.64] and [4.65] in [4.60], it can be verified that D(z) is given by:

$$D(z) = (K+1)\frac{(z - e^{-aT})}{z - 1} \qquad [4.66]$$

It can be noted that [4.8] corresponds to a digital PI controller.

4.4.2.3. *Example 3*

Let us consider this time a dynamic process that is described in the frequency domain by the z-transfer function:

$$G(z) = \frac{0.00641}{z - 0.9829}$$

The objective is to calculate the z-transfer function of a digital controller, which leads to closed-loop stability, null static error, with a real pole in the range [−0.98 0.98]. The task is to calculate the transfer function D(z) of the mentioned digital controller.

An example of transfer function F(z) that meets the desired closed-loop control specifications is written as:

$$F(z) = \frac{0.0033}{z - 0.967}$$

Indeed, the real pole of F(z) given by $z = 0.967$ is below 1 (stability condition) and the static gain F(1) is equal to 1 (condition for null static error).

Given this choice, D(z) can be calculated with [4.60]. Indeed, it can be verified that:

$$D(z) = \frac{F(z)}{(1 - F(z))} = \frac{0.0033}{z - 0.9703}$$

$$D(z) = \frac{F(z)}{G(z)\ (1 - F(z))} = \frac{0.5148\,z - 0.4268}{z - 0.9703}$$

[4.67]

4.4.3. *Conditions for the use of model approach*

The examples presented previously show that direct design of digital controllers from the model approach is not always trivial, given the multiple conditions and constraints that need to be reflected in the form of a closed-loop transfer function F(z). The basic conditions to be satisfied by F(z) are: realizability, stability, static precision and rapidity.

4.4.3.1. *Realizability condition in the strict sense of F(z)*

F(z) should be realizable in the strict sense (degree of the numerator strictly smaller than that of the denominator).

4.4.3.2. *Stability condition due to zeros of G(z)*

Relation [4.60] shows that the numerator of G(z) becomes a part of the denominator of D(z). Thus, all unstable zeros of G(z) become unstable poles of D(z). Therefore, [4.60] is not applicable if G(z) admits an unstable zero.

4.4.3.3. *Static precision condition*

Moreover, the desired F(z) function has to be stable, with a static gain equal to 1.

4.4.3.4. *Rapidity condition*

It is also possible to predict good dynamic performances by setting an upper bound of time response, overshoot, etc.

4.4.4. *Practical rules for using the model approach*

The good practices rules presented below are valuable tools that facilitate the task of direct design of digital controllers when applying the model approach.

4.4.4.1. *Rule applicable to first-order G(z)*

If G(z) is of first order, the model structures to be used are:

$$G(z) = \frac{b_0 z + b_1}{z + a_1} \tag{4.68}$$

$$F_d(z) = \frac{1 + \alpha_1}{z + \alpha_1} \tag{4.69}$$

$$D(z) = \frac{\dfrac{1 + \alpha_1}{z + \alpha_1}}{\dfrac{a_0 z + a_1}{z + b_1}\left(1 - \dfrac{1 + \alpha_1}{z + \alpha_1}\right)} = (1 + \alpha_1)\,\frac{(z + a_1)}{(b_0 z + b_1)\,(z - 1)} \tag{4.70}$$

4.4.4.2. *Rule applicable to second-order G(z)*

If G(z) is of second order, then the model structures to be used are:

$$G(z) = \frac{b_0 z^2 + b_1 z + b_2}{z^2 + a_1 z + a_2} \tag{4.71}$$

$$F(z) = \left(\frac{1 + \alpha_1 + \alpha_2}{\beta_0 + \beta_1}\right)\left(\frac{\beta_0 z + \beta_1}{z^2 + \alpha_1 z + \alpha_2}\right) \tag{4.72}$$

$$D(z) = \frac{\left(\dfrac{1 + \alpha_0 + \alpha_1}{\beta_0 + \beta_1}\right)\dfrac{(z^2 + a_1 z + a_2)}{(b_0 z^2 + b_1\,z + + b_2)}\,(\beta_0 z + \beta_1)}{z^2 + \left(\alpha_0 - \left(\dfrac{1 + \alpha_0 + \alpha_1}{\beta_0 + \beta_1}\right)\beta_1\right)z + \alpha_1 - \left(\dfrac{1 + \alpha_0 + \alpha_1}{\beta_1 + \beta_0}\right)\beta_1} \tag{4.73}$$

4.4.4.3. *Rule applicable for nth (n > 2) order G(z)*

In this case, the structures of simple and realistic models that would provide a null static error after n sampling periods can be written as:

$$G(z) = \frac{\displaystyle\sum_{j=0}^{n} b_j z^{n-j}}{z^n + \displaystyle\sum_{i=1}^{n} a_i z^{n-i}} = \frac{b_0 z^n + b_1 z^{n-1} + \ldots + b_{n-1} z + b_n}{z^n + a_1 z^{n-1} + \ldots + a_{n-1} z + a_n} \qquad [4.74]$$

$$F(z) = \frac{\displaystyle\sum_{j=1}^{n} \beta_j z^{n-j}}{z^n \displaystyle\sum_{i=1}^{n} \beta_i} = \frac{\beta_1 z^{n-1} + \beta_2 z^{n-2} \ldots + \beta_{n-1} z + \beta_n}{z^n \ (\beta_1 + .\beta_2 .. + \beta_{n-1} + \beta_n)} \qquad [4.75]$$

4.4.4.4. *Rules for validating the calculated functions F(z) and D(z)*

The validation of $F(z)$ involves the simulation of its response to an appropriate test signal, in order to verify that design specifications have been correctly interpreted.

Moreover, the validation of $D(z)$ calculated from [4.60] involves the simulation of closed-loop response of:

$$F(z) = D(z)G(z) / (1 + G(z)D(z)) \qquad [4.76]$$

in order to verify the reliability of the numerical calculation of [4.60].

This explains the inescapable importance of the numerical simulation techniques to be presented in the next chapter in the practice of direct design of digital controllers.

4.5. Discrete block diagram of digital control

The previous developments lead to the equivalent block diagram of a digital control system represented in the frequency domain.

Figure 4.4 shows the synthesis principle of the mentioned equivalent discrete block diagram, where the digital controller and the discrete dynamic process are modeled by transfer functions $D(z)$ and $G(z)$, respectively.

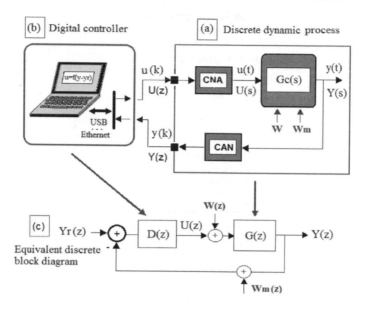

Figure 4.4. *Synthesis principle of discrete block diagram*

4.5.1. *Closed-loop characteristic transfer functions*

Direct analysis of the block diagram in Figure 4.4c under the disturbance model W(z) and the measurement noise model Wm(z) leads to:

$$Y(z) = \frac{G(z)\,D(z)}{1+G(z)D(z)}\,Yr(z) + \frac{G(z)}{1+G(z)D(z)}\,W(z) - \frac{G(z)D(z)}{1+G(z)D(z)}\,W_m(z) \quad [4.77]$$

Thus, the characteristic transfer functions of a digital feedback control system are the following:

$$- G_0(z) = G(z)D(z) \;\; \text{(loop gain)} \tag{4.78}$$

$$- G_m(z) = \frac{1}{1+G(z)D(z)} \;\; \text{(sensitivity function)} \tag{4.79}$$

$$- G_r(z) = \frac{G(z)D(z)}{1+G(z)D(z)} \;\; \text{(closed-loop transfer function)} \tag{4.80}$$

Similarly to the analog case, let us note that $G_r(z) + G_w(z) = 1$. Moreover, the following should be the case in practice:

– $G_0(z) \gg 1$ in the low frequency zone, where noise is nearly absent, in order to guarantee a proper follower behavior since $G_r(z) \to 1$;

– $G_0(z) \ll 1$ in the high frequency range, where desired output and disturbance are nearly absent, so that noise is sufficiently damped;

– stability, which corresponds to the fact that all the roots of the characteristic equation $1 + G_O(z) = 0$ must have modules below 1.

4.5.2. Sampling frequency

All the cases presented in the previous developments show that the transfer functions $D(z)$ and $G(z)$ of a digital control loop are closely dependent on the sampling frequency $f_s = 1 / T$ used. It is therefore important to know the practical conditions for choosing the range of f_s for which quantities $D(z)$ and $G(z)$ are sufficiently reliable.

4.5.2.1. Practical choices of sampling frequency

A digital controller behaves in most practical cases as a low-pass digital filter. Consequently, the bandwidth of the closed-loop transfer function $F(z) = Y(z) / Y_r(z)$ is limited to the cut-off frequency f_b for which the gain is reduced by $\sqrt{2}$ with respect to the static gain (low frequency).

Considering that the discrete output signal $Y(z)$ is therefore essentially constituted of frequency components below f_b, then the value of f_e should verify the sampling theorem expressed by the following relation:

$$f_s \geq 2\,f_b \text{ or otherwise expressed } T \leq \frac{1}{2f_b} \tag{4.81}$$

In practice, a reasonable sampling frequency is 10 to 30 times that of Nyquist, which is $2f_b$, which corresponds to the following range:

$$\frac{1}{60\,f_b} \leq T \leq \frac{1}{20\,f_b} \tag{4.82}$$

4.5.2.2. Sampling frequency of a first-order process

For a first-order dynamic process represented by $F(s) = \dfrac{1}{1 + \tau\,s}$, the following can be written as:

$$f_p = 1/\tau \qquad\qquad [4.83]$$

In practice, the sampling period T can therefore be chosen within the range:

$$\frac{\tau}{60} \le T \le \frac{\tau}{20} \quad \text{or} \quad \frac{20}{\tau} \le f_e \le \frac{60}{\tau} \qquad\qquad [4.84]$$

4.5.2.3. Sampling period of a second-order process

For a second-order process described by $F(s) = \dfrac{\omega_n^2}{s^2 + 2\,\xi\,\omega_n\,s + \omega_n^2}$, it can be proved by solving the equation $\left| F(j\omega_b) \right| = \left| \dfrac{\omega_n^2}{(j\omega_b)^2 + 2\xi\omega_n(j\omega_b) + \omega_n^2} \right| = \dfrac{1}{\sqrt{2}}$ that:

$$f_b = \frac{\omega_n}{2\,\pi} \sqrt{1 - 2\xi^2 + \sqrt{4\xi^4 - 4\xi^2 + 2}} \qquad\qquad [4.85]$$

Thus, in practice the sampling frequency can be chosen within the range:

$$20\,f_b \le f_e = \frac{1}{T} \le 60\,f_b \qquad\qquad [4.86]$$

or:

$$\frac{1}{60\,f_b} \le T \le \frac{1}{20\,f_b} \qquad\qquad [4.87]$$

4.5.2.4. Sampling period of a nth (n > 2) order process

When the model of a dynamic process has an order above 2, the exact calculation of the cut-off frequency f_b is generally not possible. In this case, an approximate value of f_b can be determined by numerical simulation, by reading the value of the frequency f_b for which the gain of the Bode diagram decreases by -3 dB with respect to the low frequency gain, which corresponds to a damping by a factor of $\sqrt{2}$ with respect to the low frequency gain.

4.6. Exercises and solutions

Exercise 4.1.

Determine the hypotheses to consider for the calculation of a transfer function in z by the discretization of the transfer function $G_c(s)$ with the step invariance technique.

Solution – Exercise 4.1.

The hypotheses to consider for the step invariance technique are:

– zero-order holder upstream of the process and sampler downstream of the process;

– existence of the z-transform of the quantities involved.

Exercise 4.2.

Explain the general principle as well as the practical interest of the discretization of transfer functions by transformation techniques.

Solution – Exercise 4.2.

The general principle and the practical interest of the transformation techniques are:

– General principle: based on a reversible criterion of passage from the complex z-space to the complex s-space;

– Practical interest: no need for a table of z-transforms.

Exercise 4.3.

A dynamic process preceded by a DAC and followed by an ADC has the transfer function $G_c(s) = \dfrac{a}{s(s+a)}$. Find the equivalent discrete transfer function $G(z)$ considering a symbolic discretization period T.

Solution – Exercise 4.3.

If $G_c(s) = \dfrac{a}{s(s+a)}$, then:

$$G(z) = \left(\frac{z-1}{z}\right) Z \left(\frac{a}{s^2(s+a)}\right),$$

or:

$$\frac{a}{s^2(s+a)} = \frac{1}{s^2} - \frac{1}{a\,s} + \frac{1}{a\,(s+a)}$$

therefore:

$$Z\left(\frac{a}{s^2(s+a)}\right) = \frac{Tz}{(z-1)^2} - \frac{z\,(1/a)}{z\text{-}1} + \frac{z\,(1/a)}{z-e^{-aT}},$$

hence:

$$G(z) = \left(\frac{z-1}{z}\right)\left(\frac{Tz}{(z-1)^2} - \frac{z\,(1/a)}{z\text{-}1} + \frac{z(1/a)}{z-e^{-aT}}\right)$$

After reduction in the same denominator, this yields:

$$G(z) = \left(\frac{1}{a}\right)\frac{\left(e^{-aT}+aT-1\right)z+\left(1-e^{-aT}-aTe^{-aT}\right)}{z^2-(1+e^{-aT})z+e^{-aT}}$$

Exercise 4.4.

A dynamic process preceded by a DAC and followed by an ADC has the following transfer function:

$$G_c(s) = \frac{Y(s)}{U(s)} = \frac{1}{s^2+2s+4}$$

a) Find the bandwidth of $G_c(s)$, then prove that a sampling period $T = 0.1$ s is satisfactory for the discretization of $G_c(s)$.

b) Find the transfer function $G(z)$ of the process for $T = 0.1$ s.

c) Validate this transfer function by the Matlab-aided simulation, then generate the graphs of step responses of $G_c(s)$ and $G(z)$ on the same Matlab figure.

Solution – Exercise 4.4.

a) Bandwidth of $G_c(s)$ and the Nyquist frequency:

$G_c(s)$ is a second-order transfer function with:

- $\omega_n = 2$ rad/s;

- $\xi = 1/2$.

Hence:

$$f_b = \frac{\omega_n}{2\pi}\sqrt{1-2\xi^2 + \sqrt{4\xi^4 - 4\xi^2 + 2}} = 0.4049 \text{ Hz.}$$

Therefore, the Nyquist minimum sampling rate is $2f_b = 0.8098$ Hz.

The sampling rate recommended in the problem statement is $f = 1/0.1 = 10$ Hz. This value is therefore practically reliable for the discretization of $G_c(s)$.

b) Transfer function $G(z)$ of the process with $T = 0.1$ s:

$$G(z) = \left(\frac{z-1}{z}\right) Z\left(\frac{1}{s(s^2+2s+4)}\right) = \left(\frac{z-1}{z}\right) Z\left(\frac{1}{s(s^2+2s+4)}\right)$$

or:

$$\frac{4}{s(s^2+2s+4)} = \frac{1}{s} - \frac{s+2}{s^2+2s+4}$$

$$= \frac{1}{s} - \frac{s+1}{s^2+2s+4} - \frac{1}{s^2+2s+4}$$

$$= \frac{1}{s} - \frac{s+1}{(s+1)^2+4-1} - \frac{1}{(s+1)^2+4-1}$$

$$= \frac{1}{s} - \frac{z+1}{(s+1)^2+3} - \left(\frac{1}{\sqrt{3}}\right)\frac{\sqrt{3}}{(s+1)^2+3}$$

Therefore:

$$
Z\left(\frac{1}{s\,(s^2+2\,s+4)}\right) = \frac{z}{4(z\text{-}1)} - \frac{z^2 - e^{-T}\left(\cos(\sqrt{3}\,T) - \frac{1}{\sqrt{3}}\sin(\sqrt{3}\,T)\right)z}{(z^2 - 2e^{-T}\cos(\sqrt{3}\,T)\,z + e^{-2\,T})}
$$

$$
= \left(\frac{z}{4\,(z\text{-}1)}\right)\left(1 - \frac{(z-1)\left[z - e^{-T}\left(\cos(\sqrt{3}T) - \frac{1}{\sqrt{3}}\sin(\sqrt{3}\,T)\right)\right]}{z^2 - e^{-T}\left(\cos(\sqrt{3}\,T) - \frac{1}{2}\sin(\sqrt{3}\,T)\right)z}\right)
$$

Several stages of term reduction in the same denominator lead to:

$$
G(z) = \left(\frac{z-1}{z}\right)Z\left(\frac{1}{s(s^2+2s+4)}\right)
$$

$$
= \frac{\left[1 - 2\,e^{-T}\cos(\sqrt{3}\,T) + e^{-T}\left(\cos(\sqrt{3}\,T) - \frac{1}{\sqrt{3}}\sin(\sqrt{3}T)\right)\right]z + e^{-2\,T} - e^{-T}\left(\cos(\sqrt{3}T) - \frac{1}{\sqrt{3}}\sin(\sqrt{3}T)\right)}{4(z^2 - 2e^{-T}\cos(\sqrt{3}\,T)\,z + e^{-2\,T})}
$$

In particular, if T = 0.1 s, the previous relation becomes:

$$
G(z) = \frac{Y(z)}{U(z)} = \frac{-0.27z + 0.0122}{z^2 - 1.7826\,z + 0.8187}
$$

c) Step responses of $G_c(s)$ and $G(z)$:

The required step responses can be simulated with the following Matlab program:

```
1    % Step responses of Gc(s) and G(z)
2    T= 0.1;  t = 0:T:6;  N= length(t);
3    Numz = [-0.0127  0.0488]/4;  Denz = [1 -1.7826  0.8187] ;
4    yz = dstep(Numz, Denz, N);
5    stem(t, yz); axis([0 6 -0.05 0.4]);
6    sysc = tf(1,[1  2  4]) ;  yc = step(sysc,t);  hold on;
7    plot(t,yc);  hold off
```

The results displayed after the execution of the proposed program are presented in Figure 4.5.

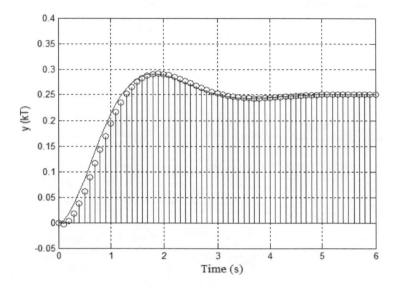

Figure 4.5. *Result of the execution of the proposed program*

It can be noted that the response of the discrete model is sufficiently close to the graphic profile that could be obtained by sampling the continuous model response. The sampling rate used for the synthesis of $G(z)$ from $G_c(s)$ is therefore practically appropriate.

Exercise 4.5.

Let us consider a phase-lead/lag controller, defined by the following transfer function:

$$D_c(s) = \left(\frac{1+(\tau_1\ s)}{1+\alpha_1\ (\tau_1\ s)} \right) \left(\frac{1+(\tau_2\ s)}{1+\alpha_2\ (\tau_2\ s)} \right);$$

with $\alpha_1 < 1$ and $\alpha_2 > 1$ or conversely.

Find the equivalent transfer function $D(z)$ using the discretization technique based on the pole(s) and zero(s) transformation.

Solution – Exercise 4.5.

For $D_c(s) = \left(\dfrac{1+(\tau_1\, s)}{1+\alpha_1\,(\tau_1\, s)} \right) \left(\dfrac{1+(\tau_2\, s)}{1+\alpha_2\,(\tau_2\, s)} \right)$

$$= \frac{1}{\alpha_1 \alpha_2} \left(\frac{s+1/\tau_1}{s+1/(\alpha_1\tau_1)} \right) \left(\frac{s+1/\tau_2}{s+1/(\alpha_2\tau_2)} \right)$$

Hence:

$$D(z) = K \left(\frac{z-e^{-T/\tau_1}}{z-e^{-T/(\alpha_1\,\tau_1)}} \right) \left(\frac{z-e^{-T/\tau_2}}{z-e^{-T/(\alpha_2\,\tau_2)}} \right)$$

In order to find K, the following equation must be solved:

$$D(z=1) = K \left(\frac{1-e^{-T/\tau_1}}{1-e^{-T/(\alpha_1\,\tau_1)}} \right) \left(\frac{1-e^{-T/\tau_2}}{1-e^{-T/(\alpha_2\,\tau_2)}} \right) = D_c(0) = 1$$

This yields:

$$K = \left(\frac{1-e^{-T/(\alpha_1\,\tau_1)}}{1-e^{-T/\tau_1}} \right) \left(\frac{1-e^{-T/(\alpha_2\,\tau_2)}}{1-e^{-T/\tau_2}} \right)$$

Finally, the result is:

$$D(z) = \left(\frac{1-e^{-T/(\alpha_1\,\tau_1)}}{1-e^{-T/\tau_1}} \right) \left(\frac{1-e^{-T/(\alpha_2\,\tau_2)}}{1-e^{-T/\tau_2}} \right) \left(\frac{z-e^{-T/\tau_1}}{z-e^{-T/(\alpha_1\,\tau_1)}} \right) \left(\frac{z-e^{-T/\tau_2}}{z-e^{-T/(\alpha_2\,\tau_2)}} \right).$$

Exercise 4.6.

List the causes that may lead to loss of properties during the discretization of a transfer function.

Solution – Exercise 4 6.

The causes that may lead to loss of properties during the discretization of a transfer function are:

– calculation errors;

– inappropriate choice of the discretization period.

Exercise 4.7.

What are the main practical difficulties encountered in the use of the model approach for direct design in the frequency domain of digital controllers?

Solution – Exercise 4.7.

The difficulties encountered are:

– preliminary demand to synthesize the transfer function G(z) of the process by discretization of continuous model (if available) or by parameter identification ARMA (if test results are available);

– transposition of the desired closed-loop specifications in the form of a transfer function F(z) to be exploited;

– availability of a tool for digital simulation of discrete dynamic models.

Exercise 4.8.

Let us consider a dynamic process described in the frequency domain by the z-transfer function:

$$G(z) = \frac{0.3678\,(z+0.7189)}{(z-1)\,(z-0.3678)}$$

The objective is to calculate the transfer function in z of a digital controller allowing a closed-loop stable behavior, a null static error and having a zero $z = -0.7189$ and two conjugated poles $p_{1,2} = 0.2380 \pm j\,0.5280$.

a) calculate the desired closed-loop transfer function F(z);

b) calculate the transfer function D(z) of the required digital controller.

Solution – Exercise 4.8.

a) A transfer function F(z) according to the desired closed-loop control specifications can be written as:

$$F(z) = \frac{0.5\,(z+0.7189)}{z^2 - 0.476\,z + 0.3354}$$

b) Direct calculation leads to:

$$\frac{F(z)}{(1-F(z))} = \frac{0.5\,(z+0.7189)}{z^2 - 0.976\,z - 0.024}$$

$$D(z) = \frac{F(z)}{G(z)\,(1-F(z))} = 1.3594\left(\frac{z-0.3678}{z+0.024}\right)$$

Exercise 4.9.

In practice, the range for choosing the discretization period of a transfer function is contained between two finite bounds: T_{min} and T_{max}. Explain why these two bounds have to be finite.

Solution – Exercise 4.9.

The reasons for which the bounds T_{min} and T_{max} have to be finite are:

– T_{min} must be finite because the maximum frequency of a real clock source that can be used to generate the required sampling period is finite.

– T_{max} must be finite because the maximum period of discretization to be used is imposed by the Nyquist minimum sampling rate with respect to the bandwidth of the process.

Exercise 4.10.

Let us consider the transfer function $G_c(s) = \dfrac{Y(s)}{U(s)} = \dfrac{1}{s+1}$ to be discretized using the step invariance technique. Find:

a) the expression of the step response $y(t)$ of $G_c(s)$;

b) the theoretical range of choice of the discretization period of $G_c(s)$;

c) the equivalent transfer function $G(z)$ for symbolic T;

d) the recurrence equation depending on T;

e) the general expression of $y(k)$ depending on T, for $k = 0, 1, 2,...$

Solution – Exercise 4.10.

Given $G_c(s) = \dfrac{Y(s)}{U(s)} = \dfrac{1}{s+1}$ to be discretized with the step invariance technique.

a) The step response:

For a step, $U(s) = 1/s$. Therefore $Y(s) = \dfrac{1}{s(s+1)}$, which yields:

$$y(t) = (1 - e^{-t})$$

b) The theoretical range of choice of the discretization period T:

The bandwidth of $G_c(s)$ is limited to $\omega_b = 1$ rad/s or $f_b = \omega_b/(2\pi)$ Hz. The theoretical range of T is $T < 2\pi/\omega_b$ or $T < 6.28$ s.

c) The equivalent transfer function G(z) for T = 0.1 s:

$$G(z) = \frac{(z-1)}{z} Z\left(\frac{1}{s\ (s+1)}\right) = \frac{1-e^{-T}}{z-e^{-T}}$$

d) The recurrence equation:

$$zY(z) - e^{-T}Y(z) = (1-e^{-T})U(z)$$

therefore:

$$Y(z) - e^{-T}z^{-1}Y(z) = (1-e^{-T})z^{-1}U(z)$$

hence:

$$y(kT) \equiv y(k) = e^{-T}y(k-1) + (1-e^{-T})\,u(k-1)$$

with $y(0) = 0$.

e) The general expression of $y(k) \equiv y(kT)$

$k = 0 \rightarrow y(0) = 0$

$k = 1 \rightarrow y(1) = 1 - e^{-T}$

$k = 2 \rightarrow y(2) = e^{-T}y(1) + 1 - e^{-T} = e^{-T}(1 - e^{-T}) + 1 - e^{-T} = 1 - e^{-2T}$

$k = 3 \rightarrow y(3) = e^{-T}y(2) + 1 - e^{-T} = e^{-T}(1 - e^{-2T}) + 1 - e^{-T} = 1 - e^{-3T}$

Assuming that:

$$y(k) = 1 - e^{-kT},$$

then:

$$y(k + 1) = e^{-T}(1 - e^{-kT}) + 1 - e^{-T} = 1 - e^{-(k + 1)T}$$

therefore:

$$y(k) = 1 - e^{-kT}, \text{ for } k = 0, 1, 2,...$$

Exercise 4.11.

A digital controller is defined by the transfer function:

$$D(z) = \frac{U(z)}{E(z)} = \frac{a\,z}{z+b}$$

Find:

a) the stability conditions of this controller depending on the values of parameter b;

b) the recurrence equation required for an implementation by a digital processor;

c) the general expression of the impulse response based on an analytical calculation of the first samples of this response;

d) the general expression of the step response based on an analytical calculation of the first samples of this response;

c) the graph of the step response identified, considering that $a = 1$, $b = -1/2$, $T = 0.05$ s (sampling period) and first $N = 11$ data samples. Any calculation and data numerical analysis tool can be used to answer this question.

Solution – Exercise 4.11.

A digital controller is defined by the transfer function:

$$D(z) = \frac{U(z)}{E(z)} = \frac{a\,z}{z+b}$$

a) Stability:

$D(z)$ admits only one pole for $z = -b$. The stability condition is then: $|b| < 1$.

b) Recurrence equation:

Let us write: $zU(z) + bU(z) = azE(z)$

Multiplying both members of the equality by z^{-1} yields:

$U(z) + bz^{-1}U(z) = aE(z)$

which drives in discrete time the relation:

$u(kT) = -bu((k-1)T) + ae(kT)$

with $u(0) = ae(0)$ and for $k = 0, 1, 2,...$

c) The general expression of the impulse response $u(kT) = \delta(kT)$, with $\delta(kT) = 1$ if $k = 0$ and $\delta(kT) = 0$ if otherwise.

$u(0) = a$;

$u(T) = -ab$;

$u(T) = ab^2$;

...

Let us assume at this stage that:

$u(kT) = a(-b)^{kT}$

In this case:

$u((k+1)T) = -bu(kT) = (-b)a(-b)^{kT} = a(-b)^{(k+1)T}$

Therefore, for any $k = 0, 1, 2,...$, the following can be written as:

$u(kT) = a(-b)^{kT}$

d) The general expression of the step response $u(k)$, with:

$u(kT) = 1$ if $k \geq 0$ and $u(kT) = 0$ if otherwise.

It can be readily verified that:

$$u(0) = a$$

$$u(T) = -a(1 - b^T)$$

$$u(2T) = a(1 - b + b^{2T})$$

$$u(3T) = a(1 - b + b^{2T} - b^{3T})$$

...

Let us assume at this stage that:

$$u(kT) = a \underbrace{\left(1 + (-b^T) + b^{2T} + (-b)^{3T} + \ldots + (-b)^{kT}\right)}_{\substack{\text{Sum of } (k+1) \text{ terms of a geometric progression} \\ \text{with first term unity and ratio} -b^T}}$$

$$= a\left(\frac{1 - (-b)^{(k+1)T}}{1 + b}\right)$$

If up to k order:

$$u(kT) = a\left(\frac{1 - (-b)^{(k+1)T}}{1 + b}\right)$$

then, at $(k + 1)$ order, it can be written as:

$$u((k+1)T) = -bu(kT) + ae((k+1)T)$$

$$= -b\, a\left(\frac{1 - (-b)^{(k+1)T}}{1 + b}\right) + a = a\left(1 - b\left(\frac{1 - (-b)^{(k+1)T}}{1 + b}\right)\right)$$

$$= a\left(\frac{1 + b - b + b\left(1 - (-b)^{(k+1)T}\right)}{1 + b}\right) = a\left(\frac{1 + b\left(1 - (-b)^{(k+1)T}\right)}{1 + b}\right)$$

$$= a\left(\frac{1 - (-b)^{(k+2)T}}{1 + b}\right)$$

It can be concluded that for any k:

$$u(kT) = a\left(\frac{1-(-b)^{(k+1)T}}{1+b}\right)$$

e) In order to represent the graph of the step response, the following Matlab program has been used for implementing and drawing the solution to the recurrence equation:

```
1    % Step response program
2    k = 0:10;           % Indices discrete time of simulation
3    a=1; b = -1/2; T= 0.05;              % Parameters
4    tk = k*T;  u = (1-(-b) .^ (k+1)) /(b+1);  % Command calculation
5    stem(tk, u);                         % Graph
6    xlabel('k T (s)');  ylabel('u (kT)');
7    title ('Réponse Indicielle');  grid;  axis([0  0.5  0  2.5]
```

The graph resulted from the execution of the proposed program is presented in Figure 4.6.

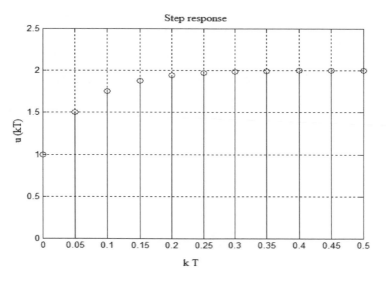

Figure 4.6. *Graph resulted from the execution of the proposed program*

Exercise 4.12.

A digital controller that admits $e(k)$ and $x(k)$ as input and output signals, respectively, is defined by a recurrence equation of the form:

$$u(k) = e^{-aT} u(k-1) + (1 - e^{-aT}) e(k-1)$$

Find:

a) the expression of the corresponding transfer function $D(z)$, then analyze the stability conditions;

b) the general expression of the impulse response based on an analytical calculation of the first samples of this response;

c) the general expression of the step response based on an analytical calculation of the first samples of this response;

d) the graph of the identified step response, considering that $a = 1$, $T = 0.1$ s (sampling period) and first $N = 61$ data samples. Any calculation and data numerical analysis tool can be used to answer this question.

Solution – Exercise 4.12.

The recurrence equation of the digital controller has the form:

$$u(k) = e^{-aT} u(k-1) + (1 - e^{-aT}) e(k-1)$$

a) Expression of the corresponding transfer function $D(z)$:

The translation in real time of the recurrence equation leads to:

$$U(z) = e^{-aT} z^{-1} U(z) + (1 - e^{-aT}) z^{-1} E(z)$$

Multiplying both members of the equality by z^{-1} leads to:

$$zU(z) = e^{-aT} U(z) + (1 - e^{-aT}) E(z)$$

hence, the searched expression:

$$D(z) = \frac{U(z)}{E(z)} = \frac{1 - e^{-aT}}{z - e^{-aT}}$$

Therefore, the stability condition is:

$$e^{-aT} < 1$$

b) General expression of the impulse response:

Considering the notation $y(k) \equiv y(kT)$, it can be written as:

$u(0) = 0$

$u(1) = (1 - e^{-aT})\delta(0) = 1 - e^{-aT}$

$u(2) = e^{-aT}u(1) = e^{-aT}(1 - e^{-aT})$

$u(3) = e^{-aT}u(2) = (e^{-aT})^2 \, (1 - e^{-aT})$

Assuming that at order k:

$u(k) \equiv u(kT) = (e^{-aT})^{n-1} \, (1 - e^{-aT})$

then, at order $k + 1$:

$u(k + 1) = e^{-aT}u(k) = e^{-aT}(e^{-aT})^{n-1} \, (1 - e^{-aT}) = (e^{-aT})^k (1 - e^{-aT})$

Therefore, for any k, the following can be written as:

$u(k) = (e^{-aT})^{k-1} \, (1 - e^{-aT})$

c) General expression of the step response:

$u(0) = 0$

$u(1) = 1 - e^{-aT}$

$u(2) = e^{-aT}u(1) + (1 - e^{-aT}) = (1 + e^{-aT}) \, (1 - e^{-aT})$

$u(3) = e^{-aT}u(2) + (1 - e^{-aT}) = (1 + e^{-aT} + e^{-2aT}) \, (1 - e^{-aT})$

Assuming that at order k:

$u(k) \equiv u(kT) = (1 + e^{-aT} + e^{-2aT} + \ldots + e^{-(k-1)aT}) \, (1 - e^{-aT})$

then, at order $k + 1$:

$u(k + 1) = e^{-aT}u(k) + (1 - e^{-aT})$

$= e^{-aT}(1 + e^{-aT} + e^{-2aT} + \ldots + e^{-(k-1)aT}) \, (1 - e^{-aT}) + (1 - e^{-aT})$

$= (e^{-aT}(1 + e^{-aT} + e^{-2aT} + \ldots + e^{-(k-1)aT}) + 1) \, (1 - e^{-aT})$

$= (1 + e^{-aT} + e^{-2aT} + \ldots + e^{-kaT}) \, (1 - e^{-aT})$

Therefore, for any k, the following can be written as:

$$u(k) \equiv u(kT) = (1 + e^{-aT} + e^{-2aT} + \ldots + e^{-(k-1)aT})\,(1 - e^{-aT})$$

$$= ((1 - e^{-kaT})/(1 - e^{-aT}))\,(1 - e^{-aT}) = 1 - e^{-kaT}$$

d) Graphs of the step response, considering the values $a = 1$, $T = 0.1$ s:

In order to represent the graph of the step response, the solution to the recurrence equation found with the following Matlab program has been implemented and drawn:

```
1    % Step response
2    a = 1;  T = 0.1; k = 0:60;  tk = k*T;
3    ustep = (1-exp(-k*a*T));
4    stem(tk,ustep);  xlabel('k T (s)');
5    ylabel('u (kT)');  title ('Step response');
6    grid;  axis([0 6 0 1.2])
```

The graph of this step response is presented below:

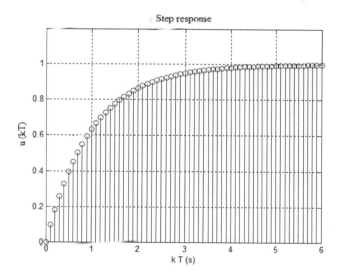

Figure 4.7. *Graph of the step response*

Exercise 4.13.

In an analog control loop, the transfer functions of the process and of the controller are designated by $G_c(s)$ and $D_c(s)$, respectively, with:

$$G_c(s) = \frac{Y(s)}{U(s)} = \frac{1/2}{s(s+1/2)}$$

$$D_c(s) = \frac{U(s)}{E(s)} = \frac{6(s+1/2)}{s+3}$$

The objective is to study this analog control loop in view of the computer-aided implementation of the analog controller.

Find:

a) the expression of the closed-loop transfer function $F_c(s)$;

b) the bandwidth of $F_c(s)$, then prove that a discretization period $T = 400$ ms to be used afterwards is satisfactory for the synthesis of the equivalent control loop in discrete time;

c) the transfer function $G(z)$ of the process, then validate the expression obtained by drawing and comparing the step responses of $G_c(s)$ and $G(z)$;

d) the transfer function $D(z)$ of the controller by the pole(s) and zero(s) transformation method;

e) the recurrence equations of $F(z)$ and $D(z)$;

f) the first samples of the step response of $F(z)$ and of the corresponding digital command;

g) the graphs of the step response and of the digital control using the first 12 samples found.

Solution – Exercise 4.13.

In an analog control loop, let us consider:

$$G_c(s) = \frac{Y(s)}{U(s)} = \frac{1/2}{s(s+1/2)}$$

$$D_c(s) = \frac{U(s)}{E(s)} = \frac{6(s+1/2)}{s+3}$$

a) The expression of the closed-loop transfer function $F_c(s)$ is:

$$F_c(s) = \frac{Y(s)}{Y_r(s)} = \frac{D_c(s)G_c(s)}{1+D_c(s)G_c(s)} = \frac{\dfrac{6(s+1/2)}{s+3}\cdot\dfrac{1/2}{s(s+1/2)}}{\dfrac{6(s+1/2)}{s+3}+\dfrac{1/2}{s(s+1/2)}}$$

The expansion leads to:

$$F_c(s) = \frac{Y(s)}{Y_r(s)} = \frac{3\,s+1,5}{s^3+3.5\,s^2+4.5\,s+1.5} = \frac{3\,(s+0.5)}{(s+0.5)(s^2+3s+3)}$$

Therefore:

$$F_c(s) = \frac{Y(s)}{Y_r(s)} = \frac{3}{(s^2+3s+3)}$$

b) Bandwidth of $F_c(s)$ and discretization period T = 1 s:

$F_c(s)$ is of second order, with $\omega_n = \omega_n = \sqrt{3}\ rad\,/\,s$, $\xi = \dfrac{\sqrt{3}}{2}$

$$f_b - \frac{\omega_n}{2\pi}\sqrt{1-2\xi^2+\sqrt{4\xi^4-4\xi^2+2}} - 0.2167\ \text{Hz}$$

or a maximum theoretical discretization period T = $1/(2f_b) = 2.3072$ s. Therefore, T = 1 ms is an acceptable value.

c) Transfer function G(z) of the process and validation:

$$G(z) = \frac{(z-1)}{z}Z\left(\frac{1/2}{s^2(s+1/2)}\right) = \left(\frac{z-1}{z}\right)\left(\frac{T\,z}{(z-1)^2} - \frac{z\left(1-e^{-0.5\,T}\right)}{0.5(z-1)\left(z-e^{-0.5\,T}\right)}\right)$$

Expansion and simplification lead to:

$$G(z) = \frac{(0.5\,T\,\text{I}\,e^{-0.5\,T}-1)z-(1+0.5\,T)e^{-0.5\,I}+1}{0.5(z-1)\left(z-e^{-0.5\,T}\right)}$$

In particular, for T = 400 ms:

$$G(z) = \frac{0.03746z + 0.03505}{z^2 - 1.819z + 0.8187}$$

The following Matlab console program allows the validation of G(z) by comparing the associated step response to that of $G_c(s)$:

```
1    % Step response
2    T = 0.4;  k = 0:6;  tk = k*T;  N = length(tk);
3    sysGc = tf(1/2, [1  1/2  0]),
4    numGz = [0.03746  0.03505],
5    denGz = [1 -1.819  0.8187]
6    yGc = step(sysGc,tk);
7    yGz = dstep(numGz, denGz,N);
8    plot(tk,yGc);  xlabel ('temps (s)');  hold on;
9    stem(tk, yGc,'o'),  grid; hold off
```

The result of the comparison is shown in Figure 4.8.

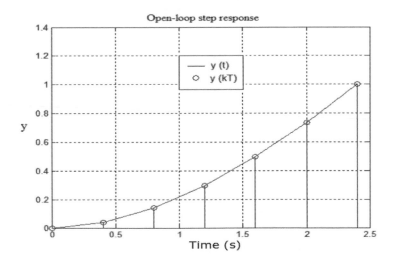

Figure 4.8. *Result of the comparison*

d) Transfer function $D(z)$ of the controller with the pole(s) and zero(s) transformation method:

Transformation refers to a zero for $s = -1/2$ and a pole for $s = -3$.

This yields:

$$D(z) = \frac{U(z)}{E(z)} = \left(\frac{1-e^{-3T}}{1-e^{-0.5T}}\right)\left(\frac{z-e^{-0.5T}}{z-e^{-3T}}\right) = \frac{3.855\,z - 3.156}{z - 0.3012}$$

e) System of recurrence equations resulting from $D(z) = U(z)/E(z)$ and $G(z) = Y(z)\,/\,Y_r(z)$:

The relations to be translated into recursive equations are:

$E(z) = Y_r(z) - Y(z)$, input quantity of the controller

$$D(z) = \frac{U(z)}{E(z)} = \frac{b_0 z + b_1}{z + a_1}, \text{ with } b_0 = 3.855; \; b_1 = -3.156; \; a_1 = -0.3012$$

$$G(z) = \frac{Y(z)}{U(z)} = \frac{\beta_1 z + \beta_2}{z^2 + \alpha_1 z + \alpha_2},$$

with $\beta_1 = 0.03746; \; \beta_2 = 0.03505; \; \alpha_1 = -1.819; \; \alpha_2 = 0.8187$

This leads to the following recursive equations:

$$\begin{cases} y(k) = -\alpha_1 y(k-1) - \alpha_2 y(k-2) + \beta_1 u(k-1) + \beta_2 u(k-2) \\ e(k) = y_r(k) - y(k) \\ u(k) = -a_1 u(k-1) + b_0 e(k) + b_1 e(k-1) \end{cases}$$

with initial conditions:

$y(0) = 0$, $e(0) = y_r = 1$ (step response)

$u(0) = b_0 e(0)$

$y(1) = \beta_1 u(0)$, $e(1) = y_r(1) - y(1)$

$u(1) = -a_1 u(0) + b_0 e(1) + b_1 e(0)$

f) The first 12 samples of *u* and *y* for a desired step response:

The following Matlab program has been used for calculating samples from the recursive equations and drawing graphic representation of the results obtained:

```
1    % Simulation for the first 12 samples
2    clear, clg
3    T = 0.4  % Sampling period
4    % Controlling parameter
5    b0 = (1-exp(-3*T))/(1-exp(-0.5*T));
6    b1 = -b0*exp(-0.5*T);  a1 = -exp(-3*T);
7    % Process parameters
8    bet0 = 0;  bet1= (-1+0.5*T+exp(-0.5*T))/0.5;
9    bet2 = (1-0.5*T*exp(-0.5*T)-exp(-0.5*T)) /0.5;
10   alp1= -(1+exp(-0.5*T));  alp2=exp(-0.5*T)
11   N = 12; yr = ones(N,1);  % Unit step set points
12   % Initial conditions
13   Temps(1) = 0;  Temps(2) = T;  Temps(3)=2*T;
14   y(1) = 0;  e(1) = yr(1); u(1) = b0* e(1);
15   y(2) =  bet1* u(1);   e(2) = yr(2) - y(2);
16   u(2) = -a1* u(1) + b0* e(2) + b1* e(1);
17   for  k = 3:N  % Processing of recursive equations
18   Temps(k) = (k-1)*T;
19   y(k) = -alp1*y(k-1)-alp2*y(k-2)+bet1*u(k-1)+bet2*u(k-2);
20   e(k) = yr(k)-y(k);
21   u(k) = -a1*u(k-1)+b0*e(k)+b1*e(k-1);
22   End
23   plot(Temps, u,'--');   hold ;   stem(Temps,y); grid
24   xlabel('Temps (s)'); title ('y(kT) et u(kT)');
```

The first 12 samples calculated are presented in Table 4.6.

k	k T	u	y
0	0	3.8551	0
1	0.4000	1.3032	0.1444
2	0.8000	-0.1745	0.4466
3	1.2000	-0.7704	0.7331
4	1.6000	-0.8151	0.9327
5	2.0000	-0.6067	1.0386
6	2.4000	-0.3462	1.0740
7	2.8000	-0.1358	1.0688
8	3.2000	-0.0060	1.0473
9	3.6000	0.0523	1.0247
10	4.0000	0.0631	1.0079
11	4.4000	0.0502	0.9984

Table 4.6. *Table of the first 12 samples*

g) The graphs of the step response and of the digital control are presented in Figure 4.9.

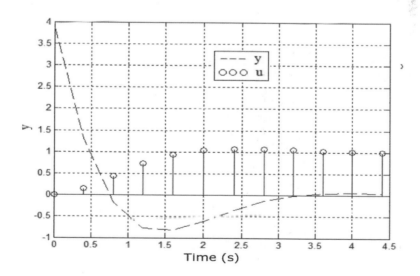

Figure 4.9. *Graphs of the step response and of the digital control*

5

Computer-aided Simulation of Digital Feedback Control Systems

5.1. Approaches to computer-aided simulation

Let us consider a digital feedback control system admitting the following quantities:

– Ref: desired output;

– U: input;

– Y: output.

Let us also consider the z-transfer functions of the process and of the controller, given by $G(z)$ and $D(z)$, respectively, as follows:

$$G(z) = \frac{Y(z)}{U(z)} = \frac{\sum_{i=1}^{n} b_i z^{n-i}}{z^n + \sum_{i=1}^{n} a_i z^{n-i}} = \frac{b_1 z^{n-1} + ... + b_{n-1} z + b_n}{z^n + a_1 z^{n-1} + ... + a_{n-1} z + a_n} \qquad [5.1]$$

$$D(z) = \frac{U(z)}{E(z)} = \frac{\sum_{j=0}^{m} \beta_j z^{m-j}}{z^m + \sum_{i=1}^{m} \alpha_i z^{n-i}} = \frac{\beta_0 z^m + \beta_1 z^{m-1} + ... + \beta_{m-1} z + \beta_m}{z^m + \alpha_1 z^{m-1} + ... + \alpha_{m-1} z + \alpha_m} \qquad [5.2]$$

Under these conditions, the simulation of the digital feedback control diagram, modeled by the transfer function $F(z) = Y(z) / \text{Ref}(z) = D(z)G(z) / (1 + D(z)G(z))$ knowing [5.1] and [5.2], involves analyzing, by means of an appropriate software, the behavior (graphic profile, dynamic and static performances) of the output quantity generated under a desired output applied over a finite time horizon.

In general, three digital simulation approaches can be considered, depending on the needs, namely:

– programming of joint recurrence equations deduced from [5.1] and [5.2];

– macro programming;

– graphic simulation.

5.2. Programming of joint recurrence equations

5.2.1. *Formulation*

Considering the expansions performed in Chapter 4, the joint recurrence equations resulting from [5.1] and [5.2] can be generalized in the following form:

$$
\begin{cases}
y(0) = 0, \ \ e(0) = y_r(0), \ \ u(0) = b_0 e(0) & (a) \\[2mm]
y(k) = \begin{cases} \displaystyle\sum_{i=1}^{k}\left(b_i u(k-i) - a_i \ y(k-i)\right), & k = 1, 2, ..., n-1 & (b) \\[4mm] \displaystyle\sum_{i=1}^{n}\left(b_i u(k-i) - a_i \ y(k-i)\right), & k = n, \ n+1, \ ... & (c) \end{cases} \\[8mm]
e(k) = y_r(k) - y(k), & k = 1, 2, ... & (d) \\[2mm]
u(k) = \begin{cases} \displaystyle\beta_0 e(k) + \sum_{i=1}^{k}\left(\beta_i e(k-i) - \beta_i \ u(k-i)\right), & k = 1, 2, ..., m-1 & (e) \\[4mm] \displaystyle\beta_0 e(k) + \sum_{i=1}^{m}\left(\beta_i e(k-i) - \alpha_i \ u(k-i)\right), & k = m, m+1, \ ... & (f) \end{cases}
\end{cases}
\qquad [5.3]
$$

with:

$$e(k) = y_r(k) - y(k), \ k = 0, 1, 2,... \qquad [5.4]$$

It is worth noting that the linear and recursive structure of [5.3] can be readily implemented in design time or in real time with any classic or Windows-oriented programming tool.

5.2.2. *Example of Matlab® programming*

Let us consider here an analog control loop represented by the block diagram in Figure 5.1.

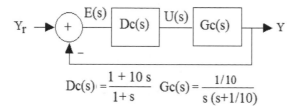

$$Dc(s) = \frac{1 + 10\,s}{1 + s} \qquad Gc(s) = \frac{1/10}{s\,(s+1/10)}$$

Figure 5.1. *Analog control loop*

The problem to solve involves:

– analyzing the behavior of the continuous dynamic model of this analog control loop;

– establishing in the frequency domain the equivalent discrete block diagram for various possible discretization techniques;

– simulating the resulting step responses of the continuous model and of the discrete models for several choices of sampling periods;

– analyzing and comparing the obtained simulation results.

5.2.2.1. *Choice of sampling period*

The analog control loop is described by the following transfer function:

$$F_c(s) = \frac{Y_r(s)}{Y(s)} = \frac{D_c(s)\,G_c(s)}{1 + D_c(s)\,G_c(s)} = \frac{\left(\dfrac{1+10\,s}{s+1}\right)\left(\dfrac{1/10}{s\,(s+1/10)}\right)}{1 + \left(\dfrac{1+10\,s}{s+1}\right)\left(\dfrac{1/10}{s\,(s+1/10)}\right)} \qquad [5.5]$$

A simple expansion yields:

$$F_c(s) = \frac{(1/10)\,(10\,s+1)}{s\,(s+1/10)(s+1)+(1/10)(10\,s+1)} \qquad [5.6]$$

Factorization followed by simplification of the common term in numerator and denominator leads to:

$$F_C(s) = \frac{1}{s^2 + s + 1} = \frac{\omega_n^2}{s^2 + 2\,\xi\,\omega_n s + \omega_n^2} \qquad [5.7]$$

with:

- $\omega_n = 1$ rad/s;

- $\xi = 0.5$.

As regards to discretization of analog models, it is worth noting that the closed-loop bandwidth of this analog feedback control system is given by the expression:

$$f_b = \frac{\omega_n}{2\,\pi}\sqrt{1 - 2\xi^2 + \sqrt{4\xi^4 - 4\xi^2 + 2}} = 0.2040 \text{ Hz} \qquad [5.8]$$

Therefore, the sampling period T can be chosen in the interval:

$$\frac{1}{60\,f_b} \le T \le \frac{1}{20\,f_b} \rightarrow 0.0817\,s \le T \le 0.2451\,s \qquad [5.9]$$

5.2.2.2. Calculation of G(z) by discretization of Gc(s)

The use of step invariance technique, combined with the results of a table of z-transforms, leads to:

$$G(z) = \frac{z-1}{z} Z\left(\frac{1/10}{s\,(s+1/10)}\right) = \frac{(z-1)}{z}\,\frac{T\,z}{(z-1)^2} - \frac{10\,z}{(z-1)} + \frac{10}{z - e^{-T/10}} \qquad [5.10]$$

After reduction in G(z) to the same denominator and arrangement of terms, the following expression is obtained:

$$G(z) = \frac{b_1\,z + b_2}{z^2 + a_1 z + a_2} \qquad [5.11]$$

$$\begin{cases} a = 1/10 \\ b_1 = (e^{-aT} + a\,T - 1)/a;\ b_2 = (1 - e^{-aT} - a\,T e^{-aT})/a \\ a_1 = -(1 + e^{-aT});\ a_2 = e^{-aT} \end{cases} \qquad [5.12]$$

5.2.2.3. *Calculation of D(z) using the step invariance method*

For $D_c(s) = (1 + 10s)/(1 + s)$, the transfer function $D(z)$ of the controller, which results from the discretization of $D_c(s)$ by step invariance, is written as:

$$D(z) = \frac{\beta_0 z + \beta_1}{z + \alpha_1}$$
[5.13]

with:

$- \beta_0 = 10;$

$- \beta_1 = -9.923;$

$- \alpha_1 = -0.9231.$

5.2.2.4. *Closed-loop simulation based on the recurrence equations*

In this case, for a programming tool that has no 0 index, the joint recurrence equations of [5.3] and [5.4] are written as:

$$k = 1,2: \begin{cases} y(1) = 0; \quad e(1) = 1, \quad u(1) = \beta_0 * e(1), \\ y(2) = b_1 u(1) - a_1 y(1), \quad e(2) = y_r(2) - y(2), \\ u(2) = \beta_0 * e(2) + \beta_1 * e(1) - \alpha_1 * u(1), \end{cases}$$
[5.14]

$$k \geq 3: \begin{cases} y(k \geq 3) = b_1 u(k-1) - a_1 y(k-1) + b_2 u(k-2) - a_2 y(k-2) \\ u(k \geq 3) = \beta_0 e(k) + \beta_1 e(k-1) - \alpha_1 u(k-1) \end{cases}$$

The "SimEquaRec.m" program allows the numerical simulation of [5.14] and the production of graphic results presented in Figure 5.2.

No.	"SimEquaRec.m"	
1	a = 1/10; tau = 1/a;	
2	T= 0.08; t = 0:T:12; N = length(t); % Time data	
3	b1= (exp(-a*T)+a*T-1)/a; b2 = (1-exp(-a*T)-a*T*exp(-a*T))/a;	
4	a1= - (1+exp(-a*T)); a2 = exp(-a*T);	
5	beta0 = 1/a , % beta0 =1/0.1;	
6	beta1 = (1/a)*(-1+ a*(1-exp(-T/(a*tau)))); % beta1= -9.923;	
7	alpha1 = -exp(-T/(a * tau)); % alpha1 = -0.9231;	
8	yr = ones(N,1); % N Samples	

9	y(1) = 0; e(1) = 0; u(1) = beta0*e(1);
10	y(2) = b1*u(1) - a1*y(1); e(2) = yr(2)-y(2);
11	u(2) = beta0*e(2) + beta1*e(1) - alpha1*u(1);
12	for k = 3:N % Simulation loop
13	y(k) = b1 *u(k-1) -a1*y(k-1) + b2*u(k-2) - a2*y(k-2);
14	e(k) = yr(k)-y(k);
15	u (k) = beta0*e(k)+beta1*e(k-1) - alpha1*u(k-1);
16	End
17	subplot(211); plot(t,y,'k'); grid; xlabel('Temps(s)'); ylabel('Y(t)');
18	subplot(212); plot(t,u,'k'); grid; xlabel('Temps(s)'); ylabel('U(t)');

Figure 5.2 presents the graphic results obtained after complete execution of the proposed program. It can be noted that, in a steady state, when the static error is nearly null, the digital control tends to zero.

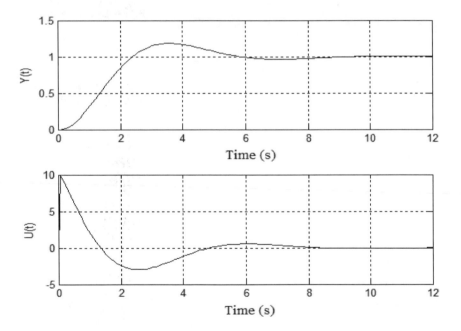

Figure 5.2. *Result of the step response simulation using Matlab programming*

5.3. Simulation using Matlab macro programming

Let us resume the example presented in the previous section, in which the transfer functions of the process and of the controller are given, respectively, by:

$$
\begin{cases}
G_c(s) = \dfrac{\alpha}{s\,(s+\alpha)} \\[3mm]
D_c(s) = \dfrac{1+\tau\,s}{s+1}
\end{cases}
\quad \text{with } \alpha = 1/10,\ \ \tau = 10
\qquad\qquad [5.15]
$$

The graphic responses of control systems in continuous and discrete time for T = 0.1 s can be more rapidly simulated using the following "MacroSim.m" macro program:

No.	"MacroSim.m" program
1	T = 0.3; t = 0:T:12; N= length(t); % Time
2	a = 1/10; tau = 10 ; ;
3	Gc = tf(a, [1 a 0]) ; Dc = tf([tau 1], [a * tau 1]);
4	Fc = feedback(series (Gc, Dc),1); % Object Fc(p)
5	yc = step(Fc, t); % Step response of Gc(s)
6	[NumGz , DenGz] = c2d(Gc, T, 'zoh') ; % Discretization
7	Gz = tf(NumGz , DenGz); % Object G(z)
8	yzBo = dstep(NumGz, DenGz,N); % Response of G(z)
9	[NumDz , DenDz] = c2d(Dc, T, 'zoh') % Discretization
11	Dz = tf (NumDz, DenDz, T) ; % Object D(z)
12	Fz = feedback(series (Dz, Gz),1); % Object F(z)
13	[NumFz, DenFz] = tfdata(Fz, 'v'); % Parameters
14	yd = dstep(NumFz, DenFz ,N); % Step response
15	plot(t,yc, 'k', t,yd, 'o'); grid ; xlabel('Temps (s)'); ylabel('Y');
16	gtext('--- Continu '); gtext('ooo Discret')

The specialized commands used in this Matlab macro program are:

– "tf": transfer function object;

– "series": algebraic operator for the serialization of transfer functions;

– "feedback": algebraic operator for the looping of transfer functions;

– "c2d": operator for the discretization of continuous dynamic models.

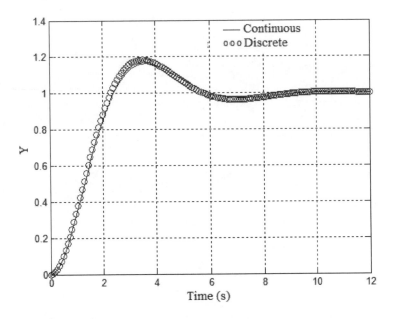

Figure 5.3. *Step responses obtained in continuous and discrete time*

The execution of the proposed Matlab macro program leads to the result in Figure 5.3, where the step responses obtained in continuous and discrete time coincide with the result in Figure 5.2, obtained using the programming of joint recurrence equations.

In the previous program, the sampling period T or the technique used for the discretization of $D_c(s)$ can be modified. In the second case, the expressions of $D(z)$ obtained and summarized in Table 5.1 all have the following form:

$$D(z) = \frac{\beta_0 z + \beta_1}{z + \alpha_1}$$ [5.16]

Methods for calculating D(z) for T = 0.1 s	D(z) for $D_c(s) = \dfrac{(1+10\,s)}{1+s}$
Step invariance	$D(z) = \dfrac{10\,z - 9.923}{z - 0.9231}$
Direct linear transformation	$D(z) = \dfrac{10\,z - 9.8}{z - 0.8}$
Inverse linear transformation	$D(z) = \dfrac{10.2\,z - 10}{1.2\,(z - 1/1,2)}$
Tustin transformation	$D(z) = \dfrac{20.2\,z - 19.8}{2.2\,(z - 1.8/2.2)}$
Transformation of poles and zeros	$D(z) = \dfrac{9.154z - 8.973}{z - 0.8187}$

Table 5.1. *D(z) for various discretization methods*

A block diagram is thus obtained, having a variable structure of the digital control loop (Figure 5.4).

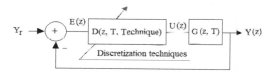

Figure 5.4. *Variable structure block diagram of the digital control loop*

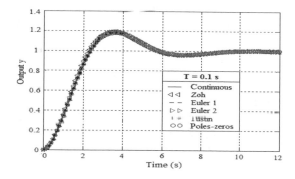

Figure 5.5. *Step responses for T = 0.1 s. For a color version of this figure, see www.iste.co.uk/mbihi/automation.zip*

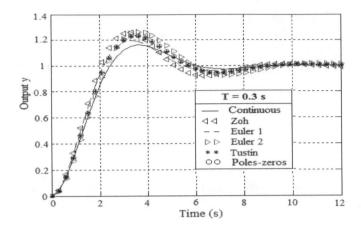

Figure 5.6. *Closed-loop step responses for T = 0.3 s. For a color version of this figure, see www.iste.co.uk/mbihi/automation.zip*

Figure 5.5 presents the simulation results of closed-loop step responses, obtained with various controller discretization methods, with the following values of the sampling period: T = 0.1 s. A nearly perfect superposition of responses can be noted, due to an appropriate choice of the sampling period T = 0.1 s. On the contrary, the results presented in Figure 5.6 show that an increase in T to 0.3 s generates significant gaps between the discretization methods used.

5.4. Graphic simulation

Graphic simulation tools provide an environment for setting up simulation diagrams based on ranges of input and output virtual components and data processing. It is the case for Simulink environment and for *Graphical User Interface* (GUI) in Matlab. In all cases, a Matlab or Simulink GUI application can communicate during execution time with specialized modular procedures, implemented using C/C++ programming or Matlab macro programming.

An example of graphic simulation results of an analog feedback control system in the Matlab/Simulink environment corresponds to Figure 5.7. This tool has been configured for simulation with the fourth-order Runge–Kutta algorithm, for a sampling period T = 0.1 s. The equivalent discrete control system can also be easily simulated using discrete operators from the Simulink toolbox.

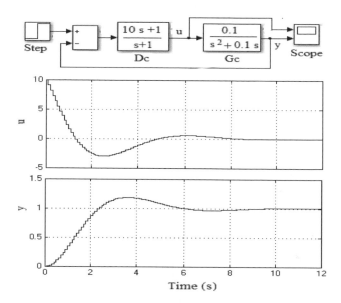

Figure 5.7. *Graphic simulation in the Simulink environment*

At this stage, it is very important to note that, despite the ease of graphic simulation without programming, the digital simulation conditions to be configured in the menus and deep submenus of the Simulink environment can prove difficult to locate, handle and interpret from the perspective of allowable adjustment ranges.

The case study presented in the next section of this chapter has been implemented and thoroughly tested with the Matlab GUIDE (*Graphical User Interface Development*).

5.5. Case study: simulation of servomechanisms

5.5.1. *Simulation of a speed servomechanism*

5.5.1.1. *Transfer function G(z) of the process*

If the transfer function $G_c(s)$ of the process is subjected to an input delay τ, the following can be written as:

$$G_c(s) = \frac{Y(s)}{U_c(s)} = \frac{K_s}{1+\tau s} e^{-\tau_0 s}$$

[5.17]

Thus, the discretization of $G_c(s)$, considering a delay index $m = \tau_0/T$ (where T is the sampling period), leads to:

$$G(z) = \frac{K_s \, (1 - e^{-\frac{1}{\tau}T})}{z^{m+1} - e^{-\frac{1}{\tau}T} z^m} \qquad [5.18]$$

It is worth remembering that in the absence of input delay, $\tau_0 = 0$, or $m = 0$, then in this case [5.18] becomes:

$$G(z) = \frac{K_s \, (1 - e^{-\frac{1}{\tau}T})}{z - e^{-\frac{1}{\tau}T}} \qquad [5.19]$$

The simulation data considered are the following:

$$G_c(s) = \frac{Y_s(s)}{U(s)} = \frac{K}{1 + \tau \, s} e^{-\tau_0 \, s} = \frac{6.8483}{1 + 0.841 \, s} e^{-0.25 \, s} \qquad [5.20]$$

For $\tau = 0.5$ s and $\tau_0 = 0.25$ s, the graph and the table of numerical values of the function $T = \tau_0 \, / \, m$ are presented in Figure 5.8.

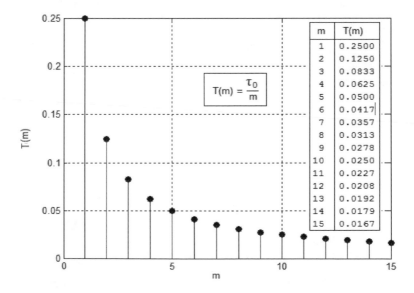

Figure 5.8. *Graph and table of values of the function $T(m) = \tau_0 \, / \, m$*

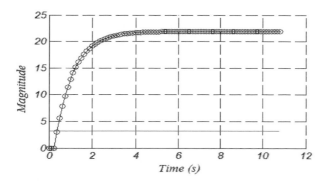

Figure 5.9. *Open-loop step responses*

Considering the means required for the real-time implementation of the sampling clock, the reasonable values of T to be used for discretization can be chosen in the range from 30 to 50 ms. Under these conditions, Figure 5.9 presents the results of the comparison of step responses, simulated by considering the transfer functions $D_c(s)$ and $D(z)$.

5.5.1.2. *Transfer functions D(z) of the PIDF controller*

The controller used here is a PIDF (proportional, integral, derivative, with first-order filter) controller. In this case, the transfer function $D_c(s)$ is written as:

$$G_c(s) = \frac{Y_p(s)}{U(s)} = \frac{K}{s\,(1+\tau\,s)}\,e^{-\tau_0\,s} \qquad [5.21]$$

Although [5.21] can be discretized directly using the Matlab command "c2d", it is more advantageous in this specific case to use a discretization approach, leading to an analytical structure of $D(z)$ with symbolic parameters.

Thus, direct application to [5.21] of the Tustin discretization technique leads after simplification of the rational structure of $D(z)$, given by relations [5.22] and [5.23] to:

$$D(z) = K_p \frac{(b_0 z^2 + b_1 z + b_2)}{z^2 + a_1 z + a_2} \qquad [5.22]$$

with:

$$
\begin{cases}
b_0 = K_p \dfrac{\left((1+\dfrac{T}{2\,T_i})\,(T+2T_f)+2\,T_d \right)}{T+2\,T_f} \\[4mm]
b_1 = K_p \dfrac{\left(\dfrac{T^2}{T_i}-4\,(T_f+T_d) \right)}{T+2\,T_f} \\[4mm]
b_2 = K_p \dfrac{\left((\dfrac{T}{2\,T_i}-1)\,(T-2T_f)+2\,T_d \right)}{T+2\,T_f} \\[4mm]
a_1 = \dfrac{-4\,T_f}{T+2T_f} \\[4mm]
a_2 = \dfrac{2\,T_f-T}{T+2\,T_f}
\end{cases}
\qquad [5.23]
$$

At this stage, knowing the transfer functions $G(z)$ and $D(z)$ leads to the representation in the frequency domain of the digital feedback control system of a lag servomechanism (Figure 5.10).

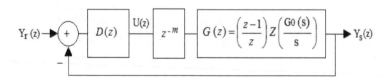

Figure 5.10. *Block diagram of a digital feedback control system of a servomechanism*

In the particular case of a PI controller with $K_p = 0.6$ and $T_d = 0.75$ s, relations [5.22] and [5.23] lead to:

$$
\begin{cases}
D(z) = \dfrac{a_0\,z^2+a_1\,z+a_2}{z^2-1} \\[3mm]
u(k) = u(k-2)+a_0 e(k)+a_1\,e(k-1)+a_2 e(k-2)
\end{cases}
\qquad [5.24]
$$

with:

$$\begin{cases} a_2 = K_p \left(1 + \dfrac{T}{2\,T_i}\right); \\[2ex] a_1 = K_p \left(\dfrac{T}{T_i}\right); \\[2ex] a_0 = K_p \left(\dfrac{T}{2\,T_i} - 1\right) \end{cases} \qquad [5.25]$$

5.5.1.3. *Closed-loop simulation of a speed servomechanism*

The results of open-loop and closed-loop simulation of a speed servomechanism for $m = 8$ and $T = 30$ ms are presented in Figure 5.11. In each case, a nearly perfect superposition of step responses of $G_c(s)$ and $G(z)$, which is obtained in continuous and discrete time respectively, can be noted. Furthermore, following a disturbance applied in a steady state from instant 4.5 s, it can be noted that its effect on the closed-loop behavior is rigorously compensated after approximately 1 s.

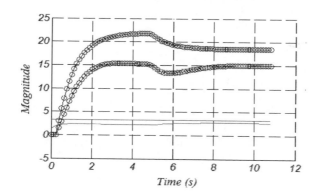

Figure 5.11. *Open-loop and closed-loop responses of a speed servomechanism*

5.5.2. *Simulation of a position servomechanism*

5.5.2.1. *Open-loop transfer function G(z)*

In this case, the open-loop transfer function is written as:

$$G_c(s) = \frac{Y_p(s)}{U(s)} = \frac{K}{s\,(1 + \tau\,s)}\,e^{-\tau_0\,s} \qquad [5.26]$$

The subsequent discretization of [5.26] by the step invariance method yields:

$$
\begin{aligned}
G(z) &= z^{-m} \, K_s \left(\frac{z-1}{z}\right) Z\left(\frac{1}{s^2\,(1+\tau s)}\right) = z^{-m} \, K_s \left(\frac{z-1}{z}\right) Z\left(\frac{1/\tau}{s^2\,(s+1/\tau)}\right) \\[2em]
&= z^{-m} K_s \left(\frac{z-1}{z}\right) \left(\frac{T\,.z}{(z-1)^2} - \frac{\left(1-e^{-\frac{1}{\tau}.T}\right).z}{\frac{1}{\tau}.(z-1).\left(z-e^{-\frac{1}{\tau}.T}\right)} \right)
\end{aligned}
\qquad\qquad [5.27]
$$

Expansion and simplification of [5.27] lead to:

$$
G(z) = K_s \, \frac{\left(T-\tau(1-e^{-\frac{1}{\tau}T})\right)z - Te^{-\frac{1}{\tau}T} + \tau\,(1-e^{-\frac{1}{\tau}T})}{(z^{m+1}-z^{m})\,(z-e^{-\frac{1}{\tau}T})}
\qquad\qquad [5.28]
$$

The simulation parameters of the open-loop transfer function [5.28] of the position servomechanism are:

– K_s = 1.2 (static gain);

– τ = 0.5 s (time constant);

– τ_0 = 0.25 s (input delay);

– m = 8 (integer index of input delay).

For a servomechanism featuring only a tachometer (speed sensor), the position quantity y_p can be numerically estimated at each sampling instant kT (with k = 1, 2,...) from speed samples y_s using the Euler algorithm given by the following relation:

$$
y_p(k+1) = y_p(k) + T \, y_s(k)
\qquad\qquad [5.29]
$$

Figure 5.12 shows the results of open-loop simulation of continuous and discrete transfer functions of the servomechanism.

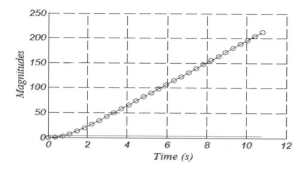

Figure 5.12. *Open-loop step response of the position servomechanism*

5.5.2.2. *Specification of the PI controller to be discretized*

The structure of $D(z)$ given by the previous relations maintains its validity, but the following updated values of the PI controller parameters should however be considered:

$-K_p = 0.445;$

$-T_i = 2000$ s.

5.5.2.3. *Closed-loop simulation of the position servomechanism*

Figure 5.13 presents the results of the comparison of open-loop and closed-loop responses. It can be noted that the controller stabilizes the system and maintains precision in a steady state (null static error).

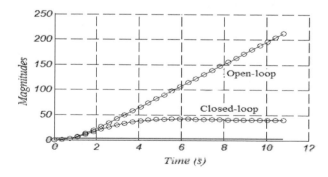

Figure 5.13. *Open-loop and closed-loop responses of a position servomechanism*

5.6. Exercises and solutions

Exercise 5.1.

Fill in Table 5.2 that compares digital simulation approaches of the following feedback control systems:

APPROACHES	COMPARISON CRITERIA	
	ADVANTAGES	DRAWBACKS
Programming		
Macro programming		
Graphic simulation		

Table 5.2. *Table comparing simulation approaches*

Solution – Exercise 5.1.

The results of the comparison of simulation approaches are presented in Table 5.3.

APPROACHES	COMPARISON CRITERIA	
	ADVANTAGES	DRAWBACKS
Programming	Code that is readily exportable into other programming tools	Heavy programming efforts
Macro programming	Rapid programming	Code non-portability
Graphic simulation	No direct programming	Great difficulties with appropriate reconfiguration of simulation conditions in various submenus

Table 5.3. *Results of the comparison of simulation approaches*

Exercise 5.2.

Use Table 5.4 as a model to describe the Matlab commands used in the Matlab macro program "MacroSim.m" provided in section 5.3.

Type	Name	Role
Numerical analysis		
...		
Graphic representations		
...		

Table 5.4. *Model of table summarizing the Matlab commands used*

Solution – Exercise 5.2.

The Matlab commands used in the "SimEquaRec.m" macro program are described in Table 5.5.

Type	Name	Role
Numerical analysis	"exp"	Exponential function of base e
	"ones"	Creation of unit vector/matrix
Graphic representations	"plot"	2D graphic representation of data
	"subplot"	Subdivision of a figure area into a basis of graphic windows "n x m"
	"grid"	Grid of the overlay plane
	"xlabel"	Writing of the X-axis label
	"ylabel"	Writing of the Y-axis label

Table 5.5. *Matlab commands used in the "SimEquaRec.m" program*

Exercise 5.3.

Use Table 5.6 as a model to describe the Matlab commands used in the Matlab macro program "MacroSim.m".

Type	Name	Role
Numerical analysis		
...		
Graphic representations		
...		

Table 5.6. *Matlab commands used in the "MacroSim.m" program*

Solution – Exercise 5.3.

The Matlab commands used in the Matlab macro program "MacroSim.m" are described in Table 5.7.

Type	Name	Role
Numerical analysis	"length"	Dimension of a data vector
	"tf"	Creation of a transfer function object
	"tfdata"	Extraction of numerator and denominator contained in a tf object
	"c2d"	Discretization of a dynamic model
	"series"	Model serialization operator
	"feedback"	Operator for looping the two dynamic models
Graphic representations	"step"	Continuous time step response
	"dstep"	Discrete time step response
	"gtext"	Writing a text from a point of the graphic zone

Table 5.7. *Matlab commands used in the "MacroSim.m" program*

Exercise 5.4.

Under what condition can the graphic simulation of feedback control systems be definitely qualified as easy?

Solution – Exercise 5.4.

The graphic simulation of feedback control systems is definitely only easy under simulation conditions based on default configuration options of menus and submenus.

Exercise 5.5.

Let us consider the "MacroSim.m" program of section 5.3.

a) what parameters should be modified in this program in order to calculate the transfer function $D(z)$ of the controller, with other discretization methods specified in Table 5.1, under a sampling period $T = 0.5$ s?

b) considering the same discretization methods indicated in Figure 5.6 with $T = 0.5$ s, generate the graphs of step responses obtained from modified versions of this macro program;

c) given these simulation results, what conclusion can be drawn regarding the choice of T value?

Solution – Exercise 5.5.

a) in the "MacroSim.m" program, T = 0.3 should be modified in line 1, as well as "zoh" in line 9;

b) the new graphs of step responses, obtained from modified versions of this program, are presented in Figure 5.14.

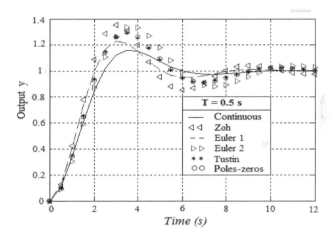

Figure 5.14. *New graphs obtained. For a color version of this figure, see www.iste.co.uk/mbihi/automation.zip*

c) compare the obtained results to those in Figure 5.6:

It can be noted that, compared to the case presented in Figure 5.6, where the sampling period is T = 0.3 s, the behavior gaps between various sampling methods are more significant in the transient state for T = 0.5 s, which is to be expected, since the new value of T is higher.

Discrete State Models
of Dynamic Processes

6.1. Discretization of the state model of a dynamic process

Applying to state space, the same reasoning used in Chapter 4 in the context of transfer functions leads to the block diagram of the sampled dynamic process represented in Figure 6.1. The input variable $u(t)$, state variable $x(t)$ and output variable $y(t)$ of the process schematically represented in Figure 6.1(a) are replaced in Figure 6.1(b) by their respective sampled quantities $u^*(t)$, $x^*(t)$ and $y^*(t)$.

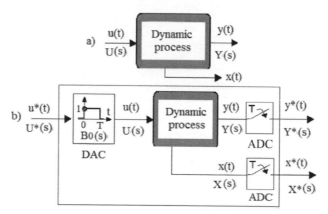

Figure 6.1. *Block diagram of a dynamic process sampled in the state space*

6.1.1. *Discretization of a state model*

Let us consider a dynamic process, described by the following continuous state model:

$$\begin{cases} \dfrac{dx(t)}{dt} = A_c \; x(t) + B_c \; u(t) \\ y(t) = C_c \; x(t) + D_c \; u(t) \end{cases} \equiv \{A_c, B_c, D_c, D_c\} \qquad [6.1]$$

Knowing that the state-transition matrix from the initial instant t_0 to instant t is written as:

$$\Phi\left(t, t_0\right) = e^{Ac(t - t_0)} \qquad [6.2]$$

then the expression of the general solution $x(t)$ is:

$$x(t) = e^{A_c(t - t0)} \; x(t0) + \int_{t0}^{t} e^{A_c(t - \tau)} \; B_c(\tau) \; u(\tau) \; d\tau \qquad [6.3]$$

In particular, if $t_0 = kT$ and $t = kT + T$, then:

$$x(kT + T) = e^{A_c(kT + T - kT)} \; x(kT) + \int_{kT}^{kT + T} e^{A_c(kT + T - \tau)} \; B_c \; u(\tau) \; d\tau \qquad [6.4]$$

or, in the presence of a zero-order holder, $u(\tau) = u(kT)$ if $kT \le \tau < (k + 1)T$, therefore:

$$x(k + 1) = e^{A_cT} \; x(kT) + \left(\int_{kT}^{kT + T} e^{A_c((k+1)T - \tau)} \; B_c \; d\tau \right) u(kT) \qquad [6.5]$$

In order to simplify the term contained in the integral, the following change in variable must be made:

$$\eta = (k + 1)\,T - \tau, \text{ or } \begin{cases} \tau = kT & \Rightarrow \quad \eta = T \\ \tau = (k+1)T \Rightarrow \quad \eta = 0 \\ d\eta = -d\tau \end{cases} \qquad [6.6]$$

This change in variable leads to:

$$x((k + 1)T) = e^{A_cT} \; x(kT) + \left(\int_{T}^{0} e^{A\eta} \; B_c \; (-d\eta) \right) u(kT) \qquad [6.7]$$

hence, the discrete state equation:

$$x((k+1)T) = e^{A_c T} x(kT) + \left(\int_0^T e^{A\eta} \, d\eta \right) B_c \ u(kT) \qquad\qquad [6.8]$$

Thus, using the simplified notations $x(kT) \equiv x(k)$, $y(kT) \equiv y(k)$, the complete discrete dynamic model of the process is given by:

$$\begin{cases} x(k+1) = A\, x(k) + B \ u(k) \\ y(k) = C\, x(k) + D\, u(k) \end{cases} \equiv \{A\ B\ C\ D\} \qquad\qquad [6.9]$$

with:

$$A = e^{A_c\, T}, \ B = \left(\int_0^T e^{A\eta} \, d\eta \right) B_c, \ \ C = C_c, \ \ D = D_c \qquad\qquad [6.10]$$

Relations [6.9] and [6.10] lead to the block diagram of the discrete state model of a dynamic process, represented in Figure 6.2, where the delay operator of a sampling period T is symbolized by z^{-1}.

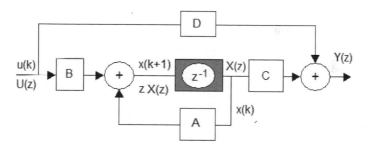

Figure 6.2. *Block diagram of the discrete state model of a dynamic process*

6.1.2. Discretization of a state model with input delay

In this case, the dynamic process is described by the following state model:

$$\begin{cases} \dfrac{dx(t)}{dt} = A_c x(t) + B_c u(t - \tau_0) \\ y(t) = C_c x(t) + D_c u(t - \tau_0) \end{cases} \qquad\qquad [6.11]$$

Knowing that the state-transition matrix from the initial instant t_0 to instant t is written as:

$$\Phi(t, t_0) = e^{Ac(t - t_0)} \tag{6.12}$$

then the expression of the general solution $x(t)$ is:

$$x(t) = e^{A_c(t - t0)} x(t_0) + \int_{t0}^{t} e^{A_c(t - \tau)} B_c u(\tau - \tau_0) d\tau \tag{6.13}$$

In particular, if $t_0 = kT$ and $t = kT + T$, then:

$$x(kT + T) = e^{A_c(kT + T - kT)} x(kT) + \int_{kT}^{kT+T} e^{A_c(kT + T - \tau)} B_c u(\tau - \tau_0) d\tau \tag{6.14}$$

For a positive integer $m = 0, 1, \ldots$, let us consider:

$$\tau_0 = mT \tag{6.15}$$

Thus, expression [6.15] becomes:

$$x(kT + T) = e^{A_c(kT + T - kT)} x(kT) + \int_{kT}^{kT+T} e^{A_c(kT + T - \tau)} B_c u(\tau - mT) d\tau \tag{6.16}$$

Let us now examine the values taken by $u(\tau - kT)$ at the integral boundaries:

– if $\tau = kT$, then $u(\tau - kT) = u(kT - mT)$;

– if $\tau = kT + T$, then $u(\tau - kT) = u(kT + T - mT)$.

Then, given the assumption of zero-order holder, $u(\tau - kT)$ is constant within the range $kT \leq \tau \leq kT + T$, and this constant is $u(kT - mT)$ at the instant $\tau = kT$.

Thus, expression [6.16] becomes:

$$
\begin{aligned}
x(kT + T) &= e^{A_c(kT + T - kT)} x(kT) + \int_{kT}^{kT+T} e^{A_c(kT + T - \tau)} B_c u(kT - mT) d\tau \\
&= e^{A_c(kT + T - kT)} x(kT) + \left(\int_{kT}^{kT+T} e^{A_c(kT + T - \tau)} d\tau \right) B_c u(kT - mT)
\end{aligned}
\tag{6.17}
$$

Now, if a change in variable is made such that:

$$\eta = (k + 1)T - \tau, \text{ or } \begin{cases} \tau = kT & \Rightarrow \quad \eta = T \\ \tau = (k+1)T \Rightarrow & \eta = 0 \\ d\eta = -d\tau \end{cases} \tag{6.18}$$

this yields:

$$x(kT+T) = e^{A_c(kT+T-kT)} x(kT) + \left(\int_{kT}^{kT+T} e^{A_c\eta} d(-\tau) \right) B_c\, u(kT-mT)$$

$$x((k+1)T) = e^{A_cT} x(kT) + \left(\int_0^T e^{A\eta} d\eta \right) B_c\quad u(((k-m)T))\qquad\qquad [6.19]$$

It can be noted that the discrete state model obtained has an input delay of m sampling periods. In order to transform [6.19] into a standard equivalent discrete model (see Figure 6.3), m new internal variables considered for the delay encapsulation are defined by:

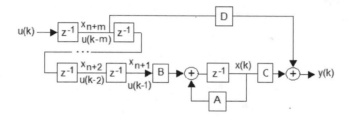

Figure 6.3. *System of m new state variables allowing the encapsulation of the pure input delay*

$$\begin{cases} x_{n+1}(k) = u(kT-mT) \\ x_{n+2}(k) = u(kT-(m-1)T) \\ \qquad\cdots \\ x_{n+m-1}(k) = u(kT-2T) \\ x_{n+m}(k) = u(kT-T) \end{cases}\qquad\qquad [6.20]$$

Under these conditions, a complete $n + m$ dimensional state model is obtained and is defined by:

$$\begin{bmatrix} x(k+1) \\ x_{n+1}(k+1) \\ x_{n+2}(k+1) \\ \cdots \\ x_{n+m}(k+1) \end{bmatrix} = \begin{bmatrix} A & B & 0 & 0 & 0 \\ 0 & 0 & 1 & 0 & \cdots \\ \cdots & 0 & 0 & 1 & 0 \\ 0 & .. & 0 & 0 & 1 \\ 0 & 0 & \cdots & 0 & 0 \end{bmatrix} \begin{bmatrix} x(k) \\ x_{n+1}(k) \\ x_{n+2}(k) \\ \cdots \\ x_{n+m}(k) \end{bmatrix} + \begin{bmatrix} 0 \\ 0 \\ \cdots \\ 0 \\ 1 \end{bmatrix} u(k)\qquad [6.21]$$

with:

$$A = e^{A_c T}, \ B = \left(\int_0^T e^{A\eta} \ d\eta \right) B_c, \ \ C = C_c, \ \ D = D_c \tag{6.22}$$

6.2. Calculation of {A, B, C, D} parameters of a discrete state model

6.2.1. *Calculation of $A = e^{AT}$*

6.2.1.1. *Calculation of $A = e^{AT}$ by the Jordan diagonalization*

Indeed, if Q is the eigenvectors matrix of A_c associated with the eigenvalues λ_1, $\lambda_2, \ldots, \lambda_p$ of respective multiplicities $n_1, n_2, \ldots, n_j, \ldots, n_p$, with $\sum_{j=1}^{p} n_j = n$, then:

$$\overline{A}_c = Q^{-1} A_c Q \tag{6.23}$$

where $\overline{A}_c$ designates the diagonal matrix of A_c according to the Jordan normal form. Under these conditions, matrix $\overline{A}_c$ is formed of p Jordan blocks $A_1, A_2, \ldots, A_p$ of the form:

$$\overline{A}_c = \begin{bmatrix} A_1 & & & 0 \\ & A_2 & & \\ & & \cdots & \\ 0 & & & A_p \end{bmatrix} \tag{6.24}$$

with:

$$A_j = \begin{bmatrix} \lambda_j & 1 & 0 & \cdots & 0 \\ 0 & \lambda_j & 1 & \cdots & \\ \cdot & \cdot & & \cdot & 1 \\ 0 & 0 & 0 & 0 & \lambda_j \end{bmatrix} \quad (j = 1, 2, \ldots, n_j) \tag{6.25}$$

Thus, knowing [6.24] and [6.25], A can be calculated as follows:

$$A = e^{A_c T} = Q \, e^{\overline{A}_c T} Q^{-1} = Q \begin{bmatrix} e^{A_1 T} & & & 0 \\ & e^{A_2 T} & & \\ & & & \\ 0 & & & e^{A_p T} \end{bmatrix} Q^{-1} \tag{6.26}$$

with:

$$
e^{AjT} = \begin{bmatrix}
e^{\lambda j T} & T e^{\lambda j T} & T^2 e^{\lambda j T} & \cdots & \dfrac{T^{nj-1} e^{\lambda j T}}{(n_j - 1)!} \\
0 & e^{\lambda j T} & T e^{\lambda j T} & \cdots & \dfrac{T^{nj-2} e^{\lambda j T}}{(n_j - 2)!} \\
\cdot & & 0 & \cdots & \\
\cdot & & & 0 & e^{\lambda j T} & \cdot \\
\cdot & & & & & \\
0 & 0 & 0 & \cdots & e^{\lambda j T}
\end{bmatrix}
\qquad [6.27]
$$

6.2.1.2. Calculation of $A = e^{A_c T}$ using the Taylor series

The expansion of $e^{A_c T}$ into Taylor series of arbitrary order M leads to:

$$
e^{A_c T} \cong I + \frac{A_c T}{1!} + \frac{A_c^2 T^2}{2!} + \frac{A_c^3 T^3}{3!} + \frac{A_c^4 T^4}{4!} + \ldots + \frac{A_c^M T^M}{M!} = \sum_{k=0}^{M} \frac{(T A_c)^k}{k!} \quad [6.28]
$$

Therefore, if:

$$
\Psi(M) = I + \frac{A_c T}{2!} + \frac{A_c^2 T^2}{3!} + \frac{A_c^3 T^3}{4!} + \ldots + \frac{A_c^M T^M}{(M-1)!} \qquad [6.29]
$$

then:

$$
\begin{aligned}
\Psi(M) &= I + \frac{A_c T}{2}\left(I + \frac{A_c T}{3} + \frac{A_c^2 T^2}{3*4} + \ldots + \frac{A_c^{M-1} T^{M-1}}{3*4*\ldots*(M-1)!} \right) \\
&= I + \frac{A_c T}{2}\left(I + \frac{A_c T}{3}\left(I + \frac{A_c T}{4} + \ldots + \frac{A_c^{M-2} T^{M-2}}{4*\ldots(M-2)} \right) \right) \\
&= I + \frac{A_c T}{2}\left(I + \frac{A_c T}{3}\left(I + \frac{A_c T}{4}\left(I + \frac{A_c T}{5} + \ldots + \frac{A_c^{M-3} T^{M-3}}{5*6*\ldots(M-2)} \right) \right) \right) \\
&= I + \frac{A_c T}{2}\left(I + \frac{A_c T}{3}\left(I + \frac{A_c T}{4}\left(I + \frac{A_c T}{5}\left(+\ldots\left(I + \frac{A_c T}{M} \right) \right) \right) \right) \right)
\end{aligned}
\qquad [6.30]
$$

It is therefore sufficient to calculate $\Psi(M)$ using algorithm [6.30], then to determine the approximate value of $e^{A_c T}$ by:

$$A = I + A_c T \Psi_M \qquad\qquad [6.31]$$

6.2.1.3. Calculation of $A = e^{AT}$ by the Laplace transform

Indeed, the Laplace transform of $e^{A_c T}$ is:

$$L\left(e^{A_c T}\right) = \left(s\, I - A_c\right)^{-1} \qquad\qquad [6.32]$$

Therefore:

$$e^{A\, T} = L^{-1}\left(\left(s\, I - A_c\right)^{-1}\right) \qquad\qquad [6.33]$$

6.2.2. Calculation of B

– If matrix $A = e^{A_c T}$ has already been calculated using the Jordan technique as a function of T, it suffices to deduce $A(\tau)$ by replacing T with τ, and then to analytically calculate the term:

$$B = \left(\int_0^T e^{A_c \eta}\, d\eta\right) B_c \qquad\qquad [6.34]$$

– If matrix A_c is reversible, then:

$$B = A_c^{-1}\ \left(e^{A\, T} - I\right)\ B_c \qquad\qquad [6.35]$$

– B can also be calculated by the previously used polynomial approximation. Indeed, knowing that:

$$e^{A_c T} = I + \frac{A_c T}{1!} + \frac{A_c^2 T^2}{2!} + \frac{A_c^3 T^3}{3!} + \frac{A_c^4 T^4}{4!} + \ldots \qquad\qquad [6.36]$$

then:

$$\int_0^T e^{A\eta}\, d\eta = I\,T + \frac{A_c T^2}{2} + \frac{A_c^2 T^3}{2!\ 3} + \frac{A_c^3 T^4}{3!\ 4} + \frac{A_c^4 T^5}{4!\ 5} + \ldots$$

$$= I\,T + \frac{A_c T^2}{2!} + \frac{A_c^2 T^3}{3!} + \frac{A_c^3 T^4}{4!} + \frac{A_c^4 T^5}{5!} + \ldots$$

$$= T\left(I + \frac{A_c T}{2!} + \frac{A_c^2 T^2}{3!} + \frac{A_c^3 T^3}{4!} + \frac{A_c^4 T^4}{5!} + \ldots\right) = T\ \Psi \qquad\qquad [6.37]$$

Therefore:

$$B = \left(\int_0^T e^{A\eta} \, d\eta \right) B_c = T\psi B_c \qquad [6.38]$$

EXAMPLE.– Let us consider the process described by the following state model:

$$A_c = \begin{bmatrix} 0 & 1 \\ 0 & 0 \end{bmatrix}, B_c = \begin{bmatrix} 0 \\ 1 \end{bmatrix}, C_c = \begin{bmatrix} 1 & 0 \end{bmatrix}, D_c = 0 \qquad [6.39]$$

The objective is to discretize this model with a sampling period T.

– Step invariance method:

$$A = e^{A_c T} = e^{\begin{bmatrix} 0 & 1 \\ 0 & 0 \end{bmatrix} T} = \begin{bmatrix} e^0 & T \\ 0 & e^0 \end{bmatrix} = \begin{bmatrix} 1 & T \\ 0 & 1 \end{bmatrix} \qquad [6.40]$$

$$B = \left(\int_0^T e^{A\eta} \, d\eta \right) B_c = \left(\int_0^T \begin{bmatrix} 1 & \eta \\ 0 & 1 \end{bmatrix} d\eta \right) \begin{bmatrix} 0 \\ 1 \end{bmatrix} = \begin{bmatrix} \int_0^T d\eta & \int_0^T \eta \, d\eta \\ 0 & \int_0^T d\eta \end{bmatrix} \begin{bmatrix} 0 \\ 1 \end{bmatrix}$$

$$= \begin{bmatrix} T & \frac{T^2}{2} \\ 0 & T \end{bmatrix} \begin{bmatrix} 0 \\ 1 \end{bmatrix} = \begin{bmatrix} \frac{T^2}{2} \\ T \end{bmatrix} \qquad [6.41]$$

$$C = C_c = \begin{bmatrix} 1 & 0 \end{bmatrix}, \quad D = D_c = 0 \qquad [6.42]$$

– Method of Taylor series of order M:

In this case, the following can be written as:

$$\Psi(M) = \begin{bmatrix} 1 & 0 \\ 0 & 1 \end{bmatrix} + \frac{\begin{bmatrix} 0 & 1 \\ 0 & 0 \end{bmatrix} T}{2!} + \frac{\begin{bmatrix} 0 & 1 \\ 0 & 0 \end{bmatrix}^2 T^2}{3!} + ... + \frac{\begin{bmatrix} 0 & 1 \\ 0 & 0 \end{bmatrix}^M T^M}{(M-1)!} \qquad [6.43]$$

$$\underbrace{}_{\begin{bmatrix} 0 & 0 \\ 0 & 0 \end{bmatrix}}$$

$$= \begin{bmatrix} 1 & 0 \\ 0 & 1 \end{bmatrix} + \frac{\begin{bmatrix} 0 & 1 \\ 0 & 1 \end{bmatrix} T}{2!} = \begin{bmatrix} 1 & \frac{T}{2} \\ 0 & T \end{bmatrix}$$

Therefore:

$$B = \psi B_c T = \begin{bmatrix} 1 & \dfrac{T}{2} \\ 0 & T \end{bmatrix} \begin{bmatrix} 0 \\ 1 \end{bmatrix} T = \begin{bmatrix} \dfrac{T^2}{2} \\ T \end{bmatrix}$$ [6.44]

$$C = C_c = \begin{bmatrix} 1 & 0 \end{bmatrix}, \quad D = D_c = 0$$ [6.45]

– Laplace transform method:

$$A = L^{-1}\left(\begin{bmatrix} s & 0 \\ 0 & s \end{bmatrix} - \begin{bmatrix} 0 & 1 \\ 0 & 0 \end{bmatrix} \right) = L^{-1}\left(\begin{bmatrix} s & -1 \\ 0 & s \end{bmatrix} \right)$$ [6.46]

$$A = L^{-1}\left(\dfrac{1}{s^2}\begin{bmatrix} s & 1 \\ 0 & s \end{bmatrix} \right) = L^{-1}\left(\begin{bmatrix} \dfrac{1}{s} & \dfrac{1}{s^2} \\ 0 & \dfrac{1}{s} \end{bmatrix} \right) = \begin{bmatrix} 1 & t \\ 0 & 1 \end{bmatrix}_{t=T} = \begin{bmatrix} 1 & T \\ 0 & 1 \end{bmatrix}$$ [6.47]

$$\begin{aligned} B &= \left(\int_0^T e^{A\eta}\, d\eta \right) = \left(\int_0^T \begin{bmatrix} 1 & \eta \\ 0 & 1 \end{bmatrix} d\eta \right) \begin{bmatrix} 0 \\ 1 \end{bmatrix} \\ &= \begin{bmatrix} \int_0^T d\eta & \int_0^T \eta\, d\eta \\ 0 & \int_0^T d\eta \end{bmatrix} \begin{bmatrix} 0 \\ 1 \end{bmatrix} = \begin{bmatrix} T & \dfrac{T^2}{2} \\ 0 & T \end{bmatrix} \begin{bmatrix} 0 \\ 1 \end{bmatrix} = \begin{bmatrix} \dfrac{T^2}{2} \\ T \end{bmatrix} \end{aligned}$$ [6.48]

6.2.3. *Calculation of C and D*

$$C = C_c \text{ and } D = D_c$$

6.3. Properties of a discrete state model {A, B, C, D}

6.3.1. *Infinity of state models of one dynamic process*

A dynamic process modeled in the discrete state space admits an infinity of discrete state representations. Indeed, let us consider the following discrete state model:

$$\begin{cases} x((k+1)T) = A\, x(kT) + B\, u(kT) \\ y(k) = C\, x(k) + D\, u(k) \end{cases}$$ [6.49]

Let P be an arbitrary regular matrix of order n; if this model is applied to the transformation law $\tilde{x}(k) = P\,x(k)$, the following is obtained in the space of variable $\tilde{x}(k)$:

$$\begin{cases} \tilde{x}((k+1)T) = P\,A\,\mathrm{P}^{-1}\,\tilde{x}(kT) + P\,B\,\,u(kT) \\ y(k) = C\,\mathrm{P}^{-1}\,\tilde{x}(k) + D\,\,u(k) \end{cases} \qquad [6.50]$$

When arbitrary matrix P is subjected to variation, an infinity of similar discrete state models can be built for a single process. Nevertheless, canonical state models, which offer a maximum of null terms, are of greatest practical interest among all possible representations.

6.3.2. Stability

Relation:

$$G(z) = \frac{Y(z)}{U(z)} = C\,(z\,I_n - A)^{-1}\,B + D \qquad [6.51]$$

shows that the eigenvalues of state matrix A and the poles of $G(z)$ are identical. Consequently, the dynamic system is stable and all the eigenvalues of state matrix A have a module below unity.

6.3.3. Controllability and stabilizability

The model of a process is controllable if there is a sequence of controls allowing the passage from an arbitrary initial state $x(k_0T)$ to an arbitrary final state $x(k_fT)$ within finite time. The controllability test that applies to matrices A and B of the discrete state model of dimensions $n \times n$ and $n \times 1$, respectively, is defined by:

$$\begin{cases} a) \quad Rank\left(\begin{bmatrix} B & AB & A^2B & \dots & A^{n-1}B \end{bmatrix}\right) = n \\ or \\ b) \quad Rank\left(\begin{bmatrix} \lambda\,I_n - A & B \end{bmatrix}\right) = n \quad \forall \text{ the eigenvalue } \lambda \text{ of A} \end{cases} \qquad [6.52]$$

On the contrary, if $Rank([A \ AB \ A^2B \ ... \ A^{n-1}B]) = \text{p} < n$, then the dynamic process is not controllable. An uncontrollable dynamic system is stabilizable if all the uncontrollable eigenvalues have modules below one. In this case, the system can be partially controlled in the state subspace generated by the controllable eigenvalues.

6.3.4. *Observability and detectability*

The model of a process is observable if the initial state $x(k_0T)$ can be reconstructed within finite time, knowing the sequences of controls and outputs obtained up to instant $t_f = k_fT$. Once more, the observability test applicable to matrices A and C of the discrete state model, whose dimensions are n^2 and $1 \times n$ respectively, is defined by:

$$
\begin{cases}
a) \quad Rank\left(\begin{bmatrix} C \\ CA \\ ... \\ CA^{n-1} \end{bmatrix}\right) = n \\
\\
or \\
\\
b) \quad Rank\left(\begin{bmatrix} \lambda \ I_n - A \\ C \end{bmatrix}\right) = n \ \ \forall \ \ \text{the eigenvalue } \lambda \text{ of } A
\end{cases}
$$

[6.53]

If $Rank([C^T \ A^TC^T \ (A^2)^TC^T \ ... \ (A^{n-1})^TC^T)^T = q < n$, then the dynamic process is not observable. This unobservable dynamic process is detectable if the unobservable eigenvalues have all modules below one. In this case, the dynamic process can be partially observed in the state subspace generated by the observable eigenvalues, although some of them are unstable.

6.4. Exercises and solutions

Exercise 6.1.

An analog process is described in the state space by parameters $\{A_c, B_c, C_c, D_c\}$ with $A_c = \begin{bmatrix} 0 & -2 \\ 0 & 0 \end{bmatrix}$, $B_c = \begin{bmatrix} 1 \\ 0 \end{bmatrix}$, $C_c = 1$, $D_c = 0$. Calculate the equivalent discrete state model for T = 1 ms (sampling period) using:

a) an analytical discretization method;

b) a Matlab® program for numerical calculation using the Taylor series method and "c2d" primitive.

Solution – Exercise 6.1.

Matrix A_c is given in diagonal form. It admits two identical and null eigenvalues.

a) Analytical discretization method:

$$
\begin{cases}
A = e^{\begin{bmatrix} 0 & -2 \\ 0 & 0 \end{bmatrix} T} = e^{\begin{bmatrix} 0 & 1 \\ 0 & 0 \end{bmatrix}(-2\,T)} = \begin{bmatrix} 1 & -2\,T \\ 0 & 1 \end{bmatrix}, \\[2mm]
B = \left(\int_0^T e^{\begin{bmatrix} 0 & -2 \\ 0 & 0 \end{bmatrix} \eta}\, d\eta \right) B_c = \left(\int_0^T \begin{bmatrix} 1 & -2\eta \\ 0 & 1 \end{bmatrix} d\eta \right) B_c, \\[2mm]
B_c = \begin{pmatrix} \eta & -\eta^2 \\ 0 & \eta \end{pmatrix}_0^T B_c = \begin{bmatrix} T & -T^2 \\ 0 & T \end{bmatrix} \begin{bmatrix} 1 \\ 0 \end{bmatrix} = \begin{bmatrix} T \\ 0 \end{bmatrix}, \\[2mm]
C = C_c = 1,\ D = D_c = 0
\end{cases}
$$

b) Taylor series method and use of "c2d" primitive:

The Matlab program below is used for this purpose, which yields the following results:

$$
A = \begin{bmatrix} 1 & -0.002 \\ 0 & 1 \end{bmatrix},\ B = \begin{bmatrix} 0.001 \\ 0 \end{bmatrix},\ C = [\,1 \quad 0\,],\ D = 0
$$

It can be verified that "c2d" yields the same result.

No.	Matlab program for the discretization using Taylor method and c2d command
1	T = 0.001; % Time
2	M = 10; Ac = [0 -2; 0 0]; Bc = [1 0]'; Cc = [1 0]; Dc = 0;
3	I2 = eye(2); % Unity Matrix of order 2
4	Psi = eye(2); % Initialization of Psi
5	fac = 1; % Initialization of factorial
6	for k = 1:M % (M) iterations within the loop
7	fac = fac * k; % Factorial function k!
8	Psiav = Psi; % previous value of Psi
9	Psi = Psi + (T * Ac)^k / (fac * (k+1)); % (k+1)! = k! (k+1)

10   Psiar = Psi;   % Updated value of Psi

11   End

12   'Results obtained using Taylor method

13   A1 = I2 + T * Ac * Psi;   B1 = Psi * T * Bc;

14   sysdTaylor = ss(A1, B1, Cc, Dc);

15   [A, B, C, D] = ssdata(sysdTaylor)   % Result Taylor

16   'Results obtained using c2d method

17   sysdC2d = c2d(ss(Ac,Bc,Cc,Dc),T);

18   [A, B, C, D] = ssdata(sysdC2d)   % c2d result

Exercise 6.2.

The linear model of a pendulum, which is valid for small variations around the functioning point, is given by:

$$\frac{dx(t)}{dt} = \begin{pmatrix} 0 & 1 \\ -2 & -3 \end{pmatrix} \begin{pmatrix} x_1(t) \\ x_2(t) \end{pmatrix} + \begin{pmatrix} 0 \\ 2 \end{pmatrix} u(t)$$

Calculate the equivalent discrete state model for $T = 1$ ms (sampling period) using:

a) an analytical discretization method;

b) a Matlab program for numerical calculation using the Taylor series method and "c2d" primitive.

Solution – Exercise 6.2.

a) Analytical method:

– calculation of A:

$$sI - A_c = \begin{bmatrix} s & -1 \\ 2 & s+3 \end{bmatrix}$$

therefore:

$$(sI - A)^{-1} = \begin{bmatrix} \dfrac{s+3}{s^2+3s+2} & \dfrac{1}{s^2+3s+2} \\ \dfrac{-2}{s^2+3s+2} & \dfrac{s}{s^2+3s+2} \end{bmatrix} = \begin{bmatrix} \dfrac{2}{s+1} - \dfrac{1}{s+2} & \dfrac{1}{s+1} - \dfrac{1}{s+2} \\ \dfrac{-2}{s+1} + \dfrac{2}{s+2} & \dfrac{2}{s+2} - \dfrac{1}{s+1} \end{bmatrix}$$

Thus:

$$A = e^{A_cT} = L^{-1}((sI - A)^{-1}) = \begin{bmatrix} 2e^{-T} - e^{-2T} & e^{-T} - e^{-2T} \\ -2e^{-T} + 2e^{-2T} & 2e^{-2T} - e^{-T} \end{bmatrix}$$

If T = 1 ms, then:

$$A = \begin{bmatrix} 1 & 0.001 \\ -0.002 & 0.997 \end{bmatrix}$$

– calculation of B:

Since matrix A_c is reversible, then:

$$B = A_c^{-1} \ (e^{A_cT} - I) \ B_c = \frac{1}{2}\begin{bmatrix} -3 & -1 \\ 2 & 0 \end{bmatrix}\begin{bmatrix} 1 & 0.001 \\ -0.002 & 0.997 \end{bmatrix}\begin{bmatrix} 0 \\ 2 \end{bmatrix} = \begin{bmatrix} 0 \\ 0.002 \end{bmatrix}$$

b) Taylor series method:

The following Matlab program is used for this purpose, yielding the results:

$$A = \begin{bmatrix} 1 & -0.001 \\ -0.002 & 0.9970 \end{bmatrix}, \ B = \begin{bmatrix} 0 \\ 0.002 \end{bmatrix}, \ C = [\ 1 \quad 0\ ], \ D = 0$$

It can then be verified that Taylor method and "c2d" yield the same result.

No.	Matlab program for the discretization using Taylor method and c2d command
1	Clear; T = 0.001; % Time
2	M = 10; Ac = [0 1; -2 -3]; Bc = [0 2]'; Cc = [1 0]; Dc = 0;
3	I2 = eye(2); % Unity Matrix of order 2
4	Psi = eye(2); % Initialization of Psi
5	fac = 1; % Initialization of factorial
6	for k = 1:M % (M) iterations within the loop
7	fac = fac * k; % Factorial function k!
8	Psiav = Psi; % previous value of Psi
9	Psi = Psi + (T * Ac)^k / (fac * (k+1)); % (k+1)! = k! (k+1)

```
10      Psiar = Psi;           %  Updated value of  Psi
11   End
12   'Results  obtained using Taylor method
13      A1 = I2 + T * Ac * Psi;   B1 = Psi * T * Bc;
14   sysdTaylor = ss(A1, B1, Cc, Dc);
15   [A, B, C, D] = ssdata(sysdTaylor)    % Result Taylor
16   'Results  obtained using c2d  method
17   sysdC2d = c2d(ss(Ac,Bc,Cc,Dc),T);
18   [A, B, C, D] = ssdata(sysdC2d)       %  c2d result
```

Appendices

Appendix 1

Table of Z-transforms

This table has been drawn up from several sources, among which [FRA 90, MBI 17].

$x(t)$, with $t \geq 0$	$X(s)$	$X(z)$
$\delta(t) = \begin{cases} 1, & \text{if } t = 0 \\ 0, & \text{if } t \neq 0 \end{cases}$	0	1
$u(t) = \begin{cases} 1, & \text{if } t \geq 0 \\ 0, & \text{if } t < 0 \end{cases}$	$u(s) = \dfrac{1}{s}$	$\dfrac{z}{z-1}$
T	$\dfrac{1}{s^2}$	$\dfrac{T_0\, z}{(z-1)^2}$
$\dfrac{t^2}{2}$	$\dfrac{1}{s^3}$	$\dfrac{T_0^2\, z(z+1)}{2(z-1)^3}$
$\dfrac{t^3}{6}$	$\dfrac{1}{s^4}$	$\dfrac{T_0^3\, z\,(z^2+4z+1)}{6\,(z-1)^4}$
e^{-at}	$\dfrac{1}{s+a}$	$\dfrac{z}{z-e^{-a\,T_0}}$
$t\, e^{-a.t}$	$\dfrac{1}{(s+a)^2}$	$\dfrac{T_0\, z\, e^{-a.t_0}}{\left(z-e^{-aT_0}\right)^2}$
$\dfrac{t^2}{2}\, e^{-a.t}$	$\dfrac{1}{(s+a)^3}$	$\dfrac{T_0^2\, e^{-a\,T_0}\, z\,\left(z+e^{-a\,T_0}\right)}{2\,\left(z-e^{-a\,T_0}\right)^3}$

$1 - e^{-at}$	$\dfrac{a}{s(s+a)}$	$\dfrac{z\left(1 - e^{-aT_0}\right)}{(z-1)\left(z - e^{-aT_0}\right)}$
$e^{-at} - e^{-bt}$	$\dfrac{b-a}{(s+a)(s+b)}$	$\dfrac{z\left(e^{-aT_0} - e^{-bT_0}\right)}{\left(z - e^{-aT_0}\right)\left(z - e^{-bT_0}\right)}$
$t - \dfrac{1 - e^{-a.t}}{a}$	$\dfrac{a}{s^2\,(s+a)}$	$\dfrac{T_0.z}{(z-1)^2} - \dfrac{\left(1 - e^{-a.T_0}\right)z}{a\,(z-1)\,\left(z - e^{-a.T_0}\right)}$
$\dfrac{1}{2}\left(t^2 - \dfrac{2.t}{a} + \dfrac{2}{a^2}\left(1 - e^{-a.t}\right)\right)$	$\dfrac{a}{s^3\,(s+a)}$	$\dfrac{T_0^2\,z}{(z-1)^3} + \dfrac{(a\,T_0 - 2)\,T_0\,z}{2\,a\,(z-1)^2}$ $+ \dfrac{z}{a^2\,(z-1)} - \dfrac{z}{a^2\left(z - e^{-a\,T_0}\right)}$
$\sin(\omega_0\,t)$	$\dfrac{\omega_0}{s^2 + \omega_0^2}$	$\dfrac{z\,\sin(\omega_0\,T_0)}{z^2 - 2z\,\cos(\omega_0.T_0) + 1}$
$\cos(\omega_0\,t)$	$\dfrac{s}{s^2 + \omega_0^2}$	$\dfrac{z(z - \cos(\omega_0.T_0))}{z^2 - 2z\,\cos(\omega_0\,T_0) + 1}$
$1 - \cos(\omega_0.t)$	$\dfrac{\omega_0^2}{s\left(s^2 + \omega_0^2\right)}$	$\dfrac{z}{z-1} - \dfrac{z\,(z - \cos(\omega_0.T_0))}{z^2 - 2z\,\cos(\omega_0\,T_0) + 1}$
$1 - (1 + a\,t)\,e^{-a.t}$	$\dfrac{a^2}{s\,(s+a)^2}$	$\dfrac{(1 - e^{-aT_0} - aT_0 e^{-aT_0})}{(z-1)\,(z - e^{-aT})^2}\,z^2 +$ $\dfrac{(e^{-2aT_0} - e^{-aT_0} + aT_0 e^{-aT_0})}{(z-1)\,(z - e^{-aT})^2}\,z$
$e^{-a.t}\,\sin(b\,t)$	$\dfrac{b}{(s+a)^2 + b^2}$	$\dfrac{z\,e^{-a.T_0}\,\sin(b.T_0)}{z^2 - 2z\,e^{-a.T_0}\,\cos(b\,T_0) + e^{-2.a.T_0}}$
$e^{-a.t}\,\cos(b\,t)$	$\dfrac{s+a}{(s+a)^2 + b^2}$	$\dfrac{z\left(z - e^{-a.T_0}\,\cos(b\,T_0)\right)}{z^2 - 2z\,e^{-a\,T_0}\,\cos(bT_0) + e^{-2\,a\,T_0}}$
$A\,e^{-\xi\,\omega_n\,t}\sin\left(\omega_n\sqrt{1-\xi^2}\,t\right)$ with $A = \dfrac{\omega_n}{\sqrt{1-\xi^2}}$	$\dfrac{\omega_n^2}{s^2 + 2\,\xi\,\omega_n\,s + \omega_n^2}$	$\dfrac{\omega_n\,e^{-\xi\omega_n T_0}\,\sin\left(\omega_n\sqrt{1-\xi^2}\,T_0\right)z}{z^2 - 2e^{-\xi\omega_n T_0}\,\cos\left(\omega_n\sqrt{1-\xi^2}\,T_0\right)z + e^{-2\xi\omega_n T_0}}$

Table A1.1. *Table of z-transforms (T: sampling period)*

Appendix 2

Matlab® Elements Used in This Book

Category	Elements	Description of elements
Specific symbols	%	Comment
	=	Assignment
	'	Transpose
	,	Argument separator/end of command
	;	No display of the result of a command
	…	Line continuation
	[,], [;]	Brackets of vector/matrix elements
	:	Separator of indices of a sequential data
	( )	Parentheses of arguments of a function
Arithmetic operators (applicable to vectors/matrices according to context)	+ and .+	Addition
	- and .-	Subtraction
	* and .*	Multiplication
	/ and ./	Division
	^ and .^	Power
Relational operators	<	Less than
	<=	Less than or equal to
	>	Greater than
	>=	Greater than or equal to
	= =	Equal to
	~=	Not equal to

General primitives	clear	Data deletion in progress
	clg	Deletion of figure content in progress
	function	Function defined by the programmer
	load	Reading in the disk object *.mat
	num2str	Conversion from number to string
	save	Storage in the disk object *.mat
Graphic management of figure object in progress	axis	Ranges of axes of a figure layout
	deploy	Deployment of the Matlab application for Windows
	figure	Figure object
	get	Recovery of the property(properties) of GUI object
	grid	Grid drawing on the figure
	gtext	Text display at a point of a figure object
	guide	Activation of the Matlab GUI editor
	hold on/off	Management of figure content memorization
	image	(GUI) image object
	imshow	Image display in progress
	plot	Graph plotting with a default pattern
	preview	Displays video data on GUI video window
	set	Writing of GUI object property
	stem	Graph plotting with a stem pattern
	subplot	Division of a figure into $n \times m$ cells
	text	Graphic display of x
	title	Titling of a figure
	videoinput	Creation of video object
	xlabel	Text display in the abscissa
	ylabel	Text display in the ordinate

Arithmetic calculation applicable to vectors/matrices according to context	cos	Cosine function
	diag	Creation of diagonal matrix
	exp	Exponential function
	floor	Rounding to nearest integer less than or equal to an element
	length	Dimension
	log	Logarithm of base e
	ones	Unit vector/matrix object
	rank	Rank of a matrix
	sin	Sine function
	sqrt	Square root
Management of dynamic models	c2d	Discretization of continuous model
	ctrb	Returns the controllability matrix
	ctrbf	Returns the controllable form
	d2c	Reconstruction of continuous model
	eig	Calculation of eigenvalues and eigenvectors
	feedback	Object creation: feedback loop
	iddata	Data of identified model
	obsv	Calculation of observability matrix
	parallel	Object creation: parallel association
	obsvf	Returns the observable form
	$p = tf('p')$	Symbolic variable for the transfer function $G_c(p)$
	series	Object creation: series association
	ss	Object creation: state model
	$s = tf('s')$	Symbolic variable for $G_c(s)$
	tf	Object creation: transfer function
	tfdata	Data of the transfer function object
	tfest	Object creation: estimator of $G_c(s)$
	$z = tf('z')$	Symbolic variable for the transfer function $G(z)$
	place	Pole placement gain

	acker	Pole placement Ackermann's gain
Synthesis of controllers	dlqg	Parameters of discrete LQG controller
	dlqr	Parameters of discrete LQR controller
	lqr	Parameters of continuous LQR controller
	lqg	Parameters of continuous LQG controller
	Bode	Bode diagram
Model simulation (default plot of data graph)	dlsim	Discrete time response
	dstep	Discrete time step response
	lsim	Continuous time response
	step	Continuous time step response
Programming structures	for ... end	Processing loop
	if ... end	Simple/multiple conditional switch

Table A2.1. *Matlab elements used in this book*

Bibliography

[ATH 13] ATHERTON D. P., *Control Engineering – An Introduction with the Use of Matlab*, 2nd ed., available at: www.bookboon.com, 2013.

[BAG 93] BAGCHI A., *Optimal Control of Stochastic System*, Prentice Hall, Upper Saddle River, 1993.

[BAK 12] BAKER K., *Introduction to Computer-Based Control Systems*, IDC Technology, available at: www.idc-online.com, 2012.

[BEN 96] BENNETT S., "A brief history of automatic control", *IEEE Control Systems*, vol. 16, no. 3, pp. 17–25, 1996.

[BIA 85] BIANCIOTTO A., BOYE P., *Informatique et Automatisation Industrielle*, Editions Delagrave, Paris, 1985.

[BOL 04] BOLTON W., *Instrumentation and Control Systems*, Newnes, Boston, 2004.

[BON 10] BONNET P., Modélisation, identification du processus, IEEA Master's course, University of Lille, France, 2010.

[BSA 94] BSATA A., *Instrumentation et automation dans le contrôle des proceed*, Editions Le Griffon d'Argile, Quebec, 1994.

[CHE 84] CHEN C.T., *Linear System Theory and Design*, Holt Rinehart and Winston, New York, 1984.

[DUR 15] DURAFFOURG L., ARCAMONE J., *Nanoelectromechanical Systems*, ISTE Ltd., London and John Wiley & Sons, New York, 2015.

[FAD 09] FADALI S., VISIOLI A., *Digital Control Engineering Analysis and Design*, Elsevier, Amsterdam, 2009.

[FOU 87] FOULARD C., GENTIL S., SANDRAZ J.P., *Commande et régulation par calculateur numérique: De la théorie aux applications*, Eyrolles, France, 1987.

[FRA 90] FRANKLIN G.F., POWELL J.D., WORKMAN M.L., *Digital Control of Dynamic Systems*, 2nd ed., Addison Wesley, Boston, 1990.

[FRI 82] FRINDEL J., *Electronique de puissance: La régulation par la pratique*, Editions Educalivre, Paris, 1982.

[GRO 08] GROUT I., *Digital Systems Design with FPGAs and CPLDs*, Newnes, Boston, 2008.

[GÜR 16] GÜRSEY H., ÜNDER EFE M., "Control system implementation on an FPGA platform", *IFAC (International Federation of Automatic Control) ScienceDirect Papers Online*, vol. 49, no. 25, pp. 425–430, 2016.

[JAS 11] JASIM O.A., MANSOOR A.Z., KHALIL M.R., "Position control of DC servo motors using soft-core processor on FPGA to move robot arm", *International Electrical Engineering Journal*, vol. 2, no. 3, pp. 555–559, 2011.

[KAT 90] KATSUHIKO OGATA, *Modern Control Engineering*, Second ed., Prentice-Hall, Upper Saddle River, 1990.

[LUE 79] LUENBERGER D.G., *Introduction to Dynamic Systems: Theory, Models and Applications*, John Wiley and Sons, New York, 1979.

[MAS 10] MASSIMILIANO *et al.*, "FPGA-based random PWM control of a buck DC/DC converter", *Journal of Electrical Systems*, vol. 6, no. 3, pp. 323–338, 2010.

[MBI 05] MBIHI J., *Informatique et automation – automatismes programmables contrôlés par ordinateur*, Editions Publibook, Saint-Denis, 2005.

[MBI 12] MBIHI J., MOTTO A., *Informatique Industrielle – Instrumentation virtuelle assistée par ordinateur: Principes et techniques, Cours et exercices corrigés*, Editions Ellipses, Paris, 2012.

[MBI 15a] MBIHI J., "A PC-based workbench for virtual instrumentation and automatic control using matlab GUI/MEX-C++ application", *WSEAS Transactions on Advances in Engineering Education*, vol. 12, pp. 52–62, 2015.

[MBI 15b] MBIHI J., "A flexible multimedia workbench for digital control of input-delay servo systems", *Journal of Computer Science and Control Engineering*, vol. 8, no. 2, pp. 35–40, 2015.

[MOH 10] MOHAMMED H., GANESH K., "Comparison between neural network based PI and PID controllers", *7th International Multi-Conference on Systems, Signals and Devices*, Amman, Jordan, pp. 27–30, June 2010.

[OBR 08] O'BRIEN R.T., "Optimal PID controller design using standard optimal control techniques", *American Control Conference*, Seattle, Washington, 11–12 June 2008.

[OGA 90] OGATA K., *Modern Control Engineering*, 2nd ed., Prentice Hall, Upper Saddle River, 1990.

[PAR 07] PARISOT F., "Guide d'achat – Informatique industrielle: Les PC industriels (suite)", *Mesures 796*, available at: www.mesures.com, pp. 94–103, 2007.

[SAL 16] SALGUES B., *Health Industrialization*, ISTE Press, London and Elsevier, Oxford, 2016.

[SHA 13] SHARMA S.R., DAHIKAR P.B., "Embedded design of temperature controlled using PIC16F876A for industries and laboratories", *International Journal of Innovative Research in Computer and Communication Engineering*, vol. 1, no. 10, pp. 2414–2422, 2013.

[TAV 03] TAVAKOLI S., TAVAKOLI M., "Optimal tuning of PID controllers for first order plus time delay models using dimensional analysis", *Fourth International Conference on Control and Automation*, Montreal, Canada, pp. 942–946, 10–12 June 2003.

[THO 96] THOMPSON M.T., Introduction to power electronics, Thompson Consulting Inc., available at: http://www.thompsonrd.com, 1996.

[THO 07] THOMPSON M.T., Introduction to power electronics, © Thompson consulting Inc., available at: http://www.thompsonrd.com, 2007.

[TRI 88] TRIGEASSOU J.C.I., *Recherche des modèles expérimentaux assistés par ordinateur*, Techniques et Documentation, Toulouse, France, 1988.

[VAI 07] VAISHNAV S.R., KHAN Z.J., "Design and performance of PID and fuzzy logic controller with smaller rule set for higher order system", *Proceedings of the World Congress on Engineering and Computer Science*, San Francisco, October 2007.

[VAM 16] VAMVOUDAKIS K., JAGANNATHAN S., *Control of Complex Systems: Theory and Applications*, Butterworth-Heinemann, Oxford, 2016.

[ZAH 11] ZAHER M.K., "Methodology for Implementing FPGA-Based Control Systeems", *Proceeding of the 18th IFAC World Congress*, Milan, Italy, pp. 9911–9916, 28 August–2 September 2011.

[ZIE 43] ZIEGLER J.G., NICHOLS N.B., "Optimum settings for automatic controllers", *ASME Transactions*, vol. 65, pp. 433–444, 1943.

Index

S, T, V, Z

Other titles from

in

Systems and Industrial Engineering – Robotics

2018

2017

ANDRÉ Jean-Claude
From Additive Manufacturing to 3D/4D Printing 1: From Concepts to Achievements
From Additive Manufacturing to 3D/4D Printing 2: Current Techniques, Improvements and their Limitations
From Additive Manufacturing to 3D/4D Printing 3: Breakthrough Innovations: Programmable Material, 4D Printing and Bio-printing

ARCHIMÈDE Bernard, VALLESPIR Bruno
Enterprise Interoperability: INTEROP-PGSO Vision

CAMMAN Christelle, FIORE Claude, LIVOLSI Laurent, QUERRO Pascal
Supply Chain Management and Business Performance: The VASC Model

FEYEL Philippe
Robust Control, Optimization with Metaheuristics

MARÉ Jean-Charles
Aerospace Actuators 2: Signal-by-Wire and Power-by-Wire

POPESCU Dumitru, AMIRA Gharbi, STEFANOIU Dan, BORNE Pierre
Process Control Design for Industrial Applications

RÉVEILLAC Jean-Michel
Modeling and Simulation of Logistics Flows 1: Theory and Fundamentals
Modeling and Simulation of Logistics Flows 2: Dashboards, Traffic Planning and Management
Modeling and Simulation of Logistics Flows 3: Discrete and Continuous Flows in 2D/3D

2016

ANDRÉ Michel, SAMARAS Zissis
Energy and Environment
(Research for Innovative Transports Set - Volume 1)

AUBRY Jean-François, BRINZEI Nicolae, MAZOUNI Mohammed-Habib
Systems Dependability Assessment: Benefits of Petri Net Models (Systems Dependability Assessment Set - Volume 1)

BLANQUART Corinne, CLAUSEN Uwe, JACOB Bernard
Towards Innovative Freight and Logistics (Research for Innovative Transports Set - Volume 2)

COHEN Simon, YANNIS George
Traffic Management (Research for Innovative Transports Set - Volume 3)

MARÉ Jean-Charles
Aerospace Actuators 1: Needs, Reliability and Hydraulic Power Solutions

REZG Nidhal, HAJEJ Zied, BOSCHIAN-CAMPANER Valerio
Production and Maintenance Optimization Problems: Logistic Constraints and Leasing Warranty Services

TORRENTI Jean-Michel, LA TORRE Francesca
Materials and Infrastructures 1 (Research for Innovative Transports Set - Volume 5A)
Materials and Infrastructures 2 (Research for Innovative Transports Set - Volume 5B)

WEBER Philippe, SIMON Christophe
Benefits of Bayesian Network Models
(Systems Dependability Assessment Set – Volume 2)

YANNIS George, COHEN Simon
Traffic Safety (Research for Innovative Transports Set - Volume 4)

2015

AUBRY Jean-François, BRINZEI Nicolae
Systems Dependability Assessment: Modeling with Graphs and Finite State Automata

BOULANGER Jean-Louis
CENELEC 50128 and IEC 62279 Standards

BRIFFAUT Jean-Pierre
E-Enabled Operations Management

MISSIKOFF Michele, CANDUCCI Massimo, MAIDEN Neil
Enterprise Innovation

2014

CHETTO Maryline
Real-time Systems Scheduling
Volume 1 – Fundamentals
Volume 2 – Focuses

DAVIM J. Paulo
Machinability of Advanced Materials

ESTAMPE Dominique
Supply Chain Performance and Evaluation Models

FAVRE Bernard
Introduction to Sustainable Transports

GAUTHIER Michaël, ANDREFF Nicolas, DOMBRE Etienne
Intracorporeal Robotics: From Milliscale to Nanoscale

MICOUIN Patrice
Model Based Systems Engineering: Fundamentals and Methods

MILLOT Patrick
Designing Human–Machine Cooperation Systems

NI Zhenjiang, PACORET Céline, BENOSMAN Ryad, RÉGNIER Stéphane
Haptic Feedback Teleoperation of Optical Tweezers

OUSTALOUP Alain
Diversity and Non-integer Differentiation for System Dynamics

REZG Nidhal, DELLAGI Sofien, KHATAD Abdelhakim
Joint Optimization of Maintenance and Production Policies

STEFANOIU Dan, BORNE Pierre, POPESCU Dumitru, FILIP Florin Gh.,
EL KAMEL Abdelkader
*Optimization in Engineering Sciences: Metaheuristics, Stochastic Methods
and Decision Support*

2013

ALAZARD Daniel
Reverse Engineering in Control Design

ARIOUI Hichem, NEHAOUA Lamri
Driving Simulation

CHADLI Mohammed, COPPIER Hervé
Command-control for Real-time Systems

DAAFOUZ Jamal, TARBOURIECH Sophie, SIGALOTTI Mario
Hybrid Systems with Constraints

FEYEL Philippe
Loop-shaping Robust Control

FLAUS Jean-Marie
Risk Analysis: Socio-technical and Industrial Systems

FRIBOURG Laurent, SOULAT Romain
Control of Switching Systems by Invariance Analysis: Application to Power Electronics

GROSSARD Mathieu, REGNIER Stéphane, CHAILLET Nicolas
Flexible Robotics: Applications to Multiscale Manipulations

GRUNN Emmanuel, PHAM Anh Tuan
Modeling of Complex Systems: Application to Aeronautical Dynamics

HABIB Maki K., DAVIM J. Paulo
Interdisciplinary Mechatronics: Engineering Science and Research Development

HAMMADI Slim, KSOURI Mekki
Multimodal Transport Systems

JARBOUI Bassem, SIARRY Patrick, TEGHEM Jacques
Metaheuristics for Production Scheduling

KIRILLOV Oleg N., PELINOVSKY Dmitry E.
Nonlinear Physical Systems

LE Vu Tuan Hieu, STOICA Cristina, ALAMO Teodoro,
CAMACHO Eduardo F., DUMUR Didier
Zonotopes: From Guaranteed State-estimation to Control

MACHADO Carolina, DAVIM J. Paulo
Management and Engineering Innovation

MORANA Joëlle
Sustainable Supply Chain Management

SANDOU Guillaume
Metaheuristic Optimization for the Design of Automatic Control Laws

STOICAN Florin, OLARU Sorin
Set-theoretic Fault Detection in Multisensor Systems

2012

AÏT-KADI Daoud, CHOUINARD Marc, MARCOTTE Suzanne, RIOPEL Diane
Sustainable Reverse Logistics Network: Engineering and Management

BORNE Pierre, POPESCU Dumitru, FILIP Florin G., STEFANOIU Dan
Optimization in Engineering Sciences: Exact Methods

CHADLI Mohammed, BORNE Pierre
Multiple Models Approach in Automation: Takagi-Sugeno Fuzzy Systems

DAVIM J. Paulo
Lasers in Manufacturing

DECLERCK Philippe
Discrete Event Systems in Dioid Algebra and Conventional Algebra

DOUMIATI Moustapha, CHARARA Ali, VICTORINO Alessandro,
LECHNER Daniel
*Vehicle Dynamics Estimation using Kalman Filtering: Experimental
Validation*

GUERRERO José A, LOZANO Rogelio
Flight Formation Control

HAMMADI Slim, KSOURI Mekki
Advanced Mobility and Transport Engineering

MAILLARD Pierre
Competitive Quality Strategies

MATTA Nada, VANDENBOOMGAERDE Yves, ARLAT Jean
Supervision and Safety of Complex Systems

POLER Raul *et al.*
Intelligent Non-hierarchical Manufacturing Networks

TROCCAZ Jocelyne
Medical Robotics

YALAOUI Alice, CHEHADE Hicham, YALAOUI Farouk, AMODEO Lionel
Optimization of Logistics

ZELM Martin *et al.*
Enterprise Interoperability –I-EASA12 Proceedings

2011

CANTOT Pascal, LUZEAUX Dominique
Simulation and Modeling of Systems of Systems

DAVIM J. Paulo
Mechatronics

DAVIM J. Paulo
Wood Machining

GROUS Ammar
Applied Metrology for Manufacturing Engineering

KOLSKI Christophe
Human–Computer Interactions in Transport

LUZEAUX Dominique, RUAULT Jean-René, WIPPLER Jean-Luc
Complex Systems and Systems of Systems Engineering

ZELM Martin, *et al.*
Enterprise Interoperability: IWEI2011 Proceedings

2010

BOTTA-GENOULAZ Valérie, CAMPAGNE Jean-Pierre, LLERENA Daniel, PELLEGRIN Claude
Supply Chain Performance / Collaboration, Alignement and Coordination

BOURLÈS Henri, GODFREY K.C. Kwan
Linear Systems

BOURRIÈRES Jean-Paul
Proceedings of CEISIE'09

CHAILLET Nicolas, REGNIER Stéphane
Microrobotics for Micromanipulation

DAVIM J. Paulo
Sustainable Manufacturing

GIORDANO Max, MATHIEU Luc, VILLENEUVE François
Product Life-Cycle Management / Geometric Variations

LOZANO Rogelio
Unmanned Aerial Vehicles / Embedded Control

LUZEAUX Dominique, RUAULT Jean-René
Systems of Systems

VILLENEUVE François, MATHIEU Luc
Geometric Tolerancing of Products

2009

DIAZ Michel
Petri Nets / Fundamental Models, Verification and Applications

OZEL Tugrul, DAVIM J. Paulo
Intelligent Machining

PITRAT Jacques
Artificial Beings

2008

ARTIGUES Christian, DEMASSEY Sophie, NERON Emmanuel
Resources–Constrained Project Scheduling

BILLAUT Jean-Charles, MOUKRIM Aziz, SANLAVILLE Eric
Flexibility and Robustness in Scheduling

DOCHAIN Denis
Bioprocess Control

LOPEZ Pierre, ROUBELLAT François
Production Scheduling

THIERRY Caroline, THOMAS André, BEL Gérard
Supply Chain Simulation and Management

2007

DE LARMINAT Philippe
Analysis and Control of Linear Systems

DOMBRE Etienne, KHALIL Wisama
Robot Manipulators

LAMNABHI Françoise *et al.*
Taming Heterogeneity and Complexity of Embedded Control

LIMNIOS Nikolaos
Fault Trees

2006

FRENCH COLLEGE OF METROLOGY
Metrology in Industry

NAJIM Kaddour
Control of Continuous Linear Systems

Printed and bound by CPI Group (UK) Ltd, Croydon, CR0 4YY